Golf Courses of Cheshire

Mark Rowlinson

Published by Sigma Leisure - an imprint of
Sigma Press, 1 South Oak Lane, Wilmslow, Cheshire SK9 6AR, England.

British Library Cataloguing in Publication Data: A CIP record for this book is available from the British Library.
ISBN: 1-85058-379-X

Typesetting and Design by: Sigma Press, Wilmslow, Cheshire.

Printed by: Manchester Free Press

Course Maps: prepared by Jeremy Semmens, from originals produced by the author.

Course Location Map: provided by Cheshire County Council, Geographical Information Unit.

Cover design: The Agency, Wilmslow

Photographs: The cover photograph was kindly provided by Shrigley Hall golf course; all other photographs are by the author.

Frederic Robinson Ltd kindly contributed to the costs of photography in this book and we are most grateful for their assistance.

Foreword

by Alan Green, Senior BBC Sports Commentator

As I'm forever being reminded, by my Boss and the many people who write to me, I have one of the best jobs in the world. BBC Radio Sport, some say with stark mis-judgement, offers me the best seat in the world's great sporting arenas and a microphone, with which to say whatever I think. For a sports nutcase who admits to having a lot to say (arguably too much!) about everything, it's the supreme indulgence.

Football is, unquestionably, my first love. I have to be passionate about the game or else my brain wouldn't survive the 130+ commentaries I do each season for Radio 5 Live. The 1993-1994 marathon began with the Charity Shield on August 7th and ended with the World Cup Final at the Rosebowl in Pasadena on July 17th ... a full year, bar 3 weeks! Yet those who listen to my commentary will know I usually find something to complain about, no matter how exotic the setting. Driving back into Los Angeles in the wake of a very disappointing game between Brazil and Italy I couldn't help but remember that by being there I had missed Nick Price's win at the Open.

If football has first call on my sporting affections, golf is a very close second. Not for the past few years in the playing sense, as my children have not unreasonably put a temporary stop to that, but, as with football, the BBC allowing me to talk about it. 1994 was the first Open I've missed in 10 years.

It's a privilege to broadcast on golf. It calls for completely different disciplines to those required in football. It has to. None of the commentary positions in football are close enough for what you say, or how you say it, to be heard by the participants. But in golf I may be only a few yards away as Faldo putts. Hence, the hushed tones of golf commentary on radio, in marked contrast to the rather more animated noises emanating from Old Trafford or Anfield.

My golf involvement has taken me to all the great courses in the British Isles but I've also been fortunate in seeing golf played abroad. I will never forget the Ryder Cup at Kiawah Island in South Carolina, and in particular, the dramatic 17th hole, where I spent three sensational hours on that Sunday afternoon in 1991.

Of course I'm lucky! But I hope I've never fallen into the trap of believing that what's available elsewhere is always better than what's right on our own doorstep. To that end Mark Rowlinson is doing every golfer a great service.

On the rare days that I'm in the office I never imagined that that quiet chap beavering away across the corridor at New

Broadcasting House in Manchester had probably left his family and home around dawn in the interest of providing this invaluable tome on Cheshire golf. While you've been dreaming of the delights out of reach at Pebble Beach, Mark was traipsing the fairways of Wilmslow or Knutsford determined that we should be informed of golfing treats available much nearer home.

Reading this book, it's obvious he's left no bunker unexplored, no greenside lake unplumbed! It's as detailed and comprehensive as it could possibly be, yet written with a lightness and humour that sees the pages turned swiftly in anticipation. Mark's was a labour of love and should be of immense benefit to anyone interested in expanding their golfing experience. I'm delighted to be associated with it.

Alan Green

Preface

Cheshire is, for the most part, a county of agriculture, its cheese rivalled only as a product of world renown by the Rolls-Royce Motor Car. Cows need a very different kind of grass from golfers and until recently there were relatively few golf courses of much standing in the county. The Rolls-Royce was Hoylake or, more properly, the Royal Liverpool Golf Club, host to ten Open Championships over the seventy years from 1897, when the amateur Harold Hilton, one of its own players, triumphed, to 1967, when Roberto de Vicenzo held off the challenge of the mighty Jack Nicklaus, a mere youngster but already at the height of his powers. Hoylake's subsequent removal from the Open Championship rota had nothing to do with the supreme quality of its golf but everything to do with the inordinate space needed for the modern 'Major'. Hoylake now finds itself in Merseyside but, from a golfing point of view, the area is still very much a part of the Cheshire scene, Wallasey and Caldy making up a formidable and miraculously varied triumvirate.

Little outbreaks of sandy heathland here and there were quickly spotted by the early golf architects, Delamere Forest and Sandiway stretching the best county players now for 60 years or more, while Prestbury, hidden away behind the exclusive village's exclusive homes, yields nothing to either. Mere, as befits its grand setting, has played host to any number of distinguished golfing visitors (and an even greater number of distinguished businessmen entertained lavishly during "Company Days") while Wilmslow has hosted a European Tour event or two within living memory.

But, for most of us, golf is confined to an occasional weekend trundle round our own home course, humble perhaps in comparison with these comparative giants but testing enough to bring us down to earth more often than we might like. These are the backbone of Cheshire golf and they form the bulk of this book.

Some of them, including a number of rather good courses such as Dunham Forest, are now technically swallowed up in Manchester and, to redress the balance, a few have migrated into the county from what used to be Lancashire, but if they have any claim at all to being or having been part of Cheshire all courses are welcome in these pages.

The priority that cows may once have held over land occupation in the county is now challenged by the interests of health and leisure, a debate stimulated by the various financial incentives to farmers to find alternative uses for their land. Suddenly deeply rural areas towards the Shropshire border are sprouting golf courses, Oaklands and Portal in their different ways entering the starting gate purposefully. The Women Professional Golfers have made their home (or at least their tour headquarters) at the Tytherington Club which occupies the farmland that once provided a buffer between the inhabitants of Macclesfield and Prestbury.

These are amongst the larger budget projects. There are others where one man and a tractor, as it were, have done it all and their courses are providing enjoyment and stimulation to a great multitude as their full membership waiting lists testify. Heyrose is just such a course, starting as nine holes to get play (and income) under way, growing in time to eighteen holes and eventually adding a fine clubhouse. Its golfers, too, have graduated. Once they hit more balls onto the fields of my uncle's farm next door than they did onto their own fairways. Now the trend is reversed and he will have to give up selling used golf balls and return to growing barley, wheat and potatoes.

Hotels, like farmers, are turning to golf to attract new money. Visitors to Mottram Hall, for instance, can enjoy the delights of a course designed by the same team that built the Belfry of Ryder-Cup fame. Guests who tackle the rigours of Shrigley Hall and survive may now swim on their backs in the old chapel where once postulant monks examined their souls on their knees. Before long the European Tour itself will make its presence felt permanently in Cheshire when its stadium complex is opened at Weston Hall near Crewe.

If this book is something of a celebration of all that is best in Cheshire golf I hope, never the less, that it may cause those of you who have been playing the same course for years to look at that course with fresh eyes if only to say, "He got it wrong". I stress the use of the word *celebration* for it has not been my intention to dwell on the less happy aspects of clubs or courses and, given the ghastly weather suffered in the summer of 1993, it would be foolish of me to make any sort of comment on their condition. While the views expressed in the book are bound to differ from the reader's from time to time they are opinions I have formed by playing the courses and I take sole responsibility for them.

Over the spring and summer of 1993 I was fortunate enough to be able to re-acquaint myself with those many Cheshire courses I already knew and loved, even if my game had in the past been properly examined by a good number of them. Completing the full collection has enlightened me greatly, not least by making me aware of the considerable architectural merits of so many relatively unsung layouts. Occasionally, as I was going round, I would begin to despair of finding something exceptional or individual to share with the reader but, miraculously, even as late as a 16th or 17th hole something invariably turned up saving me the embarrassment of writing, "There is nothing of merit to report about this course."

Having to hold down a full time job totally unrelated to golf has meant making many of these visits at 6.30 a.m., which in itself has been an education, the one disadvantage of playing so early being the universally heavy dew which makes putting almost irrelevant – another reason to avoid adverse criticism. I have had almost every course to myself, enjoyed the company of all sorts of creatures, feathered and furred, rarely taken longer than two hours for a full 18-holes, and, on the few occasions the sun has shone in an appalling summer, been granted the best light of the day for photography. Green fees for these playing visits have, in almost every case, been waived in an act of enormous kindness by the Secretaries, Managers, Captains, Chairmen, Presidents, Committees of Management, and Councils of the clubs concerned and without such benevolence this book simply would not exist. The brewers, Frederic Robinson Limited, generously assisted with the cost of photography, and a rare archive of slides covering every course in Cheshire has been assembled. Subvention, with characteristic munificence, from that connoisseur of traditional golf, Nicolas Johnston, should be associated with something appropriate and I hope he would approve that his benefaction enabled me to revisit Caldy, Delamere Forest and Wallasey.

Further benefactions not forthcoming, this book is, coincidentally, testament to the reliability of my ancient Mitsubishi *Colt*, 20-year old Fujica ST-801 camera (able to cope with the greyness of the ghastly summer of 1993 as well as my ineptitude as a photographer), 25-year old Dunlop *Bob Charles* golf clubs, and my own 44-year old frame. I no longer pretend to hit the ball out of sight and have written this book from the point of view of a middle-handicapper who only occasionally aspires to making the green of a par-5 in two shots and rather more frequently fails to reach the longer par-4s in the same number. Despite playing the game back-to-front as a left-hander I have used the words "slice" and "hook" from the point of view of the right-hander. Being a traditionalist I have eschewed metres and stuck robustly to yards throughout, quoting the men's medal card in all cases except that of Wirral Ladies', not that casual visitors are often afforded the courtesy of the white tee boxes, but it makes for uniformity and enables reasonable comparison to be made between courses.

It was as a teenager that I first discerned that the course I was playing was rather more interesting than my own performance over it. For that attitude (and my left-handed play) I have to thank my father who saw to it that I experienced the likes of Royal County Down and Southerness in my formative years. Sadly, he narrowly failed to "make the cut" before this book was published. He knew, and had sliced his way round, a number of the courses within and would have ensured that I did not go "out-of-bounds" as he read the proofs.

This book is merely a "snapshot" – Cheshire golf as it was in the summer of '93. Almost every course will have been re-measured, built a few new tees, been re-assessed for "Standard Scratch", or called in the architect for a complete rebuild by the time you read this. For that reason I have simply recorded the courses as they were when I visited. In some cases I have been given every conceivable assistance in drawing maps, sifting through historical background, being put in touch with the architect, and so on. Other clubs were less helpful or, perhaps, less informed. If I have given the reader short shrift occasionally it must not, therefore, be assumed that the course concerned is less satisfactory. In order to be reasonably fair to the pitifully few municipal courses within, I have had to impose a rule for them of no maps and the briefest of descriptions. I simply have neither the time nor the patience to queue for hours and then find myself irredeemably frustrated as I trudge along behind a four-ball unable (or unwilling) to realise that a competent single player (no status though he may have) moves round the course very swiftly indeed. I have in these cases unashamedly dragged up whatever I can from notes made perhaps a good number of years ago.

Lastly I should record my particular gratitude to my wife, Lavinia, who could be a very low-handicap player but steadfastly refuses to take her clubs out of their bag. Never the less, she and our three children have been remarkably tolerant of my auroral departures and crepuscular addiction to word-processing.

Mark Rowlinson

Locations of the courses

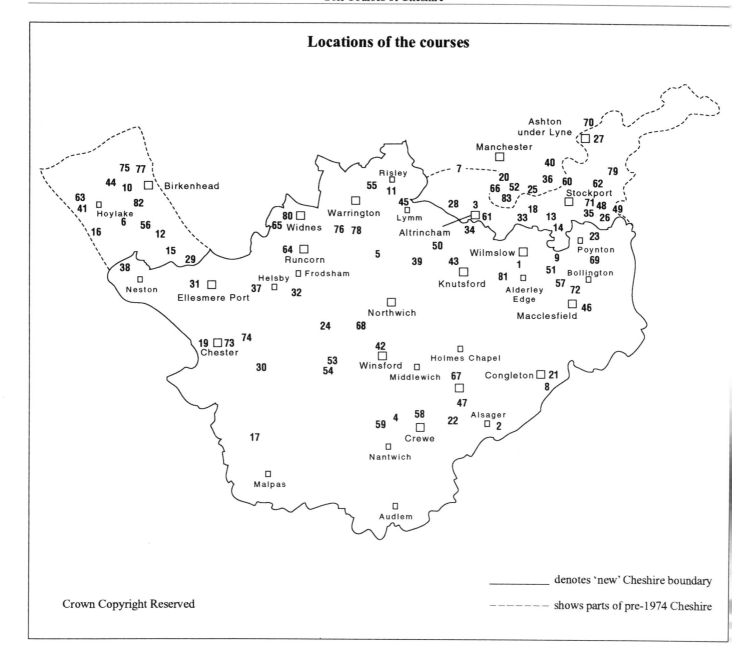

_____ denotes 'new' Cheshire boundary

- - - - - - shows parts of pre-1974 Cheshire

Course Locator

Contents

Alderley Edge

5823 yards; par 68; s.s.s. 68

To set the agenda, to lay down a standard against which all else is measured, is a considerable responsibility. That such an onerous burden should fall upon Alderley Edge is entirely reasonable, for it encompasses so many of the virtues to be found in each course which follows. That it does so in nine holes is hardly inappropriate, either: Cheshire's best half-dozen 9-hole layouts would give any other county's select six a good run for their money, if not a sound hiding.

The site allotted to Alderley Edge is now tightly constrained by roads and housing, though that was hardly the case when T.G. Renouf laid it out in the first decade of the century. Never the less, one is bound to admire the way in which every advantage is taken of the natural features of hills and a stream to separate the goats from the sheep and, as the course now stands, there is a splendid variety to the nature of problems posed.

The Swilcan Burn at St Andrews is immediately brought to mind as the 1st green is approached after an encouraging downhill drive. At Alderley Edge the green is about 40 yards further away than its Fifeshire equivalent but the effect is not dissimilar.

Sadly I am bound to declare my waning powers at an early stage for uphill holes of 450 yards on lush inland grass are no longer within the compass of two of my Sunday-best shots. The 2nd at Alderley is not only uphill but that second shot is played over a substantial depression ruling out the slightest possibility of a kindly extra roll even in dry weather. Real insult is added to perceived injury in the form of a venomous little pit just to the right of the green. That in itself might be sufficient but it was deemed necessary to balance this pit with two bunkers on the left.

The 3rd and 12th, though played to the same green, differ significantly, the former more or less straight away, the latter a left hand dog-leg over trees. Again the second shot is played over the stream, but this time it interferes only with a sickly second. There ends the big hitting for the time being.

At not even 150 yards the photogenic 4th is gentle, but again the stream interrupts proceedings just before the green, four bunkers abut the green, and trees and a fence do for the wildly erratic. A route march is now in order, the 5th tee up on a hillside far beyond, the 14th right back alongside the tee from which we have just played. The 5th then involves a healthy carry over a field (in bounds, according to the local rules) to reach the fairway, the 14th a tight tee shot with a tree-covered hill on the right and the field (now out-of-bounds) on the left. From these different beginnings the end is the same, abruptly up over a ridge to a green set behind a couple of bunkers.

The narrowest of entrances, between tall trees, gives access to the steeply sloping 6th green. Bunkers surround the said trees and a third, in the form of a cross-bunker, effectively ensures that only a crisply struck aerial shot will reach the relative sanctuary of the putting surface.

From a high tee the 7th drive is, yet again, heartening, down to the bottom of a valley. The second shot, however, must surmount a steep hill, with the slightest directional inaccuracy magnified embarrassingly by the convex nature of the fairway. Tucked in a corner over the hill is a narrow green, hard up by the fence, with three attendant bunkers.

The 8th green is the start of the best sledge run in Wilmslow — down the bumpy slope towards the stream and then, *Domine, dirige nos*, over the narrow wooden bridge and up the other side. Fortunately usable snow is infrequent here and no lasting damage seems to have been done to this green perched up on top of a pinnacle with a bunker tight in on the left and two trees keeping guard on the right. The vengeance of hell is wreaked on those who fail to make the carry.

The 9th, given a comfortable passage through the trees and over the stream directly in front of the tee, is more a matter of preventing the ball from sliding off down the hill towards the car park on the left. That slope is distinctly pronounced near the green, a couple of bunkers rounding things off on the right.

Card of the course:

1.	418 yards	par 4	10.	418 yards	par 4
2.	444	4	11.	444	4
3.	439	4	12.	439	4
4.	146	3	13.	143	3
5.	331	4	14.	371	4
6.	124	3	15.	130	3
7.	473	5	16.	473	5
8.	171	3	17.	175	3
9.	368	4	18.	342	4

Out:	2914 yards	par 34
In:	2909 yards	par 34
Total:	5823 yards	par 68

s.s.s. 68

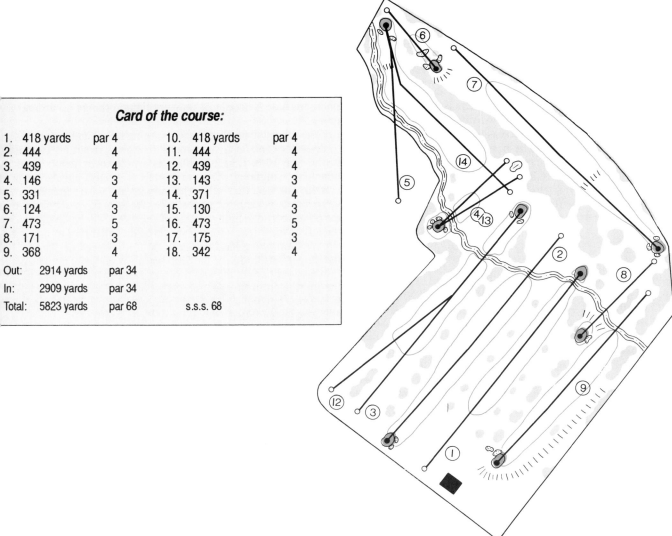

Opposite: the 8th hole at Alderley Edge

Alsager

6206 yards; par 70; s.s.s. 70

In the south-east of the county Cheshire stops abruptly and The Potteries begin just as suddenly. It is as if there is a distinct barrier keeping towns and countryside of totally different characters apart. The "border town" of Alsager (all too easily missed on one or other of the main roads which seem to by-pass it) somehow manages to maintain an air of its own, neither Crewe nor Stoke, neither Sandbach nor Newcastle. It is all about "feel". Approach the golf course over the level crossing from the centre of Alsager and you are firmly in Cheshire. Do it from the A500 motorway link and you might still be in the "Five Towns".

The course is a modern one, founded as recently as 1976, but it is not overindulged with the lakes, sleepered bunkers and Mackenzie greens that can all too readily proliferate. For the most part it is quite a gentle layout waiting for the newly-planted trees to grow, allowing social golf to flow amiably with few interruptions. But there *are* traps for the unwary, one or two rather demanding holes, and a heart attack inducing hill giving one of the finest views in all Cheshire golf. As a left-hander who occasionally slices I am tempted to describe this as a course which might suit a long-hitting right-hander with the ability to fashion a controlled fade.

From the front nine I have fond memories of the 6th, 7th and 8th. The 6th is stout stuff even from the yellow markers with a downhill drive required to pull up just short of a gap in the hedge which grows in from either side. Miscalculation results in choosing the best dropping place after lifting out of the ditch which runs at the bottom of that hedge. This green, unusually, is a two-level affair.

The same ditch and a number of trees must be carried from the 7th tee and there is the possibility of tangling with overhead power lines (not the only occasion on which this might happen). It is the 8th, though, which, to my taste, stands out with a tricky tee shot required to open up the green. The right side of the fairway, close to trees, must be held if the second shot is not to be played high over the trees which constrict the fairway just where the ubiquitous ditch crosses. A couple of bunkers tighten things up around the green.

The 9th is longer than it seems, being uphill and the other side of three bunkers. Its greatest merit, though, is in getting us rapidly to the fine 10th. Like the 8th it is a hole to be demolished by potential champions, but mere mortals will relish the challenge of clearing the lone tree left in the fairway just where that wretched ditch makes yet another appearance. We, too, have to be aware of the potentially damaging effects of another ditch which runs along the left of the fairway for the whole of the latter part of its length.

What climbing has been done so far has been negligible, but the long uphill trudge of the 12th warns of things to come. As the fairway approaches the green it narrows between a steep hill on the right (clad in savage long grasses) and a hedge on the left, in the cutting beyond which once ran one of the branch lines of what H.C. Casserley called "either one of the largest and most important of the lesser railways, or one of the smallest of the major ones", the *Knotty* or North Staffordshire.

It is now dreadfully apparent that the hill must be climbed and it is done for the first time on the par-3 13th, at 189-yards uphill about as far as most of us can hit along and up at the same time. The view from the summit green is unrivalled, a 360-degree panorama taking in the hills of the Pottery Towns, the more rural parts of Staffordshire and Shropshire, the distant Welsh hills, the Cheshire plain with its occasional sandstone outcrops, the foothills of the Pennines, and that extraordinary confection, Mow Cop. Golfers will also note that we are required to play down the hill again on the 14th (an exhilarating experience), up it on the 15th (thoroughly debilitating), and back down again on the 16th. Those whose constitutions grant them the luxury of choosing how they play these holes should note the pond into which it is easy to drift from the 14th tee and over which the 15th is played. A hedge running the length of the 16th is almost as penal.

It is not these days fashionable to put greens tight up against hedges, but it was not unknown for the ancient Scots, from whom all golf has been bequeathed (*pace* the Dutch), to park their greens tight next to stone walls, railway tracks, graveyards and pubs. Alsager's par-5 17th finishes in a green dangerously close to a hedge, with the added Scottish flavour of five bunkers several of which are small enough and deep enough to qualify for the adjective, "pot".

The course ends with a short par-4 that is no pushover, the drive needing to clear yet another stretch of ditch, avoid trees to left and right and a couple of spectacle bunkers on the direct line. Then, and only then, is one given relatively free access to the domed green.

Below: The 15th Hole

This page shows a map of the Alsager course with, below, its vital statistics:

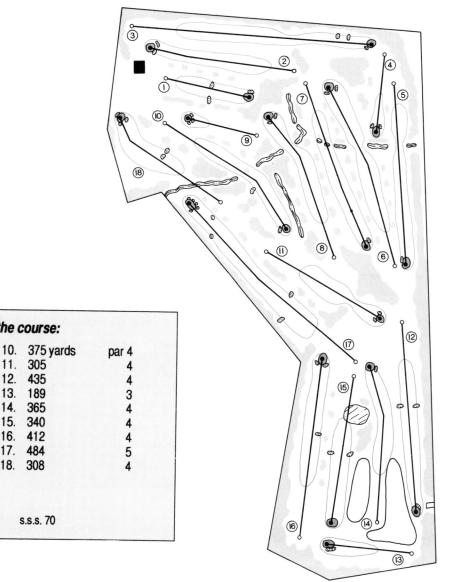

Card of the course:

1.	198 yards	par 3	10.	375 yards	par 4
2.	334	4	11.	305	4
3.	502	5	12.	435	4
4.	179	3	13.	189	3
5.	416	4	14.	365	4
6.	453	4	15.	340	4
7.	391	4	16.	412	4
8.	361	4	17.	484	5
9.	159	3	18.	308	4

Out:	2993 yards	par 34	
In:	3213 yards	par 36	
Total:	6206 yards	par 70	s.s.s. 70

Altrincham: 14th hole

Altrincham

6162 yards; par 71; s.s.s. 69

Perhaps Altrincham's grandest claim to fame is that it caused one of the finest courses in the county to be created. From the late 19th century Timperley Golf Club, very much a leading Cheshire club, had played on this site. However, when the owner died, in the mid-1930s, the members were unable to buy the land for their own use, being outbid by Altrincham Borough Council. They acquired instead Mere New Hall and the golf course subsequently built there is famed and described in detail later in this book.

What of Altrincham Borough Council's acquisition? Well, it is not going to challenge Mere for supremacy, but then what modern borough could justify spending a modern country club's budget for maintenance and grooming? In fact there is a serious shortage of public golf provision in this part of Cheshire (the neighbouring Borough of Macclesfield, for instance, has *no* municipal golf course) and Altrincham's course is, by the present bureaucratic arrangement of local government boundaries, one of several in the Borough of Trafford, an oasis in an otherwise barren and overpopulated desert.

Inevitably it is a very busy course. Golf is bound to be slow, particularly where holes run parallel, separated only by the narrowest of strips of rough, and play is frequently impeded by uninvited visitations from elsewhere and one has heard the occasional horror story of the victims of frostbite acquired during winter weekend overnight queues. I have to say that on the occasion of my only visit I was pleased to concede the match on the 15th tee having first queued for an hour and then completed only fourteen holes in just over four hours, relieved that we should no longer have to recite a litany before each time addressing the ball, terrified of being struck by a wayward shot from a yet more unlikely corner.

These, sad to relate, are the symptoms of the unenlightened golfing priorities of boroughs other than Trafford to whose care this course now falls. Under less hazardous circumstances the course would be seen as a fairly typical pre-war layout with a high proportion of shortish par-4s, few trees, plentiful bunkers, occasional hedges and ditches to liven up proceedings, any number of out-of-bounds restrictions and a pair of decently long par-5s. The last four holes make a rather curious circuit of a little field between the Stockport Road and the *Old Hall Hotel* and, fun though it may be to flip a shot over the road (and wire netting) onto the 15th green, I cannot help thinking that the 14th would make a sterling finishing hole, with its tight uphill drive between out-of-bounds on the left and bunkers on the right, holing out eventually on a green right in front of the clubhouse. This alteration might also give a slightly better balance to the disposition of the par-3 holes, the first of which comes as late as the 10th.

Card of the course:

1.	326 yards	par 4	10.	160 yards	par 3
2.	454	4	11.	429	4
3.	318	4	12.	525	5
4.	361	4	13.	328	4
5.	367	4	14.	363	4
6.	346	4	15.	134	3
7.	309	4	16.	334	4
8.	301	4	17.	384	4
9.	558	5	18.	165	3
Out:	3340 yards	par 37			
In:	2822 yards	par 34			
Total:	6162 yards	par 71		s.s.s. 69	

Alvaston Hall

2526 yards; par 54; s.s.s. 49

I love the idea of a committee deliberating for hours on whether the standard scratch at Alvaston should be 49 or 50. The plain fact is that few of us will have the "up-and-down" game to save par when we fail to make the putting surface with our tee shots. All this will soon be irrelevant as the course is expanded to take in genuine par-4s, for the beginning of the 1994 season, it is said.

If I said that eight of the 1993 holes average 130 yards and the 9th runs to 230 yards I can spare myself the need for a map, given that water is a hazard on many holes, either in the form of ponds or a stream. Otherwise, as it stands, the course is entirely a matter of adding to or subtracting from a notional 9-iron to take account of the hilly nature of the site and the effects of the wind. Despite its being apparently a mere "executive" course it has the air of a private club, with appropriate standards of dress and etiquette required allied to befitting course maintenance. We can but wait for the 1994 version.

Card of the course:

1.	124 yards	par 3
2.	123	3
3.	138	3
4.	130	3
5.	133	3
6.	121	3
7.	141	3
8.	123	3
9.	230	3
Out:	1263 yards	par 27
Total (18 holes):	2526 yards	par 54 s.s.s. 49

Alvaston Hall, 8th hole

Antrobus

6688 yards; par 74

In my pedantic way I, truthfully, give Antrobus as my place of birth – if nothing else it gives an interview board a first question with which to break the ice. Even locals will tell you it is the sort of perplexing place in which you can drive round in circles for ages without ever finding a village. Fortunately for the Antrobus Golf Club, just creeping into this book by opening at the end of August 1993, it is only just off the A559 between Northwich and Warrington behind the *Birch and Bottle*. Fishermen will know the spot, the piscatory contents of dozens of little ponds and pools being jealously guarded by innumerable angling societies. Water is the principal feature of the new golf course, too, ensuring for the Professional prolific sales of golf balls, at least until the members have lit upon the pragmatic method of remaining dry.

A ditch crosses the strong 1st hole, on the diagonal at that, a pool on the left and pond on the right sorting out the second shots of mice and men. The 4th is a double water-crossing, a dog-leg to the right, too. Only the strong drive clear of the stream on the 5th, and only they stand any chance of reaching the green on the brow

of a hill in two shots. I reserve judgement on the nature of the green itself (although I have commended just such a green in print) until it survives the first course rebuild. It is on three levels, sloping down, away from the player, and dreadfully close to the hedge which has been an ever-present factor throughout the hole.

If there is a "Signature Hole" at Antrobus it is surely the 7th, no more than a *wedge* or 9-iron away, yet punitive enough for most. The problem is not so much the forced water-carry, all the way to the green, as in stopping the ball on a very shallow putting surface beyond which there is the gentlest of hummocks. Overshoot that and you have the most treacherous of chips back. At the moment, with newly-seeded and woolly greens, it may be acceptable to overshoot. In time, this will be no place for frayed nerves.

A single water-carry on the 8th and a moated island around which the 9th bends are the remaining hazards as of August 1993, but in a year or two's time there will be a further nine water-bound holes in play and those who survive to putt out the final green with the same ball with which they drove the 1st will be good golfers indeed.

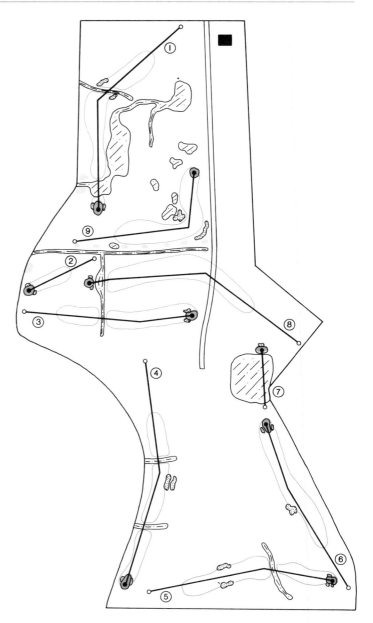

Card of the course:

1.	490 yards	par 5
2.	166	3
3.	362	4
4.	527	5
5.	403	4
6.	397	4
7.	120	3
8.	505	5
9.	374	4
Out:	3344 yards	par 37
Total (18 holes):	6688 yards	par 74

Opposite: the 7th hole

Arrowe Park

6435 yards; par 72; s.s.s. 70

I shall say it again, and it ought to be said again: the Wirral is splendidly provided with municipal golf courses. Not only are they good courses for their purpose, enabling the inexpert to survive in public while providing a decent test for the proficient, but they are wondrously varied, from the wind-swept primaeval links at The Warren to this most congenial of parkland courses. What is more, there are enough of them not to be too overcrowded in the manner of those further east.

I cannot dissociate Arrowe Park from my musical predecessor at the BBC, one Stephen Wilkinson, who, some time before the war, lost his last golf ball here, and from that moment an extraordinary character disappeared from the game. Somehow I always expect to find that ball. The course must have been newly opened in his day – 1932 I believe – yet I do not expect it was significantly different. The trees which provide such a noble backdrop to play were magnificent centuries ago, not merely 50 years ago. For the most part the golf is straightforward, but there are occasional ponds, several dog-legs (2nd, 5th, and 14th, for instance), and the odd raised green. Well mown surrounds ensure that missing a green does not hold up play for those following too long.

Card of the course:

No.	Yards	Par	No.	Yards	Par
1.	300 yards	par 4	10.	493 yards	par 5
2.	315	4	11.	213	3
3.	394	4	12.	487	5
4.	150	3	13.	202	3
5.	458	4	14.	476	5
6.	396	4	15.	192	3
7.	391	4	16.	445	4
8.	168	3	17.	340	4
9.	505	5	18.	510	5
Out:	3077 yards	par 35			
In:	3358 yards	par 37			
Total:	6435 yards	par 72		s.s.s. 70	

The 14th hole

Ashton-on-Mersey

6146 yards; par 72; s.s.s. 69

Leaving Sale by the most suburban of roads and turning down the most suburban of streets, suddenly all is cobbles, stone gate posts and wooden bell turrets. The world changes to that of the Ashton which existed long before the commuter caused the Sale of modern times to exist. In the shadow of St Martin's turret, only re-erected after the Second World War but far more in keeping with the anti-Napoleonic fervour recorded in the ancient parish records, the little golf course occupies a riverside site running down between stables on the right, a cricket pitch beyond, and the Mersey self on the left.

Nine holes run over a level plot, a stream — no more than a ditch causing what anxiety there is to be caused over the first three holes. Called *The Ash Tree*, that 3rd hole bends slowly left until a few yards in front of the green the fairway is split by that tree. Copious tree planting was undertaken sufficiently long ago for the benefits to be felt now and this green, like several to come, is framed in a semicircle of trees.

At St Andrews the Old Course has only one par-3 and a single par-5 on each half, and thereby the overall length is considerable despite the very modest length of several of the par-4s. Much the same happens at Ashton-on-Mersey where the lone par-3 is the heavily bunkered 4th, a hole on which it is possible to go out-of-bounds onto the neighbouring cricket ground.

In theory you could go out-of-bounds into the River Mersey on the 5th but it is a much more likely event on the tricky 6th where a good drive finishes somewhere about a ridge splitting the fairway where the river is at its closest and trees on the left at *their* closest, too. The pitch is made down towards a motorway bridge in front of which the green is long and narrow, copiously bunkered to boot.

The prize for the most individual hole on the course would go unquestionably to the short par-4 8th with a tee shot threatened on the left by a stream which cuts through the fairway just short of the green, but it does so behind a big artificial rampart worthy of Hadrian and a number of river-bank trees. The green itself is angled across the line and treacherously cambered making putting a potentially dangerous pursuit. The return to the impressive clubhouse may be made by the direct route, keeping to the high ground, but the slightest error brings the threat of disaster in the hedge running the length of the hole. It is much simpler to aim for the 3rd tee, trundle down onto lower ground and leave a perfectly reasonable pitch up over a modest ridge.

Card of the course:

1.	366 yards	par 4
2.	432	4
3.	476	5
4.	195	3
5.	361	4
6.	365	4
7.	314	4
8.	269	4
9.	295	4
Out:	3073 yards	par 36
Total (18 holes):	6146 yards	par 72 s.s.s. 69

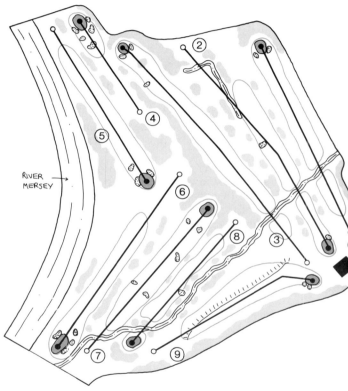

RIVER MERSEY

Left: Ashton-on-Mersey, 5th hole

Astbury

6403 yards; par 72; s.s.s. 70

'I can understand that you can write interesting accounts of 10 r 15 courses, but what do you do for all the rest?"

It was asked by a man who knows his Cheshire golf well and is own course, Astbury, intimately. He knew, naturally enough, nat there would be no problem with the account of Astbury, for it s not short of characterful holes, challenging for the tiger yet not npossible for the golfer who might be said to be in decline, and leasurably rural as recreational courses should be.

Writing authoritatively of the magnificent church of St Mary, ne of the most inspiring in Cheshire, Raymond Richards mentions ie "unimpaired loveliness" of the old village green and that is very iuch in keeping with the golf course a few hundred yards up the ttle road, over the canal bridge. There, perhaps, the comparison hould end for, while the nave and chancel would hardly be out of lace as a Cambridge college chapel, the golf course is more at the :vel of a parish church, even if rather a decent one.

There may have been a golf club in Astbury before the First Vorld War but records are only available for the present club which egan its life in 1922 as 9 holes occupying a site either side of the anal. In more recent times the club expanded its course first to 13 oles (some of those 13 holes forming the present, enviably pacious, practice ground) and then to 18 holes, the ubiquitous lawtree family being the only recognised architects officially ssociated with the expansions. Essentially those 18 holes, as urrently organised, can be divided into two distinct (and unequal) alves: 8 holes on fairly level ground up by the present clubhouse nd the main Manchester-London (via Macclesfield) railway, and ie remainder on rather more rolling terrain on the far side of the anal. Those further holes are, inevitably, more complex.

After a gentle two-hole start we are thrown into the thick of iings with a devilish 3rd. There is nothing more welcoming than ie drive, downhill between lines of trees, but then an agonising decision is called for. Is it possible to clear the deep gully in front and make it up the other side, if not actually onto the green then, at least, onto a civilised lie? If not, it is no more than a 9-iron to keep to the high ground without tumbling down the walls of the ravine and into the stream which not only runs through this course but also trundles underneath the main street of Congleton before eventually merging into the anonymity of the River Dane. Having made it to the far side in two shots is not quite the end of the story with the green no more than the narrowest of ledges on a sharply sloping hillside. As you leave the green take a sneak preview from the 12th tee, either to stiffen the sinews or to throw in the towel now.

A lenient short hole leads to the par-5 5th running alongside the canal, though newly planted trees may help to keep persistent slicers out of it. Now the main problem is avoiding pulling the ball with the slope into a pond with the second shot, the earth dragged out in creating the pond serving to raise the 5th green sufficiently to make it an elusive, and panoramic, target. From a tee nearby the 6th begins its treacherous journey down the perimeter fence, three bunkers on that side turning the hole into a slight dog-leg. A little depression before the green effectively cuts out the running approach yet there is sufficient trouble beyond to caution against overclubbing. Not for the first time are we made aware of one of Astbury's architectural features, that there are many occasions on which humiliation awaits those who charge thoughtlessly through the green. Certainly that is the case on the engaging 7th with its views out to the left over adjacent fairways and the distant Mow Cop.

Another recurring feature of golf at Astbury is being asked to place a drive accurately between fairway trees and this we are asked to achieve on the succeeding three holes, the 9th with a pleasing second shot directly on the line of Astbury's detached spire, the 10th with a moderately forbidding drive ideally drawing round alongside, but not into, the out-of-bounds ditch on the left.

Astbury, the 3rd hole

All this is but child's play compared with the sinister 12th with its drive out over the Hellespont, probably little more than 120 yards but seemingly 120 miles, to reach a fairway running uphill to the right alongside the canal. Even after a good drive there remains the possibility of a second death in a vexatious ditch crossing the fairway shortly before it climbs past a couple of bunkers on the last leg of the route to the green. That, at least, is the end of the savagery, the main problem from here on being the magisterial trees constricting the fairways in the ideal driving position. Such trees dictate play on the 14th, 16th and 18th, while a pond, home to the tamest of ducks, provides a threat on the right of the long par-4 17th as it moves gently to the right and downhill.

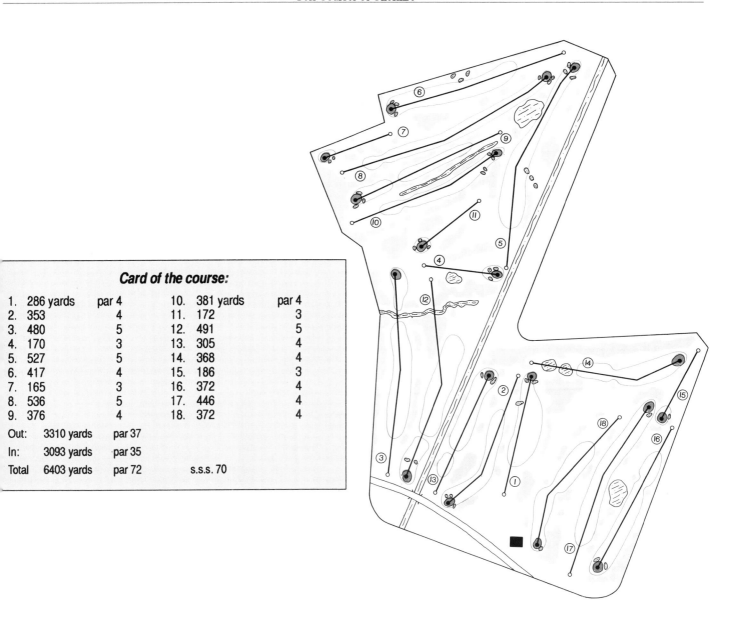

Card of the course:

1.	286 yards	par 4	10.	381 yards	par 4
2.	353	4	11.	172	3
3.	480	5	12.	491	5
4.	170	3	13.	305	4
5.	527	5	14.	368	4
6.	417	4	15.	186	3
7.	165	3	16.	372	4
8.	536	5	17.	446	4
9.	376	4	18.	372	4

Out: 3310 yards   par 37

In: 3093 yards   par 35

Total 6403 yards   par 72   s.s.s. 70

Avro

5745 yards; par 69; s.s.s. 68

It would seem a reasonable assumption that if you are going to build an airfield you do it on level ground and, on the strength of having once played at the course within the perimeter fence at RAF Waddington, I would assume that any related golf course would be similarly flat. Waddington once flew *Vulcan* bombers and already the connection with Avro is made – when I played at Waddington the left-hand boundary of the 9th hole was indeed a *Vulcan* (used for crash repair practice), and an unforgettable sound it made when it was hit! The nearest you get to a *Vulcan* at Avro is well beyond par-rating and the golfing ground is anything but flat. In fact it is one of the best surprises I have had in researching this book, a little gem started by the members of the A.V. Roe Golf Society on outlying land back in 1962 and gradually extended and improved through the years. Evocative names, such as *Vulcan, Shackleton,* and *Lancaster*, are given to the holes and the visitor – at least one of my vintage – is immediately transported back to the skies of his youth.

The 3rd hole at Avro

An escarpment runs through the course in much the same fashion as that splendid specimen that determines the best holes at Chester and so there are holes on higher and lower ground quite different in character, those on the upper level being open heathland, those below more meadowland in feel, though the aeroplane, if usually out of sight, is never far distant with the imaginative use of what to the amateur look like nose-cones as shelters on the tees. Above all, the condition of the course indicates that this is not merely a field mown when the chaps have a few hours to spare, nor simply whatever convenient holes could be found on congenial land. The evidence points to professional maintenance and thoughtful construction of greens and teeing grounds.

The escarpment threatens significantly on the left of the 1st drive, but even more on the delicate pitch which must be made over a cross-bunker to a two-level raised green. Down below is the tee for the 2nd, one of those curiosities that must regularly confound the members but charm those who visit only occasionally with a drive through the narrowest of gaps between a hillside on the left and bushes on the right. Fairway bunkers must be cleared before the fairway itself turns sharply left, over a pond, and in to a raised rectan-

gular green. After a lengthy walk round to the far side of the clubhouse, the 3rd offers the best views over the airfield, though it is the most straightforward of the holes, up alongside the boundary fence to the highest point on the course.

Most golfers will fancy their chances of getting on the 4th green in two with the hole running gently downhill over crisp heathland turf. In the distance a wind sock indicates not only the likely effect of the wind but also the best line. The second shot, however, needs to curl round slightly behind the clubhouse before fading gently onto the green, invitingly contoured in a corner of the course.

There is trouble aplenty through the back of the 5th, though few will overhit into the prevailing wind even from such an elevated tee. From the tee the views are splendidly panoramic, yet the hole itself appears dull and pedestrian. Wrong! The green is down in a saucer of its own, gathering the perfectly struck tee shot, and with four finely positioned bunkers awaiting the shot which drifts away from its intended line.

It is not uncommon on 9-hole layouts occasionally to provide alternative greens for the first and second circuits of the course. At Avro the 6th and 15th greens are 140 yards apart, the former a genuine par-5, the latter a

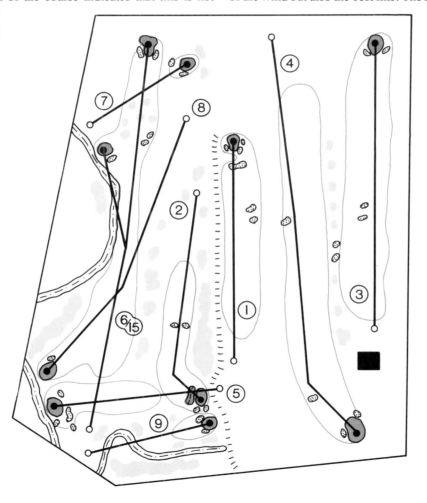

medium-length par-4. Both are good holes, the most intriguing on the course. In each case the drive is made towards a bend in the fairway where a fence (and its associated out-of-bounds) closes in uncomfortably from the left. On the second time round the pitch is then made over low trees and a bunker, avoiding a ditch on the left, to the shallowest of raised greens, only 17 yards across. On the first circuit, however, a long second shot must be played over, through, or around those trees and then over a couple of bunkers set into a ridge to leave a tight pitch to a tricky green raised up above bunkers left and right, narrowing the entrance considerably.

Only a pitch of immaculate length climbs to the ledge green on the 7th, alongside which the 8th tee looks out invitingly over the 6th fairway which must be played now in the opposite direction. Again the Curzon Park course at Chester is brought to mind (specifically the 7th hole), though this particular hole dog-legs gently to the right to the most generous green on the course. From a spot down in the wetlands beyond the 6th tee the final hole is played to a green under the escarpment alongside the 2nd, the major hazard being the out-of-bounds fence awaiting the shot that drifts away to the right. 9-hole layouts may have their limitations,

but so often they seem to pack into those nine holes as much character as an average 18-hole course.

Card of the course:

1.	293 yards	par 4		10.	293 yards	par 4
2.	287	4		11.	300	4
3.	389	4		12.	389	4
4.	511	5		13.	511	5
5.	220	3		14.	220	3
6.	525	5		15.	383	4
7.	155	3		16.	155	3
8.	390	4		17.	390	4
9.	167	3		18.	167	3
Out:	2937 yards	par 35				
In:	2808 yards	par 34				
Total:	5745 yards	par 69			s.s.s. 68	

Right: the 18th at Bidston

Bidston

6140 yards; par 70; s.s.s. 69

The course at Bidston first came into being because of over-crowding on the Warren links, that admirable municipal course on high ground overlooking the Promenade at Wallasey. That was back in 1913, 9 holes being played. From 1925 18 holes were available and they served the club well until the M53 interfered with things back in the late '70s with, it seems, some loss of character. What is left, after rearrangement, is perhaps slightly congested in the area of the clubhouse but, in the wind which habitually blows in this exposed area, not quite the joy-ride one might expect from a cursory glance from on high, passing at great speed on the motorway.

There is a new entrance to the club, a little lane leading off the dual-carriageway, and it gives an early introduction to the rivers and ditches defining the boundaries of play. The land is flat, the turf springy, the wind insistent, and one could almost be in the Fens. To these are added the additional threats of a railway, that most traditional of seaside companions – working, at that – and white posts, littering the landscape, informing the player of innumerable internal out-of-bounds.

Bidston teases from the start with a short – very short – par-4, but one on which the over-ambitious can easily perish in a pond on the right, out-of-bounds on the left, and a big bunker in the middle. The green nestles in an embankment high on which stands the 2nd tee, the green only a push-shot away, yet the other side of a deep and ruinous ditch. The 3rd pits a railway, left, against bunkers, right, with the additional peril of white posts entering play

in both directions on this piece of ground, the 4th running back parallel to a tiny green with the narrowest of entrances between bunkers and a stand of stunted trees on the right.

Reducing the 7th from a short par-5 to a long par-4 increases the player's awareness of the proximity of the stream to the left (and of the tiny area of green available to hold the longest of approach shots). It is good practice for the spiteful 8th, its drive needing to clear a hedge and ditch, yet not carry into the pond which so threatened the 1st. Even after a decent drive the second shot must carry a good deal of rolling ground, avoid a bunker on the right and a hollow to the left, yet pull up short of the trees which back the green or, *monstrum horribile*, the watery grave in wait beyond.

The card indicates a good variety of length of hole and, given the exposed nature of the course, only a mile inland from the sea, the wind will ensure a lively round despite the flattish ground. In any conditions the 15th will cause some concern with its deviously sunken green round to the left behind a shoulder of land and with a reach of The Fender only just through the back, beyond the marker post. So commences the pernicious finish, with a testing little shot over an S-bend of river to reach the refuge of the 16th green.

While the 17th may offer a breather on the drive, its green is hard to hold, a modest target beyond custodial bunkers. The final hole enjoys the benefits of ample bunkering.

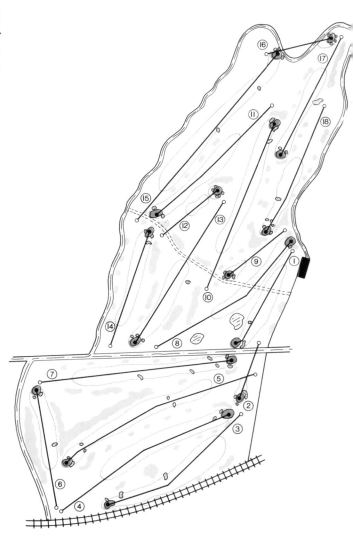

Card of the course:				
1.	268 yards	par 4	10. 439 yards	par 4
2.	144	3	11. 398	4
3.	367	4	12. 179	3
4.	410	4	13. 409	4
5.	509	5	14. 302	4
6.	300	4	15. 514	5
7.	462	4	16. 164	3
8.	427	4	17. 326	4
9.	176	3	18. 346	4
Out:	3063 yards	par 35		
In:	3077 yards	par 35		
Total:	6140 yards	par 70	s.s.s. 69	

Birchwood

6727 yards; par 71; s.s.s. 73

Pebble Beach, Pine Valley, Gleneagles — names of golf courses can be most evocative as well as practically descriptive. (I often think how appropriate the name, Western Gailes, is for an exposed links on the Ayrshire coast!). It would be misleading to expect Birchwood to live up to its name: it will not be trees which destroy the card but, rather, water in abundance.

The course itself is found in the midst of a Science Park, just off the M62 (the roar of traffic reminds us of its proximity though there are no views of it from the course), a modern creation by the Irish architect, T.J.A. Macauley. The notably flat land with which he had to work could not have been immediately conducive to natural golf course construction. What he has built, then, might be equally at home in Florida, with alligators exchanged for moorhens, the speedy greens conforming to a USGA specification.

Unusually for a contemporary course it is not made up of two loops of nine holes each beginning and ending at the clubhouse. Rather, it is more in the nature of the old links courses running out and back on three separate tracts of land separated by a road. At first glance the course map shows a superficial similarity with the famous *Shepherd's Crook* of the Old Course at St Andrews, and the use of colourful names for the holes is entirely in the spirit of Turnberry or Gleneagles — and at all three courses a good many of the names are clearly fanciful! Birchwood's are taken from Bunyan.

It is interesting to note that a number of quite separate winter greens have been constructed, not being merely a mown area in the middle of the fairway. A permanent two-green system is common in Japan where different grasses are employed for winter and summer greens in order to cope with the climate. Clearly there is not room for this on every course and bunkering can be problematic but it might give more acceptable playing conditions for more golfers more of the year on one or two muddy or frost-bound courses. It is also interesting to observe how frequently the medal

tees at Birchwood are built some distance from the yellow ones, not only altering the angles of play and varying the wear and tear on the course but also ensuring that the big hitters who might be expected to frequent these tees do not run out of fairway on the many holes where a drain or stream cuts across the hole.

The start is gentle, water coming into play progressively more threateningly as the round evolves so that by the time the 5th green is reached it is no surprise to find a lake tight in on the left for the last 100 yards of the hole, its banks shored up with boarding in best Pete Dye style. By now, too, the greens have become more interesting, so, while I am not too sure what a *Forgetful Green* may be, I *am* sure it is not *forgettable*. Entitled, *Plain of Ease* and *The Hill Called Error*, the next two holes might be thought to have escaped from a Greek legend rather than *Pilgrim's Progress*.

To my taste the course moves up several gears when the road is crossed for a second time and Birchwood's *Loop* begins (further shades of St Andrews). The 8th is a striking par-5 with a tricky drive over a little ridge, narrow between young trees. Far ahead can be seen the green but directly in line is a stand of fine old pine trees over, round, or even through which the second shot must pass. Beyond, still 175 yards away, the ground rises steeply to the two-level green, kidney-shaped and curling round behind a bunker.

From its high tee the 9th, appropriately called *Prospect*, gives much cause for concern on the drive. Not only is it necessary to clear a stream but, on the left, a big lake must be avoided. The fairway narrows and bears left around this lake so there are no soft options for those who would prefer to get there in easy stages. The view over this part of the course from the houses on the right of the fairway must be enviable but their proximity greatly restricts the golfer's freedom.

From that 9th fairway there is a good view of the short hole to come, and of the lengthy carry over water needed to reach the gently raised green. In its way, though, it is something of a respite before the horrors of the *Valley of Humiliation*, the 11th. From the tee there is no inkling of its later ordeals, a drive it would seem that must simply make progress in the general direction of the distant green-keeper's house. But, little by little, the plot thickens as not one but two streams cut across the fairway, joined by a lake eating into the left of it. This double crossing is, in its way, similar to the formidable second shot required on the *Cardinal*, Prestwick's famous 3rd hole. Notices prominently displayed around these streams forbid golfers taking a pot-shot at the green until that second stream is crossed. The reason is presumably to reduce the insurance claims of the houses just to the right of the fairway, but it seems hard on those who have to lift out of the second stream under penalty and are then allowed only to chip to the other side thereby effectively incurring a second penalty stroke. However,

even if we are safely across the second stream in two, the pitch demanding, over a third part of the stream and past a little por into the bargain. The 11th is quite a hole!

The 12th asks little, but the 13th teases engagingly with chance to get into two lakes. How many of us can bring ourselve to be sensible and play the hole conservatively? To carry th fairway bunker on the direct line is possible – it is about 190 yard out – but trees and an out-of-bounds fence on the right are dange ously close and a second lake begins on the left just beyond th bunker. *Sic itur ad astra.*

The 5th green from the 13

And so, crossing the road for the last time, play returns to the [la]nd shared with the opening three holes. There is one horror still [to] come: the second shot on the 14th. For most of us this will be [w]ith a long iron or even wood and there is no alternative to flying [al]l the way to the putting surface, a lake (thankfully the last) [cr]eeping in from the left horribly close to the green, a tree and [o]ut-of-bounds stifling any thoughts of a right-hand route in. A big [m]ound through the back of the green suggests that this is where [th]e spectators might profitably bay for blood if ever the modern [gl]adiators brought their circus here — not forgetting, of course, that [o]ur Pro Derrick Cooper is associated with Birchwood.

There is still length, plenty of it, to come but the golf is plainer [fr]om here on. The wicked final green, with its vicious borrows, [m]ight prolong the torture, doing so under the unsympathetic eyes [of] those queuing to start their round on the 1st tee.

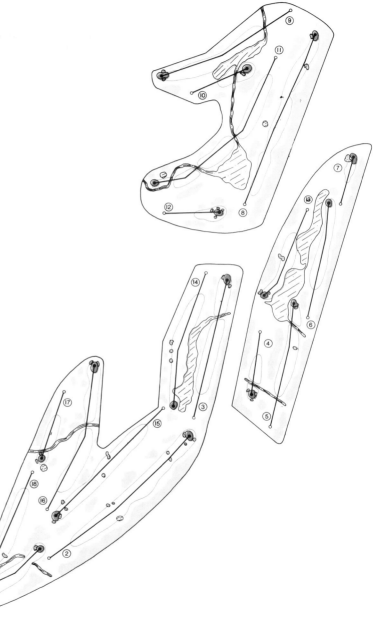

Card of the course:

1.	357 yards	par 4	10.	184 yards	par 3
2.	563	5	11.	569	5
3.	438	4	12.	168	3
4.	195	3	13.	301	4
5.	385	4	14.	423	4
6.	363	4	15.	466	4
7.	150	3	16.	464	4
8.	540	5	17.	217	3
9.	443	4	18.	501	5

Out:	3434 yards	par 36	
In:	3293 yards	par 35	
Total:	6727 yards	par 71	s.s.s. 73

Brackenwood

6285 yards; par 70; s.s.s. 70

Taking an illustrious place in the honourable company of Wirral municipals, Brackenwood encourages sturdy striking with its broad fairways and expansive layout, wide open to the wind. Several greens are uncommonly large for public golf, and many of them roll and swell significantly. At all levels, and from whichever tee play takes place, there is an encouraging variety in the lengths of the holes and the shot-making they demand.

Card of the course:					
1.	336 yards	par 4	10.	202 yards	par 3
2.	137	3	11.	343	4
3.	424	4	12.	561	5
4.	473	4	13.	190	3
5.	325	4	14.	409	4
6.	197	3	15.	331	4
7.	516	5	16.	433	4
8.	362	4	17.	293	4
9.	350	4	18.	403	4
Out:	3120 yards	par 35			
In:	3165 yards	par 35			
Total:	6285 yards	par 70		s.s.s. 70	

Bramall Park

6214 yards; par 70; s.s.s. 70

The more northerly of the two Bramhall courses, Bramall Park roams through gently wooded parkland bounded by the railway on one side, deep woodland on the second, and houses on the third side of an essentially triangular site. For all Bramall Park may be, in theory, a suburban course there are really only two holes on which it is possible to stray into neighbouring gardens, the first two holes. Those gardens are a part of the sort of houses into which one would be only too honoured to stray if only one had dressed correctly. There is a respectability about Bramall Park, and its surroundings in particular, which seems quaintly out of keeping with the informality of the BBC staff who have for many years been offered the shelter and succour of Five-Day Membership here. In this guise it has been one of my golfing homes on and off for the past thirteen years and not only have I grown immensely more attached to the place but also a little more respectful of its architectural merits – if one is going to be humiliated in public one may as well learn from the experience.

A stream dominates the 1st hole. With those big houses to the left and trees and a bunker to the right, the opening drive must be taken seriously and anything feeble or frail leaves a desperately risky second shot over the stream running at the bottom of a gully (at its widest and deepest just here into the bargain). I have in my time lost the short par-4 2nd to a 2-net-1! It offers hope to all players.

The real fun begins with the lengthy 6th, a genuine par-5. Tales are told of tigers reaching this green in two shots but I have never witnessed anything approaching it. Out-of-bounds runs all the way down the right side of the hole, entering the consciousness of the striker on every shot. Trees and a pit await the hooked drive. Bunkers, left and right, threaten the second shot. The third, which ordinarily may still be substantial, needs to be aimed at (or even phill of) a trench of a bunker running all down the left of the green. It takes courage to aim so far wide but there is a huge left-to-right break on the ball in front of the green.

The 7th is a tricky par-3 uphill across the slope, making it seem several clubs longer than the card suggests and making considerable demands on straightness. The 8th, too, always seems much longer than its measured yardage, for after a drive over, or just skirting, a cross bunker it takes a good deal of club to carry the stream (flowing through the gully shared with the 1st) to the green raised up on the far side. The 9th tee is far enough back to involve another river crossing.

The 10th and 11th are strenuous holes by any reckoning. Little or no roll seems forthcoming on the 11th drive meaning that it will take two Sunday best shots to reach the distant green perched up on a ledge. Most of us, indeed, have to take care that *our* two best shots do not finish in a line of cross-bunkers some 40 yards in front of the green. Trees to the left and a railway to the right can make a real mess of a score card at this point.

My hopes are always raised on the 14th, a par-5 but only just. The drive is inspiring over rolling fairway to pass a shoulder of land around which the hole bears right. Even if this is not cleared there is a good prospect of decent progress if a line is taken on a pair of poplar trees on the skyline. Beneath them a narrow, undulating green is raised between bunkers.

From here on the card looks manageable but there are pitfalls aplenty over the next three holes. On the 15th there is no alternative to hitting the green and sticking. Anything short or right will bumble off down the hill into thick rough, while missing on the left is likely to involve a desperate recovery pitch from a tight lie on well-trodden turf downhill over a ridge or bunkers onto the green at its narrowest.

A hook or pull from the 16th tee can leave no hope of reaching the green, with the second shot having to clear a wide depression (which I long to fill with water!) if it is to reach the tricky green angled across the line from right to left. Line from the tee is all important on the 17th, too. A hole of this length ought to be no

The 7th green

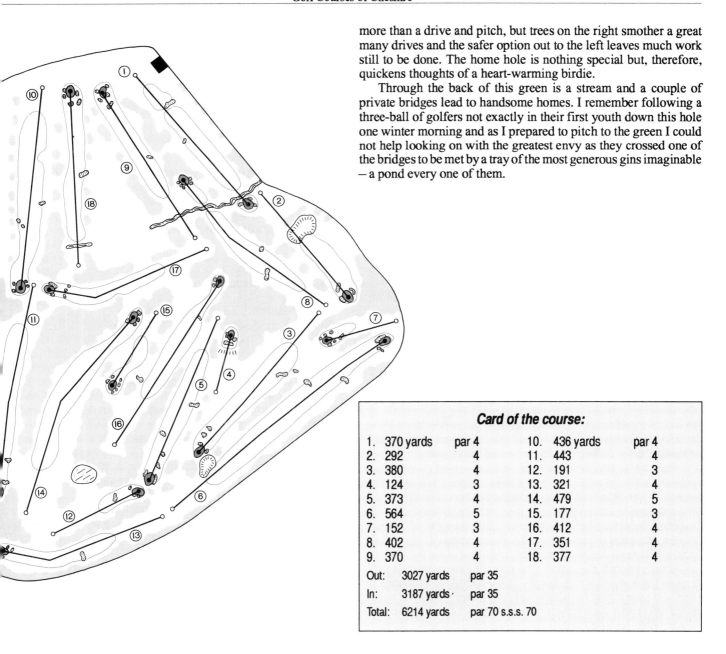

more than a drive and pitch, but trees on the right smother a great many drives and the safer option out to the left leaves much work still to be done. The home hole is nothing special but, therefore, quickens thoughts of a heart-warming birdie.

Through the back of this green is a stream and a couple of private bridges lead to handsome homes. I remember following a three-ball of golfers not exactly in their first youth down this hole one winter morning and as I prepared to pitch to the green I could not help looking on with the greatest envy as they crossed one of the bridges to be met by a tray of the most generous gins imaginable – a pond every one of them.

Card of the course:

1.	370 yards	par 4	10.	436 yards	par 4
2.	292	4	11.	443	4
3.	380	4	12.	191	3
4.	124	3	13.	321	4
5.	373	4	14.	479	5
6.	564	5	15.	177	3
7.	152	3	16.	412	4
8.	402	4	17.	351	4
9.	370	4	18.	377	4
Out:	3027 yards	par 35			
In:	3187 yards	par 35			
Total:	6214 yards	par 70 s.s.s. 70			

29

Bramhall

6280 yards; par 70; s.s.s. 70

The village of Bramhall is fortunate indeed to possess two golf courses of character, Bramall Park and Bramhall. While there are similarities they also differ sufficiently to generate a good deal of locker room debate about the comparative merits of both.

For sure, depressions characterise many holes at Bramhall and are apparent enough on the 1st hole, a sturdy opener which requires the drive to skirt a young plantation on the right or a long approach to draw to the left round a tree in the fairway and a generous pit to the front left of the green. The first four holes form a loop back to the clubhouse and then the 5th runs away alongside the railway. Its green is set amongst the conifers and there are bunkers in all the right places such as on the left of the drive (and therefore on the side away from the railway), further down more or less slap bang in the middle of the fairway, and on the front left of the green. Few amateurs will overshoot the green on a hole of this length, but if they do they will have to contend with a depression on the left.

The club's entertaining 70th anniversary booklet chronicles in detail the trials and tribulations of the acquisition and loss of various tracts of outlying land, particularly in the years between the two World Wars. It is fascinating to see the piecemeal manner in which a golf course can arrive at the form in which we know it. It frequently explains why one or two holes can seem to have a character quite different from the rest of the course.

The 7th is full of individual character, leading off into the country with a tricky drive to a narrow, leaning fairway. It turns sharply right about 240 yards out past a bunker set into the hill and, from the tee at least, apparently unavoidable. If it is successfully avoided, however, the next shot must clear a couple of substantial fairway bunkers beyond which the ground drops away slightly to a rather flatter piece of fairway from which it is not too difficult to pitch accurately to the green. That green is narrow, angled slightly across the line, breaking sharply to the right, and separated from the 12th green only by a series of little hummocks — an accurate pitch being mandatory, therefore. Distinctive qualities are readily discernible, too, on the 8th, a fine right-hand dog-leg needing a big, accurate drive to give a sight of the green protected by tree on the right and by a sizeable gully in front.

The longer irons, the *spoons* and *brassies* can probably b rested on the back nine, though the card shows it to be only 7 yards shorter, the 13th alone calling for really stout hitting. Give good drives only medium irons will be needed for the par-4s whil the one-shot holes are both gentle drop-shots. The condition, must be said, is a good drive and that is particularly so on the 10th Here the tee shot is slightly uphill (over a stream and hedge in i early flight) towards a mound in which a bunker has been set. pond lurks just beyond. The hole then swings to the right (almo all the dog-legs are right-handed at Bramhall) to a kidney-shape green handsomely set off against the trees.

It is a modest stroll through the trees and across the 18 fairway to find the 11th tee. A line of trees separates the fairwa from the 17th but it is a lone tree a couple of hundred yards o which determines whether or not there will be any sight of th green. The gentle downhill approach must clear a cluster of bun kers around and in front of the green. Beyond it the mild 12th dro through an avenue of trees to the well-bunkered green shared wit the 7th.

The golf hereabouts is notably rural, pasture-land immediate over the fence, the hills of the Peak District beckoning not f beyond. That fence is a threat on the right for much of the earlie part of the long 13th, trees on the left forming a complementar hazard.

The 17th is both handsome and bold, demanding a carry ove a gully with the drive and then a solid thump with the approach t clear a grassy hollow immediately in front of the domed green. Th 18th is an amiable way to return home, as long as a pond, dark an deep on the right, and three cross-bunkers in range of big drive are successfully negotiated.

Opposite: Bramhall, the 7th ho

Card of the course:

1.	400 yards	par 4	10.	377 yards	par 4
2.	314	4	11.	410	4
3.	167	3	12.	157	3
4.	336	4	13.	537	5
5.	411	4	14.	150	3
6.	207	3	15.	323	4
7.	500	5	16.	377	4
8.	400	4	17.	375	4
9.	440	4	18.	393	4

Out:	3175 yards	par 35		
In:	3105 yards	par 35		
Total:	6280 yards	par 70	s.s.s. 70

This page: course map and card for Bramhall

Bromborough

6650 yards; par 72; s.s.s. 73

There has been a golf club at Bromborough since the first decade of the century, and its parkland layout did adequate service until, like so many courses in this book, the coming of a motorway threatened to end civilisation as known there. As so often, a virtue was created out of necessity, new land acquired and a completely new course designed.

In the main the golf is that of wide open spaces, broad skies, far horizons and unspoiled views, but there is a change of character starting at the 9th when the play moves to a tightly wooded stretch behind the clubhouse. But let us tee off on the other side of the car park, uphill, not excessively so, past a couple of prominent bunkers to the big 1st green close by the hedge. The beginning is welcoming, as is the sweep of the 2nd fairway sprinkled at intervals with bunkers to trap the wayward drives of golfers of all strengths. The aim, though, is in clearing a gully to reach the green and, as this interrupts a good number of fairways to come, we may as well take the opportunity of zeroing our sights.

A fair clout is needed to pass over it cleanly from the back tee on the 3rd, too, an otherwise generously broad par-5 returning us to the top of the course and the first short hole. Only 151 yards long from the very back, the 4th is, none the less, tight with a hedge close in on the right, umpteen bunkers and, most visibly, a large pond surrounded by trees to be cleared. The 5th drive is made out over a further stretch of water towards two rows of bunkers forcing play over to the left. Then a long, slow fade is required to pierce first the gap between two distant trees and then that between a pair of bunkers constricting the entrance to an already narrow green. On the strength of the mauling it gave me I would not quibble with the stroke rating of this hole – 1.

A feature of the par-3s at Bromborough is their capacity to make you think, to force you to shape your shot according to the particular tee in use, the wind speed and direction, and so on. The 6th is in essence a moderate prod over a gentle valley and half a dozen bunkers yet, watching others play the hole from the relative security of the 13th green, I was conscious of just how frequently the sound of ball on wood indicates the additional threat posed by the surrounding trees.

The 7th and 8th make plainish, if lengthy, progress along the perimeter before the 9th tee and the sudden change of mood I mentioned earlier. A long-iron may be the prudent club to take here in order to clear the pond in front, stop short of the next minor chasm and find a position from which the green is not obscured by tall trees. The second shot is very much a dummy run for the tee shot on the 10th which is a sterling all-or-nothing hole between trees, over a deep valley and two or three bunkers, with the added imperative of ensuring that the ball does not roll off the back of the green into a sunken wilderness. The putting surface, thank heaven, is generous and not too exacting. It must be a wicked alternative starting point.

I suppose it is possible to generalise by saying that the short par-5s here are rather more strategic than the longer ones, but that is how it should be, the 11th being quite narrow with trees on both sides, a wild valley off to the left, and a boggy pit around which the fairway moves to the right. I should not like to have to play too long an approach to the green, either, with hedges rapidly encroaching on both sides.

There should not be too much heartache on the 12th and 13th, and the 14th, despite its length, is not overly daunting, that is provided the drive manages to find that elusive spot which is far enough right to open up the green yet not so far right that it puts it out of reach. The finish from here is vigorous but entirely fair.

On the 15th it pays to drive down alongside the 2nd green to give a view of the green round to the right past a lofty tree, the second shot passing over the same gully which made life so exciting on the 2nd. The short 16th continues the uphill journey to a green surrounded by bunkers, the most voracious of which is a menacing specimen to the front left.

During my early morning forays to the furthest corners of Cheshire it was inevitable that I should see more than a few dawn foxes, of which the one crossing Bromborough's 17th fairway at 8.25 a.m. was by far the latest in the day, and this not in darkest winter but mid-August. Even without the handsome red gentleman the hole is attractive, running gently downhill for two thirds of its length, giving a fine panoramic view of the rest of the course as it does so. The main problem is in deciding whether or not the ubiquitous gully can be cleared sufficiently with the second shot to leave a gentle pitch to the green, failure resulting in a long blind approach very possibly from a hanging or soggy lie. It is then apparent just why the marker post behind the green is so very tall.

While the 18th runs parallel to the 9th, it is both longer and yet, more humane, with no watery graves waiting, and only a pair of trees to be avoided at the lowest point of the fairway. A long approach shot, however, can easily drift off to into the long bunker zealously guarding the entire right side of the green.

The 10th at Bromborough

Card of the course:

1.	312 yards	par 4	10.	160 yards	par 3
2.	427	4	11.	486	5
3.	535	5	12.	354	4
4.	151	3	13.	335	4
5.	435	4	14.	457	4
6.	176	3	15.	448	4
7.	540	5	16.	157	3
8.	409	4	17.	486	5
9.	383	4	18.	419	4

Out:	3348 yards	par 36
In:	3302 yards	par 36
Total:	6650 yards	par 72	s.s.s. 73

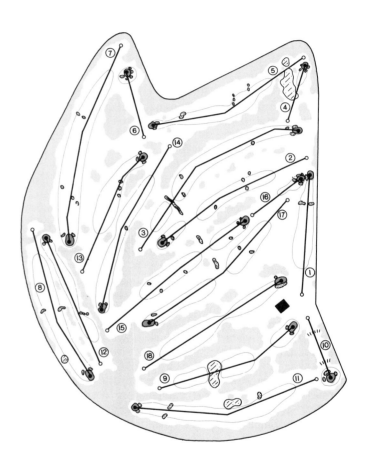

Caldy

6675 yards; par 72; s.s.s. 73

Some years ago, in an attempt to cure some persistent malaise such as shanking or topping, I took a few lessons from a ken-speckled professional at one of Cheshire's senior clubs. We fell to comparing notes on the different courses we knew, trading 600-yard par-5s for 240-yard par-3s.

"But have you ever played Caldy?" he asked.

My respect for his wise judgement led me to make a number of visits to Caldy in the late 1970s and early '80s, easily sufficient to acquire a high regard for the course. Even since then it has changed, with new 17th and 18th holes, but this is a place of constant evolution, beginning in the early years of the century with 9-holes laid out down by the beach following the advice of the Hoylake professional, John Morris. In those days trains on a single-track branch line trundled down this coast and in due course further holes were constructed inland of the railway, holes themselves changed many times before, during, and after the last war. The course we play today is (the 17th and 18th apart) that which was formalised when the clubhouse down near the beach was abandoned (about twenty years ago) in favour of a new structure about as far away from the sea as is possible on this site. Caldy now enjoys the advantages of three totally different kinds of terrain: downland, almost heathland, up near the clubhouse, parkland down towards houses to the north, and something approaching genuine linksland on that original tract on the far side of the railway.

Play begins with a stout par-4, a double dog-leg no less, running first downhill to the left, then uphill to the right, and immediately two of Caldy's characteristics are made abundantly apparent: this is a spacious layout with plenty of spare ground and little likelihood of finding refuge on an adjoining fairway, and rough here is just that, deep, grasping, soul-destroying stuff putting a great premium on straight hitting. As well as the dog-legs the hole possesses further defences in the little ridge that gives the green

the appearance of being much nearer than it is in fact, and the triangular shape of the green itself. There is no need of bunkers, yet it is a hole worthy of Ganton.

The 2nd is not long – none of the short holes is – and, therefore, runs to devious humps and hollows off the green and one or two tricky borrows on it. It has a wonderfully old-fashioned feel, yet can only date from 1929, when the ground inland of the railway was acquired, or later. In those days were they Wirral Railway 0-4-4 or 0-6-4 tank engines or Great Central refugees (courtesy of the Cheshire Lines Committee) clanking down the line from Hoylake to Hooton? One can almost sense their steamy presence to this day as the bridge is crossed leading to the 3rd tee, and here the golf moves into top gear.

From the back tee there is a huge carry over the 10th green and rough to a fairway moving all the time downhill to the right towards the immediate hazard of a couple of bunkers (and the sea in the far distance). Past the bunkers the fairway swings further to the right to a handsome green perched on a plateau above the beach with a pond to the right and Formby-like firs to the left. With the poignant cry of waders it is hard to resist a silent humming of "Mary, Call the Cattle Home" as a stretch of three holes running the length of the beach is begun. Each time we play these holes we should also offer up a silent prayer of thanksgiving that the club here has had the courage to tackle the constant erosion of the coast-line which, left to its own devices, might well, by now, have reduced these holes to additional mooring for fishing boats.

The 4th is no more than a drive-and-pitch, but the drive must avoid finishing on the beach or (almost as final) in the rough, and the pitch needs notable precision, the fairway narrowing towards the green, itself surrounded by six bunkers, wind blown trees, and a nasty little pond. Then it is genuine seaside stuff with the 5th fairway bouncing over crinkled turf, creeping ever nearer the beach as the hole develops, finally ending at a narrow green, well nkered particularly on the right. The 6th could almost have been fted from Pebble Beach with a long carry needed on the drive wards the beach and a wicked second shot over a ditch to a allow green at the far end of the course. It is no surprise to find at this hole rates as Stroke 1.

At 557-yards the 7th is, from the white tees, the longest hole, it from the yellow tees things are very different and, I suggest, easier. From the back, few will need to do more than keep out the hedge with their drives, and the pit and bunker on the right ith their seconds. Then the pitch flows gently past trees on the ght and a big mound on the left. Taking the 70-yard advantage of ing the yellow tee implies that the long second shot will be quired to land in the narrow neck of land between those trees and e hillock. It is a good hole, none the less, and for me the more markable for a little contribution I made, unwittingly, to nature nservation at just past 7.00 a.m.. From that hedge darted a rabbit, common enough occurrence here, and a few moments later a fox merged, about 15 feet from me. He took one look at me and ected to forgo breakfast in favour of the safety of the under-owth. May I hope that members whose drives finish in a rabbit rape on this hole do not curse me too loudly?

e 3rd hole

A gentle drop shot from the hillock finds the narrow 8th green surrounded by all manner of humps and hollows and a ring of bunkers. The 9th is very attractive, with a drive past a spinney (and a pond, too, for that matter) before the fairway bends significantly to the right running in to a narrow green set off against another spinney and protected by bunkers on the right and a pond just through the back of the green. Reluctantly we leave this uplifting part of the course with a straightforward short hole over the pond to a little green just below the railway bridge. There is an enormous temptation not to cross that bridge at all but instead to sneak round the eight holes from the 3rd just one more time, like that last glass of wine left in the bottom of the bottle: it will not be quite so good tomorrow, will it?

Returning inland, the 11th is almost claustrophobic in comparison with its predecessors. The drive is tight, with the fairway curving sharply right past a stand of tall trees, yet further trees on the left and one actually in the fairway itself insist that the drive is both long and unerringly straight. As the fairway proceeds to the right it crosses two deep hollows before unwinding to the left uphill to a green that is very difficult to locate from any distance. It goes without saying that it is heavily bunkered.

The 12th takes us off into the parkland, less atmospheric holes but testing enough. The 12th, for instance, with its out-of-bounds

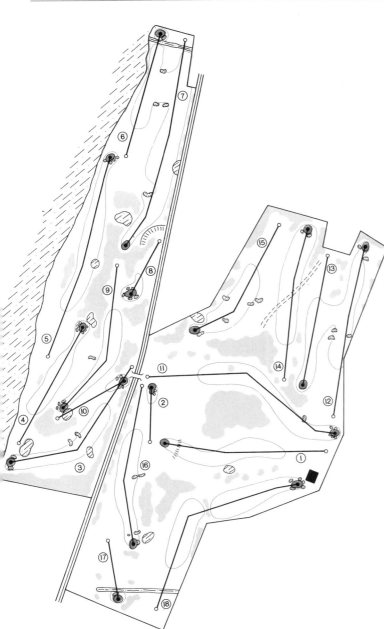

fence close in on the right and the rough allowed to grow in to narrow the fairway on the approach to the green is tough enough to rate as the 2nd Stroke Hole. A line of hummocks interrupts the 14th fairway, and the 15th dog-legs very sharply to the right around a host of bunkers, but the spirits of the old-fashioned golfer are lifted again on the 16th tee as play returns to the wide open spaces and the singing of the skylark. After a drive alongside the old railway the fairway moves gently left past a curious sandstone "rubbing stone" which is probably a more unpredictable hazard than either of the bunkers on the left of the cunningly domed green.

It is target golf on the 17th, a ditch in front of the green taking care of anything dropping short on this steeply downhill hole, before the shoulders are opened for a last time on the unusual 18th. The drive is obvious enough, needing to make the high ground in the distance on a line given by a marker post. Big hitters seem to have no advantage here, for extra length or an attempt to cut the corner will only lead to an uncertain lie at the bottom of a valley. Three trees still grow there and most of us will be hitting our second shots over them trying to make as much progress as possible as the fairway climbs gently but persistently towards the green. The ominous presence of white posts on the right for the length of this hole indicate that this is no place to develop a late slice. No fewer than five greenside bunkers await those of us whose waywardness is less drastic.

It is not hard to see why that wise professional thought so highly of Caldy and why so many championships at both county and national level have been played here.

Card of the course:

1.	405 yards	par 4	10.	188 yards	par 3
2.	156	3	11.	528	5
3.	389	4	12.	437	4
4.	342	4	13.	355	4
5.	538	5	14.	393	4
6.	377	4	15.	346	4
7.	557	5	16.	416	4
8.	157	3	17.	149	3
9.	411	4	18.	531	5
Out:	3332 yards	par 36			
In:	3343 yards	par 36			
Total:	6675 yards	par 72		s.s.s. 73	

Carden Park

6828 yards; par 72; s.s.s. 73

The south-west part of Cheshire is something very special, a corner of England as unspoiled today as it was at the turn of the century — rolling hills, sandstone cliffs, idyllic villages, handsome ancient churches, huge dairy farms, a number of historic houses with their vast estates, and several of England's oldest landed families. One such was descended from John Leche who was granted lands at Carden as long ago as 1346. His son became leech or surgeon to King Edward III and for six successive centuries the family lived around Carden, described by Herbert Hughes as "an historic site and commanding an incomparably beautiful vista of wood and water and hill. Here the Broxton ridge of the Beeston-Peckforton-Bickerton heights and Carden Cliff provide the backdrop and in the foreground lie the park lake and beyond that the valley of the Dee and the Welsh uplands." In the early 16th-Century Carden Hall was built, and according to Ormerod's definitive *History of the County Palatine* it was a "venerable mansion, embossed in timber, and presenting a very perfect specimen of the ancient timber buildings of the county." The Leches prospered, served their county faithfully as High Sheriffs, and Carden received the noblest guests: King George V visited while still Prince of Wales and the Empress of Austria stayed at the Hall on a number of occasions. But on 16th September 1912 all was changed irrevocably. A fire destroyed the house, a fire of such ferocity that even many of the house guests' jewels in the great iron safe were melted.

Although the house had gone, the estate remained, partly farmed, a good deal of it frequent host to the traditional English field sports. Now with a new owner, there are no fewer than fourteen sports on offer at Carden Park, each at a level commensurate with the noble standing of the estate. One of these, naturally enough, is golf, in the form of a Golf Academy, 9-hole short course and splendid 18-hole course of championship proportions with the added bonus of a staff headed by John Garner, ex-Ryder Cup golfer and, as coach to the victorious Solheim Cup team amongst others, one of the most respected teachers in the sport.

The course was opened at the end of August 1993, the very last of the 83 I visited, yet right from the beginning the fairways are lush, the greens immaculate, there is an established feel and the playing condition impressive in a course so youthful. Fairway watering, still a rarity in these parts, is installed. Arboriculturists will purr with delight at the variety of stately trees through and around which the course roams and inevitably that implies as much delight for the botanist and ornithologist even if those of us whose sight is diminishing will have to make do with the more visible charms of the pheasant which strut about the whole estate in such plentiful and tempting numbers.

The best golf course architects take risks, going for the most adventurous use of the available resources to create those holes which remain vividly in the mind long after play has finished. It helps, of course, if you have the abundance and variety of natural features Alan Higgins had at his disposal when he laid out Carden Park. He might have crammed a course of 10,000 yards into the space but has restricted himself to 6,828 yards, in the process ensuring a good balance between hole lengths. There are long and short par-3s, par-4s from 278 to 461 yards, a short par-5 on which many of us will hope for a birdie and three on which we will be flat out to get there in regulation at all. To this constant change of pace is added the mix of open parkland, water, coniferous forest and a sandstone cliff. When, as surely they must, the giants of the game come to Carden Park it will be the simplest of matters to provide them with their own special tees unthinkable yards behind the present white plates.

Higgins's originality and confidence is displayed as early as the 1st hole, a gentle uphill par-3. There is a theory that a par-4 must begin a round to enable play to flow. As there has been no rush to expunge the par-3s which commence proceedings at Royal Lytham and Royal Mid-Surrey there are clearly distinguished precedents. His next innovation is to bring into play a ha-ha, that archetypal feature of every English country house estate. This walled ditch must be cleared on the 2nd drive, though the greater problem may be in keeping out of a number of ponds on the left, a bunker on the right assisting the process.

Carden's greens are, for the most part, of considerable area. On the 3rd we see the advantage of this luxury, it being perfectly feasible to play unhindered to a pin position on the left and jolly difficult to attack the flag when the hole is cut on the high ground behind the two bunkers on the right. A third bunker at the back adds to the excitement.

We are out in the wide open spaces here, with broad views deep into the Welsh Marches, but it may need only a single tree to determine the strategy of a complete hole. One specimen not 100 yards in front of the 4th tee has that effect. Those with the game of a Nicklaus might hit the ball sufficiently high and long to contemplate going straight over it. The rest of us must calculate our angles to go round, hoping to find a central position in the fairway from which to hit an exacting second shot over ponds and between trees to find the distant green on a plateau above a vineyard, astonishingly flourishing so far north and all the more agreeable for it. Over a little road, the 5th continues downhill, its second shot played over bumpy ground at best and a prominent pond if things are less propitious from the tee.

Below: the 12th hole

In conversation with Alan Higgins I was delighted to learn that he will go to extreme lengths if necessary to avoid uprooting trees if at all possible. Many architects would have removed the lone tree standing proudly in the middle of the 6th fairway, three-quarters of the way to the green, and dominating proceedings. As the way to play a par-5 is to think back from green to tee perhaps I should start at the green, which is guarded by a single bunker over which all normal shots must pass to reach the putting surface. 100 yards short of that is the famous tree, therefore at the length of most players' good second shots. Serious thought must then be given to whether or not to attempt to carry the tree, lay up sufficiently short to get over it next time, or try to squeeze past it on one side or the other. In turn, the answer to that depends on the placing of the drive which is further complicated by hedges intruding first on the right and then on the left. For good measure it is quite possible to ruin the whole thing by slicing out-of-bounds on any or all shots.

The next two holes test our long hitting, both near the limits of their par, the 8th uphill to boot. A stream crosses this hole but that is perhaps not as serious a threat as the depressions short and left of the green waiting to thwart those who failed to take sufficient club. Back over the road the 9th quickens thoughts of a stroke to be gained, starting from a tee down by the vineyard, running over a narrow, hog's-back fairway to a green sheltering behind twin bunkers.

But we are dawdling! The real excitement is yet to come and the 10th gets us there leniently. Walk up a little woodland path beyond and the view from the 11th tee shows the golf to be both overwhelmingly beautiful and severely penal. We are actually on top of the sandstone outcrop, tall conifers to either side and the narrowest of fairways in front. The prudent will take a mid-iron from the tee to avoid the single fairway bunker the purpose of which is less to punish and more to prevent the unduly vigorous shot from bounding off down the chasm which rends the fairway asunder just beyond. A wedge will then suffice to climb to the little hilltop green in a clearing in the trees. It is well beyond my dwindling powers to drive this green, but I should dearly love to be present when it is done!

Equally handsome, the 12th returns downhill through the trees to a green on the far side of a couple of generous bunkers. It is then back out into the open for a couple of holes stretching almost 2/3 of a mile between them. On the 13th all depends on the drive's

successfully skirting the trees on the left if the second shot is to clear the ha-ha. Even then there are bunkers aplenty and watery horrors on the right, shared with the 2nd. From the next tee the prospect is deceptive, seemingly a long beat uphill. Get to the top of the hill, though, and the fairway turns left through 90-degrees to a green low down and protected by a tree on the left and a bunker on the right. Next time round you are wiser and contemplate cutting the corner, at which point you become very aware of just how tall and forbidding is the stand of trees on the left over which your ball must surely fly.

Trees are at least as threatening on the 15th, narrowing the fairway abruptly at the length of a reasonable drive. Then it is steeply uphill through the narrowest of gaps to a thin, angled, hilltop green, its three bunkers, like that on the 11th, serving as much to prevent the overhit ball from disappearing for ever down the steep slopes to the right as to penalise. A little way beyond, the high, platform tee of the 16th looks out, once again, over rural Cheshire and onto the little green on the far side of deep bunkers and alarmingly close to an out-of-bounds fence.

Enjoy the thrill of the 17th as it is now, if you can, for it calls for another of those tigerish drives high and long over an immense tree. For the benefit of the less accomplished I suspect a less demanding teeing ground may yet be considered or a branch or two removed from the tree, though I sincerely hope neither is found to be necessary. To complicate matters the fairway tosses like an ocean swell and the green itself is perched on a lofty plateau adequately protected by further big trees on the right and the sandstone cliff to the left. At the far end of it is the final tee, again graced with the loveliest of views and, for once, not too intimidating a tee shot. The pitch, however, is compelled to clear a pool and avoid bunkers to the left front. The overzealous will find that there is a further bunker, deeper and steeper-faced than the others, Muirfield-like, through the back of the green on the right.

A lengthy essay, perhaps the longest in the book, but for me it was immensely satisfying to end this pilgrimage, which had begun round the corner at Wilmslow in March, with a visit to Cheshire's newest course, Carden Park, already to be numbered amongst its finest.

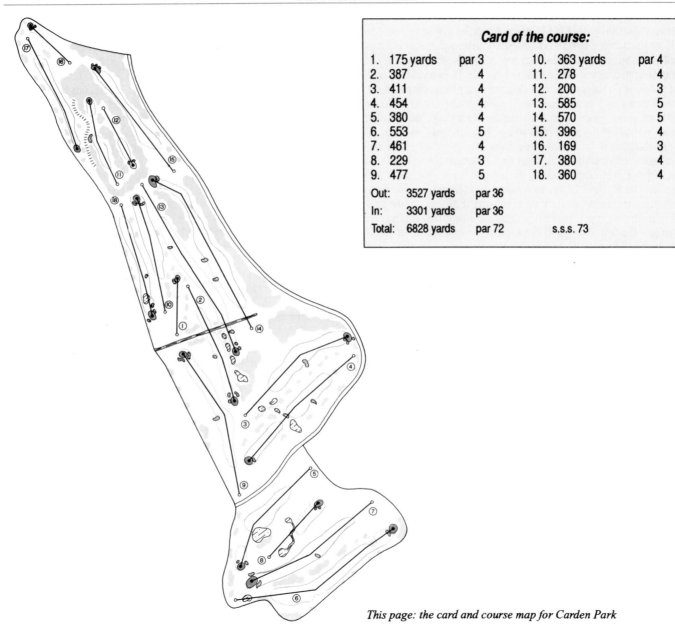

Card of the course:

1.	175 yards	par 3	10.	363 yards	par 4
2.	387	4	11.	278	4
3.	411	4	12.	200	3
4.	454	4	13.	585	5
5.	380	4	14.	570	5
6.	553	5	15.	396	4
7.	461	4	16.	169	3
8.	229	3	17.	380	4
9.	477	5	18.	360	4

Out:	3527 yards	par 36		
In:	3301 yards	par 36		
Total:	6828 yards	par 72	s.s.s. 73	

This page: the card and course map for Carden Park

Cheadle

5006 yards; par 64; s.s.s. 65

.f my assumptions are correct I think this must be the second ldest surviving club in the county (founded 1885), and it will have een established on its present site for 100 years in 1995. Laid out, pparently, by R. Renouf (a relation of "Tommy"?) on a very onstricted site there is, never the less, absolutely no skimped eeling, despite a crossing hole or two, and, surprisingly, rarely a nse of being overlooked by adjoining housing. Instead, the emories that one takes away are those of the magnificent avenues f trees through which the fairways stretch, of the little stream hich enters play on no fewer than six of the nine holes. I shall lso treasure the memory of two of the boldest urban foxes I have et encountered who stood about 20-feet from me in the rough

beside the 3rd tee to watch my drive (for once actually worth watching) and reappeared over on the 5th green as I played to it, remaining on the adjoining 9th tee as I putted out (this time rather ineffectually).

The trees, even those planted in the lifetime of the present course, are tall, handsome and splendidly varied and they provide an inspiring strait along which to drive, climbing just a little, on the 1st hole. The downhill pitch might easily bumble through onto the neighbouring 7th green. Then it is time for a first encounter with the stream, the 2nd being a short hole across it, narrow between the trees, to a sloping green.

The 5th hole

The 3rd will be familiar to regular travellers on the Cheadle-Cheadle Hulme road, clearly visible through the gaps in the hedge and an attractive hole it is, despite the eminent possibilities of driving out-of-bounds. The well-bunkered green is located in a corner next to the hedge and is not one to be missed.

A couple of big trees dominate proceedings on the 4th. Can we avoid driving behind them and thus blocking ourselves out for the approach to the green? Then, after the seductive and exceedingly short 5th, there is another splendid long two-shotter, the 6th. The question here is simply whether or not we can clear the stream with our second shots.

Two consecutive tees side by side suggest a little work study (on social occasions only, of course!), driving from both tees before putting out on the 7th green banked up at a rakish angle on the far side of the stream. The 8th would get my vote as favourite hole, though there are a couple of close challengers. The drive is quite tight between trees, over the stream, it hardly need be said, with something of a pit amongst the trees on the right. Then it is more or less blind over three cross-bunkers so thorough in their duty that there is absolutely no way around them: you *have* to go over. They are some way short of the green and, for that reason, not quite as intimidating as they look. The round ends with quite a gentle par-3 over a cross-bunker, but there is plenty of room on the far side and already the 1st tee calls, that fine tree-lined fairway beckoning irresistibly.

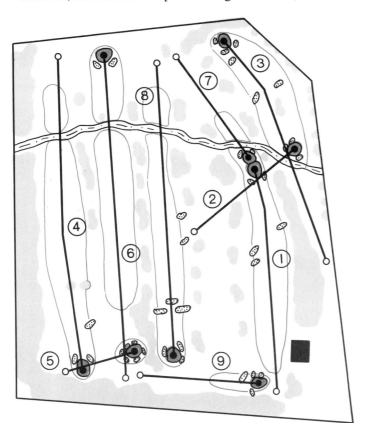

Card of the course:

1.	306 yards	par 4
2.	173	3
3.	335	4
4.	421	4
5.	95	3
6.	440	4
7.	176	3
8.	398	4
9.	159	3
Out:	2503 yards	par 32
Total (18 holes):	5006 yards	par 64 s.s.s. 65

Chester

6508 yards; par 72; s.s.s. 71

o many of us living in the east of the county Chester conjures images of its Cathedral, City Walls, the Rows, Summer Music estival and its Roman remains. There are marvellous views of the ty from the high ground around the clubhouse of Chester Golf ub and a splendid view of the race course from the car park. The ad leading to the club weaves its way through some of Curzon rk's most impressive houses. Yet Chester is not without its dustry and from the higher ground of the golf course there is mple opportunity to assess its scale, running it would seem almost ntinuously from Chester to the Welsh Hills. Like a number of

more famous courses, Chester also keeps company with a railway for a couple of holes early in the round.

The course is laid out on two tracts of flat ground, one up by the clubhouse, the other down by the canalised river, most of the holes running in roughly parallel lines separated by trees. If that sounds a little routine, even dull, it must be added that a number of holes make very considerable use of the cliff dividing the higher and lower ground and, hardly surprisingly, these are the holes which are most likely to remain in the memory.

Below: the 12th hole

As early as the 2nd hole the cliff makes its first appearance, quite spectacularly, with a tumbling drive over a little ditch to a curving fairway. It bends round a copse alongside the railway, the green being tucked away in a corner behind the trees. For almost everyone the approach to it is blind over those trees and very exacting.

After such excitement the next few holes seem very flat, as indeed they are, but from the long par-5 4th, with its charming concave saucer green, three holes run in a line alongside the river bank. The last of these, the 6th, reintroduces us to the cliff. The drive itself is simple enough but then the second shot must bear sharp right over a plantation to land in the narrowest part of the fairway. From there the pitch is steeply uphill to an undulating plateau green perched precariously on the end of the cliff.

No sooner have we made the climb than we are expected to descend immediately, the drive from the 7th tee, high above the previous green, plummeting down in similar fashion to the 2nd, but this time the approach is simpler to a wide open green. Not content with getting us back to the lower ground the architect of torture sends us back up a steep path to the 8th tee and a short hole which would be no more than a simple prod over a cross-bunker if it were not for the presence of the steep drop to the left of it. After these trials the pond over which the drive at the 9th must be made is but a trifle.

The big drop is there again, this time on the right, on the 11th, but in regulation play we should not descend it until we tee off from the 12th. A notice by the tee advises that it is out-of-bounds to the right of the ditch plainly visible far below. That ditch adds considerably to the spice of the hole (especially when it is realised that steep drops of this kind greatly magnify the effects of directional error) and must prove difficult to negotiate into a stiff wind. It impinges uncomfortably until by the green it is only a yard or two off the putting surface.

I have a soft spot for short par-4s and there are two in succession in the closing stages at Chester. The drive at the 15th is nothing to speak of (one large bunker excepted) but the pitch to the narrow, raised green and the tribulations of putting on it are unique here. Similarly, the 16th puts few demands on the drive other than opening up a view of the green beyond the trees, but again the pitch is testing, this time over an abundance of bunkers.

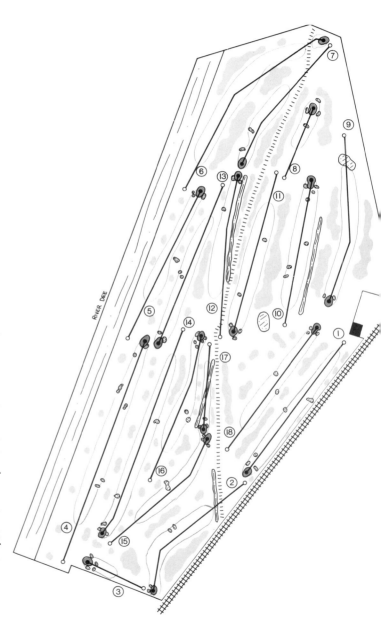

Chester has not quite finished its examination of us for at the 17th a ditch runs more or less down the middle of the fairway for its entire length forming a lateral water hazard. For sure, we are supposed to take the aerial route all the way to the putting surface but water has magnetic powers, science notwithstanding. The bush-covered hill on the left is uncomfortably close for left-handed slicers. Another climb awaits us, thankfully the last, to reach the 18th tee, but the hole itself is quite forgiving.

If I may be allowed a slight personal indulgence, I first came here back in the late 1960s as a guest of an uncle who was a member. We were snowed off after four holes. I did not return until 1993. As I walked to the 16th green on this recent visit it occurred to me that I was playing with the very clubs that same uncle had bought from the professional here at Chester in about 1970 and had used very successfully until he died a couple of years later. Perhaps those clubs knew the secrets of this course for they served me particularly favourably.

Card of the course:

1.	373 yards	par 4	10.	374 yards	par 4
2.	350	4	11.	391	4
3.	150	3	12.	392	4
4.	539	5	13.	400	4
5.	390	4	14.	514	5
6.	494	5	15.	340	4
7.	355	4	16.	358	4
8.	184	3	17.	205	3
9.	355	4	18.	344	4

Out:	3190 yards	par 36	
In:	3318 yards	par 36	
Total:	6508 yards	par 72	s.s.s. 71

Chorlton-Cum-Hardy

6024 yards; par 70; s.s.s. 69

Since the arrival of Mottram Hall and Shrigley Hall on the Cheshire golfing scene the architectural merit of its clubhouses is greatly improved. Mere may have been impressive before its destruction by fire, Royal Liverpool is undoubtedly imposing, if verging on the *Gothic*, and there is a certain dignity to Sale and Upton-by-Chester, but to the best of my knowledge the earliest building in golfing use in the county is that at Chorlton-cum-Hardy. Barlow Hall was a fine 16th and 17th century half-timbered house partially burnt in 1879, what remains incorporated in the comfortable clubhouse rarely failing to surprise when it is encoutered in an otherwise drab suburbia.

Fortunately there is almost no contact with domesticity on t course itself, a place of remarkable seclusion running down t wards the same River Mersey which flows past or through so ma courses in this book. A hedge, thick and tall, cuts off the 1st ho from the outside world and forms the principal hazard, the 2 being a mere drive and flip as long as you keep out of the strea on the left, the better side from which to approach the angled gree

The 11th ho

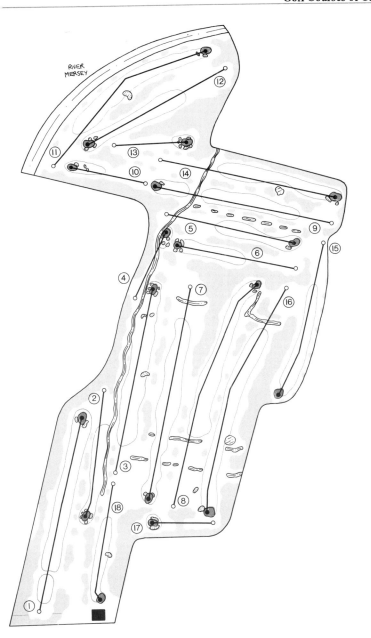

RIVER MERSEY

Matters are altogether tougher on the 3rd, running, like the 1st, along the hedge, but there is now a ditch contained therein and, with a single bunker splendidly placed on the right, the drive is demanding. The approach is no easy matter, either, with cross bunkers 60 yards short of the green, ditches left and right and no fewer than five greenside traps. It is already apparent that this is not a course to suit the left-handed slicer (or right-handed hooker, for that matter) with severe trouble on the left of a great many holes.

A rickety bridge leads across the deeper of the ditches to the white tee on the short 4th, from which the green is a difficult target, the ditch accounting for anything the least bit to the left, a couple of fairly cavernous bunkers dealing with underclubbing, and further sand around the narrow green itself. The 5th and 6th run up and down a hill, but hardly strenuously.

Most of us will be at full stretch on the 7th, though, a par-4 right on the limit at 475 yards. As the second shot must climb steeply to a plateau green we are bound to consider it a bogey-5. From a high tee up alongside another big drive is called for on the 8th, a pleasing hole gradually curving to the right as the latter stages of the fairway climb towards a hilltop green.

The main hazard on the 9th is the ditch which makes a reappearance though it should not really be of any concern, being easily out of driving range yet plenty short of the green. We are now down on the flattest part of the course and the short 10th takes us down to the banks of the Mersey. It does so in cruel fashion. From the tee it looks drearily flat but, almost invisible from there, two venomous little pot bunkers lurk just short and right of the green and, with the hedge terribly close on the left, there is in fact almost no latitude at all. Incidentally, the flags on the back nine at Chorlton are, unusually, coloured blue.

As we play the curving 11th we are separated from Sale Golf Club only by the muddy waters of the river running between high banks. As with the 3rd, a single fairway bunker is all that is needed to dominate play. While the 12th and 13th are quieter there is another tough drive from the back of the 14th, needing a carry of 160 yards simply to clear the deep ditch which has entered play on so many holes. At least we are now clear of it for good. The rest of the 14th is no give-away with a boggy pit enclosed in trees and bushes further up the right and the green hard up against a hedge.

Leaving aside the 15th on higher ground up by a cricket field, the next excitement comes with the 16th drive from a high tee out over an escarpment. A pond and incursions of trees and hedges yet again threaten the left until, right at the end, the fairway swings steeply uphill to the left. Up on top the green is a two-level affair, the ridge, uncommonly, running from front to back, so that the entire left side is at a distinctly lower level. Up behind it is the 17th tee and, unless the green keeper has been benevolent, the tee of the day may give you no sight of the tiny green at all, somewhere beyond a line of trees and a shallow valley, in its own semi-circle of trees and bushes. The *Home* hole may not be strenuous but it is pretty, overlooked by stately trees and giving the first sight of the welcoming clubhouse since leaving its security a couple of hours earlier.

Card of the course:

1.	435 yards	par 4	10.	170 yards	par 3
2.	285	4	11.	430	4
3.	416	4	12.	342	4
4.	165	3	13.	162	3
5.	284	4	14.	393	4
6.	265	4	15.	350	4
7.	475	4	16.	528	5
8.	527	5	17.	135	3
9.	395	4	18.	266	4
Out:	3248 yards	par 36			
In:	2776 yards	par 34			
Total:	6024 yards	par 70		s.s.s. 69	

Congleton

5103 yards; par 68; s.s.s. 65

Queen Victoria still had four years to reign when Congleton Golf Club was established, its emblem a shield bearing no fewer than three barrels of what one presumes to be ancient claret or cognac. Surely no golf club of this vintage would aspire merely to ale! The shield is held upright (a necessary precaution after the barrels) by a smiling Bruin of a bear, whose provenance lies in borough folk-history.

As a course Congleton is, by yardage alone, decidedly short. In character it is generous, its fairways leaping over strikingly hilly land, almost violently so on occasion. This is not mountain golf, though the terrain itself is mountainous enough. It is parkland golf set off in the foreground by handsome woods and in the distance by the foothills of the Pennines. Like so many 9-hole layouts it is given variety by alternative teeing grounds for first and second times round. More importantly it is given a number of alternative greens, of which more anon.

The opening hole is not fierce, though there are no fewer than six bunkers in the vicinity of the green, the brevity of our tenure of the links emphasised by the green's proximity to the neighbouring little church. The 2nd tee is right by a gate leading directly into the churchyard but, on the lay side of the hedge, life is rosy, a downhill drive leading inevitably to a charming green wholly developed in not so much an upturned saucer, more a vast pudding bowl, so comprehensive are the mounds all around.

The first of two short but uncompromising par-3s follows, between tall trees to a domed green on top of very sloping ground, and particularly testing in a swirling wind. Then it is downhill, very sharply so, on the 4th with every chance of pulling the ball into a vast upland valley shared with the 9th. Trees on the right are a more definite alternative, and for those with ability there is a narrow band of higher ground which is the preferred line. From there the pitch is downhill, though the green is itself raised above all kinds of perils: trees to the left, a sharp downslope on the right, and something of a cliff straight on.

From a tee down there the 5th drive is played over a venomous gully to a fairway angled to the right, and falling away distinctly in that direction, too. This is the first of the holes with alternative greens, one being down in a hollow to the right, guarded by plentiful bunkers, the other a ledge cut in the hillside some yards further on additionally protected by a broad cross-bunker. In between the greens is at least one of the tees for the 6th, its green similar to that on the 3rd in its hill-top situation with a ditch worthy of Offa on the left and dense woodland to the right.

If the 4th was very sharply downhill the 7th is spectacularly so. The drive, particularly from the back tees, appears to be nothing more than a big clout over the immediate obstacles of scrubby bushes and Offa's Dyke to a marker post on the brow of a hill. In all probability the ball will clear that brow easily to race away down the other side towards one of two greens set out side by side, the 7th on the left, 16th on the right.

From that 16th green the prospect of the next drive is alarming, seemingly a huge carry through the narrowest of gaps between a hill on the left and trees on the right. Those few yards forward to the tees make all the difference with the pressure quickly removed and a decision possible on line, with two separate greens again available for play. That on the left is raised up at a jaunty angle beyond a lily pond.

The longest hole is saved for last and, the fairway running stoutly uphill, plays materially longer. The main problem is in estimating how much club will be needed to gain the three-level green perched up on its high ground and surrounded by bunkers, particularly if the drive leaks left into the low ground shared with the 4th.

Congleton: 3rd ho

Card of the course:

1.	278 yards	par 4	10.	278 yards	par 4
2.	303	4	11.	303	4
3.	132	3	12.	132	3
4.	344	4	13.	344	4
5.	307	4	14.	268	4
6.	139	3	15.	139	3
7.	353	4	16.	358	4
8.	340	4	17.	341	4
9.	372	4	18.	372	4

Out: 2568 yards par 34

In: 2535 yards par 34

Total: 5103 yards par 68 s.s.s. 65

Crewe

6229 yards; par 70; s.s.s. 70

Truly rural golf courses are becoming harder to find as housing and industry change the nature of Cheshire from a mainly agricultural economy to one hardly different from those of all other English counties. As a town, Crewe has played its part in this conversion, its industry embracing in its time the manufacture of railway locomotives and motor cars of the highest quality. No one would quite suggest that the golf course at Crewe is a Rolls-Royce but it is not without quality and remains attractively countryfied, roaming gentle parkland outside the village of Haslington.

A recurrent strategic factor of golf at Crewe is that quite frequently a decision has to be made on the tee on whether to aim to the left or to the right of a solitary oak standing bang in the middle of the fairway. The first nine holes enjoy the delights and perils of land running in and out of a valley, handsomely wooded on the far side, but bounded by a little brook nearer to hand. Over the back nine the ground is generally flatter. The round includes no fewer than fourteen par-4s, yet such is their variety and change of pace that there is no danger of monotony. With may blossom out, the odour of wild garlic filling the air, a threatening sky and occasional shafts of sunlight picking out distant targets this was indeed a congenial spot for my early morning golf.

The first fairway tree comes into play on the downhill opening hole, well within reach of everyone's drive. The important thing to achieve, as well as avoiding finishing smack up against its trunk, is a line in to the flag from the right, thus avoiding having to flirt with the little pond covering the left half of the canted-up green. It is an inviting opening.

All seaside golfers will immediately recognise the charm of the 2nd hole – while those of an inland disposition may think differently – with drives of a good length carrying into an area of old-fashioned tumbling fairway with any number of uncertain lies. It is a long hole, seemingly longer as it plays uphill, and few who duck the challenge of the long drive will stand much chance of reaching the green, further uphill, in two shots. Extra spice is adde by the gradual right-hand bend as the hole progresses, calling f directional accuracy as well as length.

Equally appealing is the parallel 3rd, downhill this time. Th drive is once again determined by a stout tree dominating th fairway and for those who do not make good length from the te there will be a bit of guesswork about the approach shot playe rather steeply downhill to a green beautifully situated in a de framed by trees, the rural scene completed by the little brook whi winds a sinuous course at the foot of the hill. The 4th involves drive up the steep hill down which we have just pitched, the sho 5th drops us down again, and the 6th sends us back up, *Grand O Duke of York* fashion.

With the 7th there is a change of direction, driving out acro the previous fairway, avoiding another fairway oak. It pays consult the yardage chart here for big drives might carry into a dee gully crossing the fairway 100 yards short of the green. It all loo so innocent from the tee, which is far from the case with successor, the 8th green being the only level ground on top o conical hill, and an attractive spot it is, too, if you do not mis Once again we are asked to drive long and straight on the 9th te but it is seriously uphill for the last time.

The 10th and 11th are flattish holes divided by a hedge whi plays out-of-bounds in both directions, though the short 12th tak my fancy, offering big hitters the chance to play a slow draw in the green and the threat of out-of-bounds on the right and a sta of trees on the left awaiting miscalculation. Its green adjoins th of the 14th, a fine hole that I suspect may once have been playe as a par-5, and yet again play is completely dictated by a sing tree left growing in the middle of the fairway about 250 yards ou On this occasion bunkers, two on the left and another on the rig constrict the landing zone and, of no concern to me but very mu in the thoughts of the giants, there is another of those infuriati

The 1st hole

gullies crossing the fairway just beyond the tree. Hardly surprisingly, this hole is rated Stroke 1.

At last comes a par-5, the only one, and it is quite a teaser, easy enough in three middling shots. After a drive of good length, however, the narrowness of the fairway on the approaches to the green becomes apparent. A ditch on the right turns into a pond and three bunkers on the left take care of the lily-livered. With the fairway by now bending to the right the landing area is effectively halved, while the pond itself must be cleared if attempting the direct route to the green.

A couple of holes take play out onto open land by the practice ground, the memorable feature being the agonising little pitch to the 17th. As at the 1st, those who approach from the right have the simplest route in, a big tree and dark pond possibly needing to be cleared on the direct line. The 18th, though nearly 100 yards longer, is altogether gentler, with a downhill pitch over a couple of bunkers to end the round.

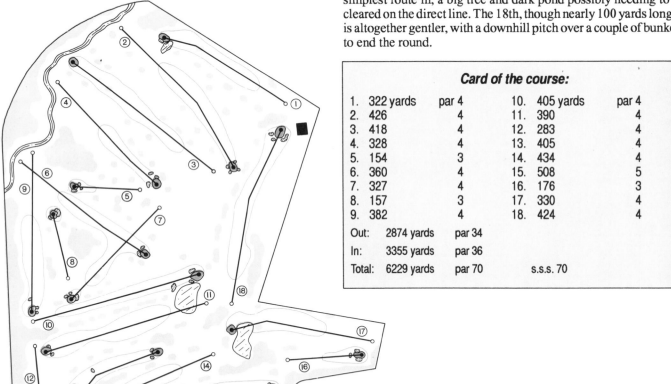

Card of the course:

1.	322 yards	par 4	10.	405 yards	par 4
2.	426	4	11.	390	4
3.	418	4	12.	283	4
4.	328	4	13.	405	4
5.	154	3	14.	434	4
6.	360	4	15.	508	5
7.	327	4	16.	176	3
8.	157	3	17.	330	4
9.	382	4	18.	424	4

Out:	2874 yards	par 34	
In:	3355 yards	par 36	
Total:	6229 yards	par 70	s.s.s. 70

Davenport

6065 yards; par 69; s.s.s. 69

..rouble occasionally recurred. There were complaints of dogs ealing golf balls, the horse (which had mowed the long grass) ed, and the club had to join forces with the Stockport Anglers ho fished the ponds within the club's boundaries) to fight off the espassers. Such was life in the pioneering days of the golfers of arners Lane. They had started out as *The Niblicks*, 35 gentlemen minally devoted to pitch-and-putt, back in 1913. Amongst their les was one which allowed members to "introduce only one lady aying member each, who must be a member of his family or usehold". Perhaps, today, a rule should be invoked at every club mpelling each member to introduce at least one female playing ember.....

Their 9-hole course lasted until 1973 when the potential of a te on the road leading from Poynton to the snowline proved more tractive than the continued battles to preserve their tenure in ockport. It cannot have been the most easily converted of poten- l golf courses but after twenty years a good deal of it has already quired the aura of a rather more ancient foundation. As a loca- n, with splendid views out over miles of countryside, it is mensely attractive in clear weather.

I am easily diverted from the task in hand and my imagination on occasion seized by the associated implications and ideas of dividually named holes. Several of Davenport's holes sport naval les, such as *Anson, Nelson,* and *Resolution* and one which mediately revived an extraordinary memory: some years ago, hile working in the north-east, I stayed in a rather superior untry house hotel with a wine list to match the antiquity of the rniture. It had once been Captain Cook's home and the bed- oms, instead of being numbered, were named after Cook's ships. here was a certain irony in being the single occupant of a bedroom titled *Adventure*. The 9th at Davenport is so named, but there is uch golf to be played before that point.

The course is in two parts, either side of the road. Neither is

short of interest or character and both are full of movement, although my fancy is caught more by the personality of those holes running round Worth Hall and the clubhouse. Take the 2nd, for instance, only 340 yards from the white tee buried deep in the woods and a mere 283 yards from the front, but a potential card-wrecker. 200 yards out the hole veers sharply to the left around trees which offer no prospect of recovery and no sight of the green if you fail to make the distance. A pair of bunkers on the outside of the dog-leg add to the intimidation on the drive and the green itself completes the task, a very ungenerous affair cocked up at a jaunty angle above a steep drop.

Over the road most of the holes run in parallel up and down a rolling meadow, the more immediately attractive being the par-3 5th, downhill with fine views out over the Cheshire plain and Manchester conurbation, and the distinctive 7th, snaking its way past a spoil tip on the right with a long second shot over low ground and a pond to a hilltop green. Stroke 1, though, occurs on the aforementioned 9th, technically a par-4 but plenty long enough to be out of reach of two shots for nearly all of us even though the final approach is downhill over a knobbly hummock.

It is about the 13th that Davenport takes on its own distinctive flavour with a funny little hole by the practice ground along a furrowed fairway to the tiniest of greens (only 22 yards deep) hard up against a stone wall and a hedge. Another tight pitch follows, this time to the short 14th, its green raised up above a ridge with trees through the back and an out-of-bounds fence to the left. But these merely warm us up for the fun to come.

On the 15th the drive ought to run the gauntlet of a pond, or at least its marshy surrounds, in order to gain maximum distance and what advantage is available from shortening the dog-leg, for the final 175 yards are steeply uphill and far round to the right. In the trees beyond is the tee for the 16th from which it is said the Great Orme, nearly a hundred miles distant, is visible on a clear day. The

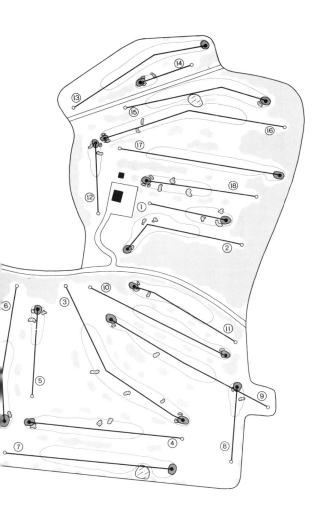

fairway sweeps down the same hill up which we have just panted, past the same pond, now low down to the right, then bearing left over second-shot cross-bunkers, until, and only until, we are close to the green we are permitted to see the object of our endeavours, a narrow green raised up between a pair of bunkers. Only recently has the hole played as a par-5 from the yellow tees and in its former guise must have yielded very few points in Stableford and Bogey competitions.

There is more to come, too, with the 17th climbing gently, but remorselessly, for more than 400 yards, the green shielded on the right by a clump of trees, and sheltered from the wind and wayward golf by a rather deeper belt of forest. Despite its lateness in the round this hole is, never the less, considered difficult enough to be nominated Stroke Hole 2. The final hole is very much less strenuous, a mid-iron and pitch or a drive followed by either a putt for an eagle or an embarrassing escape from one of the plentiful bunkers put there to test our resolve.

Card of the course:

1.	206 yards	par 3	10.	394 yards	par 4
2.	340	4	11.	306	4
3.	493	5	12.	186	3
4.	403	4	13.	385	4
5.	236	3	14.	144	3
6.	357	4	15.	369	4
7.	412	4	16.	488	5
8.	178	3	17.	413	4
9.	469	4	18.	287	4
Out:	3094 yards	par 34			
In:	2972 yards	par 35			
Total:	6065 yards	par 69		s.s.s. 69	

Opposite: 5th tee/6th green

Delamere Forest

6305 yards; par 69; s.s.s. 70

It will be apparent enough from these essays that I am an old-fashioned traditionalist responding warmly to distinctive qualities. At Delamere Forest tradition, in the clubhouse formality and adherence to the bogey system for course rating, and distinctiveness, in the inspirational layout of W.H. Fowler, put it immediately somewhere near the top of my list. Fowler's first venture into course architecture was nothing less than the Old Course at Walton Heath. The catalogue of subsequent achievements is modest in size but outstanding in quality. (Beau Desert, haunt of deer and nightjar up on Cannock Chase in Staffordshire, is the nearest of his other creations, a fine test of golf in an equally handsome setting.) Delamere Forest is out of the same top drawer, dating from 1910 and I suspect you and I would rather play it to a bogey of 72 than a par of 69.

At an early stage it should be understood that, despite the word "Forest" in the title, this is a heathland course. For sure, trees are a part of the strategy on several holes but in general the forest provides a glorious backdrop to the panoramic views from the higher parts of the course. Like all great architects Fowler made the most of what nature provided, and here that means vigorously undulating land, Fowler having no qualms about asking the golfer to undertake a number of blind drives, carry some considerable distances, and enjoy the healthy exercise of hill-walking. Overall there is plenty of variety in hole lengths and every kind of shot will be called for, but the opening five holes really stretch the average player, and immediately the relevance of the bogey system is abundantly clear. The club feels that "Par" is only appropriate to professional golfers and those who hit the ball similar prodigious distances. They recognise that few of the rest of us stand any chance of getting up in two on a number of their par-4 holes.

Stout hitting is the order of the day on the 1st, the fairway encouragingly wide but rolling a good deal and climbing steadily to a green raised just sufficiently above its surroundings to repel all but the straightest of approaches. The standard has been se Incidentally, a terrace of grassy platforms just outside the clul house gives the impression that this might be a teeing ground fo special occasions. The carry from there to reach the sanctuary the first hump of fairway is alarming. Another big carry is calle for on the 2nd, not only to clear the big depression immediately i front of the tee, but, more particularly, because the second (an third for most of us) shots continue to climb until eventually th twin guardian bunkers are passed giving access to the green backe by a stark row of dark firs.

Fowler sought to examine your golf rather than your mountain eering and there is a chance to recuperate on the downhill 3rd, an a first chance to savour the lovely views it affords. There is plent of room on the drive encouraging a full turn of the shoulders, an maximum advantage should be taken for the approach can t difficult to hold up against the slope if played from some distanc The 4th green is up on a little ledge behind bunkers, the slight ris being enough to add one or two clubs to the already substanti; distance.

Bunkering so far has been restrained but on the 5th, again long uphill hole, there are five in driving range and no marks fo dropping short with the need to cross another valley to make th putting surface. Up here is the place to catch up with the fortune of the other matches out on the course with the 6th and 16th tee alongside each other and the feel of each nine changing swiftly; this point.

The 6th is no more than a pimple of a green at the end of a mer drop shot. Immediately around the green is a ring of bunkers. I you have to miss do it on the right where the ground simply fall away. To miss on the left means three off the tee, even though th view is enticing – a pond below the green on the left and lovel views over woods and fields in all other directions.

Opposite: the 14th ho

After the broad fairways of the early holes the drive at the 7th is notably tight, the fairway a narrow plateau falling away into trees on the left and uncertainty on the right. This is as nothing compared with the drive at the 8th, a terrifying prospect to the average golfer who cannot guarantee to clear the chasm and bunker on the direct line. Aiming off to the right may appear safer but then the hole is lengthened substantially and three bunkers await the drive which is caught just right. The fairway seems to become ever narrower as it approaches the green, a narrow and wobbly affair perched on the edge of the abyss.

To return to the clubhouse a short par-4 is provided, nothing more than a couple of mid-irons. All that is needed is a line slightly right of centre on the drive, blind over trees, to open up the elevated green rolling about on the far side of yet another gully.

That is the end of the big hitting – over 3200 yards for a par of 34 (pace Delamere's bogey rating) is stern stuff – and, as if to compensate, everything is tighter from here on and the ground markedly hillier. On the 10th, for instance, the fairway, rising steeply in the far distance, is both narrow and convex. Hit it on an angle and there is every chance of the ball's bounding off into the perdition on either hand. The climbing is only just beginning, the pitch continuing the steep rise until the sloping green is reached. At least the drive on the 11th is downhill – spectacularly so – to a valley fairway far below. Unfortunately another climb is demanded immediately with the second shot played blind over a marker post on the crest of the hill in front. The green is a sunken affair adequately protected by the lie of the land and three bunkers.

The 12th is a nondescript hole, or, rather, would seem to be until you miss on the right. By the same token the 13th would appear to be no more than an iron from the tee and gentle pitch but somehow we always seem to strive for maximum length and then it becomes apparent just how much the fairway leans to the left and just how well positioned are the bunkers on that side.

One of my favourite holes is the 14th which, after a drive to the crest of a hill (and yet another marker post), involves a most appetising approach shot downhill to a picture-postcard green raised up behind bunkers and with the most majestic of forest backdrops completing the scene. It is the prelude to the most characterful (or most eccentric, depending on the outcome of the tee shot) hole on the course. Again the drive is blind over a marker and that is the line to take, with a bunker and boggy ground down to the left to frustrate those who would attempt to shorten the hole.

Assuming the first part of the operation is accomplished successfully the pitch is then a delight, up onto a ledge green, narrow and angled.

It is time for a second skirmish with the pond that made the 6th so beautiful. From the 16th tee the line to the green is directly over the abyss at the bottom of which lurks that pond. In reality only a really dreadful shot would end up down there and the real threat to par or bogey are the sloping approaches to the green likely to divert weak shots into one of the greenside bunkers.

The 17th is not difficult despite the big drops beyond the green and provides a moment's respite before the final challenge. If we were willing to accept a bogey-5 we should not be called upon to do more than clear the end of the trees in front, make reasonable distance with our seconds towards a boggy patch allowed to interrupt the fairway short of the green, then run the ball up to the flag. Tigers who aspire to reaching the green in two shots must bite off a huge chunk of (out-of-bounds) forest and then run the gauntlet of ever encroaching trees.

Somehow, reading back through my notes, it is this tactical difficulty which makes a bogey of 72 seem so much more realistic than a Standard Scratch of 70. Maurice Bembridge's course record 63, achieved while qualifying for the 1967 Open Championship, merely serves to exemplify the huge gulf that divides the real players from those who can only dream about it. My dreams, though, will be of an early morning round when mist still hung in the valleys, the higher fairways bathed in the clearest sunlight, the distant hills rising from the mists like fairytale castles, and "The Lark Ascending" distracting the mind, filling it with snatches of Vaughan Williams's masterpiece, as evocative of its era as Herbert Fowler's gem at Delamere Forest.

Card of the course:

	429 yards	par 4	10.	381 yards	par 4
	442	4	11.	498	5
	414	4	12.	149	3
	213	3	13.	312	4
	428	4	14.	373	4
	147	3	15.	304	4
	445	4	16.	197	3
	418	4	17.	360	4
	333	4	18.	462	4

ut:	3269 yards	par 34
:	3036 yards	par 35
tal:	6305 yards	par 69	s.s.s. 70

Didsbury

6273 yards; par 70; s.s.s. 70

At the beginning of this century the river alongside our course saw more tranquil days, when droves of wagonettes used to drive from Manchester. Their occupants picnicked on the river banks, hired rowing boats and even took trips on a small steamer, up to Simon's bridge and back to Northenden. (From Didsbury Golf Club's Centenary Booklet). Previous, less peaceful, visitors had included King Charles II's Scottish troops after their routing at Worcester and Bonnie Prince Charlie's *fierce looking, long haired rough Highlanders* on their way to defeat in 1745. The long-haired rough golfers of Didsbury only began their occupation in the first decade of the century having played a 9-hole circuit in School Lane since 1891.

George Lowe laid out the first holes at Ford Lane, and this was later altered and extended by Alister Mackenzie and, despite occasional floodings and a World War, it provided a good test of golf until the 1970s when work began on construction of the M63, leading, incidentally, to yet another severe flood. The motorway severed the old course and a substantial rebuild was necessary, Peter Allis and David Thomas landing one of their earliest contracts. What they had to work with was a somewhat restricted site, what remained of the original course bounded by the retaining walls of the river, a detached *Promised Land* containing five holes on the far side of the motorway, with a lake and the Altrincham-Stockport railway as additional boundaries.

A level par-3 provides a gentle start, but muscle is called for as early as the 2nd, a stout par-4 curving gently to the right with first a bunker and, later, trees to restrict freedom on the side away from the river bank. The river is a constant companion on the long 3rd, too, the fairway bending sharply right before climbing steeply to the green. To get on here in two shots is quite a feat. The 4th is tight, with a drop to the 10th fairway on the right and purgatory on the left with a tree-covered slope and the Mersey beyond.

Over the motorway bridge the course is relatively cramped, with a degree of common sense allied to skill needed to avoi interference between matches. The 5th is another sharp righ handed dog-leg with an exacting pitch to a green with a pro nounced hump on the right and the lake close at hand on the lef The 7th, too, runs close to its shores, the angled green favourin an approach from that side.

There will be very few birdies achieved on the fine 8th hol Only a drive of prodigious length holding the very right side of th fairway offers a view of the green, secreted away in a sylvan glad the fairway curving to the left around trees over the final 100 yard or so. It is only a stone's throw from motorway, railway an industrial buildings yet admirably screened from their presence.

Back on the original tract the 10th is an unfortunate hole, s close to the motorway that a rule is imposed forbidding the use o wooden clubs, a sadness when the fairway is so inviting at th bottom of a hill. Running back up that hill, the 11th plays far longe than its official 199 yards, and with bunkers either side of th narrow entrance and a huge Mackenzie-style ramp dividing th green into very distinct upper and lower levels there is no alterna tive to flying the ball all the way to the pin. Inevitably, the groun inside the river being so flat, there is less character to the remainin golf but the 12th is good fun with a decision to be made on th second shot: will it clear three fairway bunkers?

Almost every golf club seeks sponsorship in the form o advertising on its tee markers. They will usually be local garage insurance companies, hotels and restaurants that go in for this kin of promotion: it rarely seems to be tallow chandlers or cleric outfitters, though I know of several holes sponsored by funera directors. The 13th at Didsbury deserves special mention as it sponsored by my old friend, Martin Locke, in an act of commend able generosity as his eyesight, unhappily, prevents any possibili of his ever playing golf. His exceptional powers of hearing, fortu nately, make him one of the finest piano tuners in the north.

The 14th hole

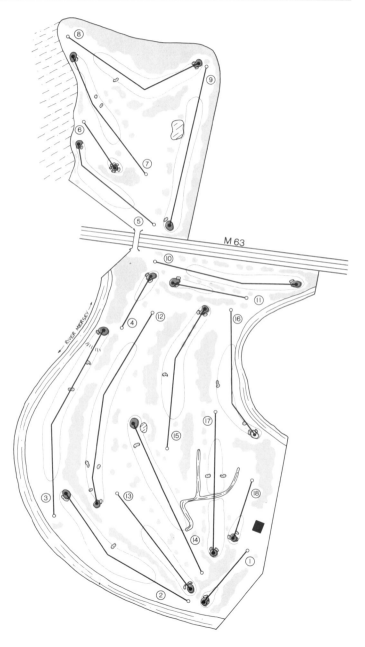

The 14th is no pushover with a pond just to the right of the green. A lone tree in the middle of the fairway (in the style familiar to those who have enjoyed the Spanish courses of Javier Arana) adds spice to the drive at the 15th, the fairway rising attractively at the length of a good drive. From there the approach shot must be faded gently to curve in to the green past a prominent tree on the right.

As befits a short par-4, the green at the 16th is small and tightly bunkered at the end of a curving fairway. The 17th would be nondescript if it were not for a ditch crossing the fairway 200 yards out. How many of us can guarantee to clear that every time? The course ends as it began with a gentle par-3, not perhaps its most memorable hole.

Card of the course:

1.	176 yards	par 3	10.	383 yards	par 4
2.	451	4	11.	199	3
3.	534	5	12.	546	5
4.	162	3	13.	328	4
5.	307	4	14.	437	4
6.	148	3	15.	409	4
7.	378	4	16.	348	4
8.	424	4	17.	377	4
9.	498	5	18.	168	3
Out:	3078 yards	par 35			
In:	3195 yards	par 35			
Total:	6273 yards	par 70		s.s.s. 70	

Disley

6015 yards; par 71; s.s.s. 69

Royal Liverpool carried Cheshire's flag alone for twenty years from its foundation in 1864 until a number of clubs emerged towards the end of the 1880s, in which noble company Disley can counted. It straddles a hilltop site above Lyme Park and as might expected there is a certain amount of climbing to be done hough it is a good deal gentler than its near neighbour and fellow nturion, Mellor. Inevitably there are many sidehill lies and during the round the golfer will be called upon to maintain his balance while taking wood or a long iron from hilly stances. Accuracy of approach work will also be tested with almost all the greens in the form of a ledge or plateau, the ground falling away on at least one side, very often through the back.

The 8th green

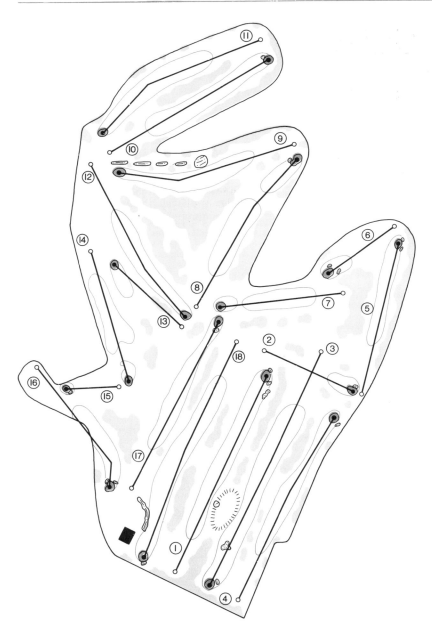

James Braid is credited with the layout and on a si[te]
of this nature perhaps his outstanding achievement is i[n]
having plotted a route which asks for few blind shots t[o]
be played and on which a well struck tee shot has a fa[ir]
chance of finishing in a favourable lie. The openin[g]
sequence is encouraging, for sure, with a short par-
climbing gently past the smoke shaft of the old Midlan[d]
Railway tunnel underneath, followed by an invitin[g]
downhill shot across a meadow to the 2nd green, a ledg[e]
at the foot of the hill.

The 3rd and 4th are strong holes, the former [a]
genuine three shotter climbing back uphill to a platea[u]
green just below the 1st tee, the 4th making amends b[y]
running downhill for its 423 yards. There is some temp[-]
tation to attempt to carry the corner of the out-of-bound[s]
hedge on the right to give a slightly uphill approach t[o]
the green for it is not one on which to hope that a lon[g]
shot from the left will stick.

The course then climbs from the 5th tee sunken in [a]
glade below the 2nd green over the next three holes unt[il]
the 8th tee is reached. This is not quite as spectacular a[s]
the remarkable 12th at Mellor but it is similar in i[ts]
tumbling fairway where a straight drive will run for eve[r.]
Here, however, the green is tucked away to the righ[t]
protected by trees and by a little ridge crossing th[e]
fairway 50 yards in front. The 9th, too, is an attractiv[e]
hole, again dog-legging to the right, but this time uphi[ll]
and with a nasty little pond right in the angle of th[e]
dog-leg.

For the moment the golf is parkland in nature, bu[t]
with the blind tee shot at the 13th the character change[s]
to that of moorland. It is a disconcerting hole to play fo[r]
the first time for nothing can be seen over the brow o[f]
the hill other than a marker post. When you get over th[e]
brow you are amazed to find the post some way to th[e]
left of the green, such is the slope down to the right.

The 14th, too, is guesswork until you know it, wit[h]
a blind tee shot smartly uphill and a testing pitch over [a]
yawning chasm to an angled green. The 15th, no mor[e]
than a coffee table on top of a hill, is real target golf, an[d]
then we are invited to gamble. From an elevated te[e]
nothing of the challenge of the 16th is concealed. A ston[e]

ll surrounds the practice ground and the fairway curves round
n a big right-handed arc. You bite off as much as you think you
n chew and jolly well have to get it right. Now that the lovely
d 17th on the Eden Course at St Andrews has been ploughed up
admirers will simply have to come to Disley instead.

One demanding drive remains, that on the 17th, tight to a
ping fairway with out-of-bounds on the right and high ground
the left. The final hole raises hopes of a birdie, being generously
de and not too hilly.

Card of the course:

1.	449 yards	par 5	10.	379 yards	par 4
2.	202	3	11.	385	4
3.	528	5	12.	388	4
4.	423	4	13.	190	3
5.	322	4	14.	285	4
6.	169	3	15.	109	3
7.	257	4	16.	305	4
8.	375	4	17.	391	4
9.	373	4	18.	485	5

Out:	3098 yards	par 36	
In:	2917 yards	par 35	
Total:	6015 yards	par 71	s.s.s. 69

Dukinfield

5303 yards; par 67; s.s.s. 66

In those civilised days when matchplay was the thing, Cheshire extended to the north-east well past Stockport, indeed up to a short boundary with Yorkshire. A number of the golf clubs in this area have remained staunchly proud of their Cheshire ancestry and, ignoring the relocation efforts of the bureaucrats, remain defiantly in the Cheshire Union. Dukinfield is one of these.

Simply scanning yardages or Standard Scratch ratings in a guide book, the eye would not be caught by Dukinfield — not much over 5000 yards for 18 holes — and, as I have discovered so frequently in researching this book, a great many of the little courses are full of surprises: who, for instance, would have suspected that such a short course could boast a 592-yard par-5, not perhaps, the longest hole in the county from the competition te but almost certainly the longest a visitor will play, the yellow te no more than 5 yards in front of the white when I visited? But I an jumping the gun, for that is the 16th hole.

The 4th hole

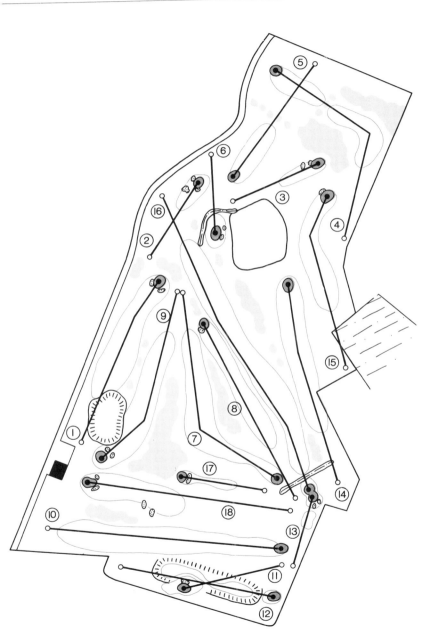

Almost all the course is on a west-facing slope giving admirable views of rain clouds racing in from the west and of the Jumbo Jets descending from the heavens on their way to Ringway, but also, it must be admitted, of the proximity and abundance of that industry which over the years has provided the wealth simply to play golf. One of these factories produces cigarettes and is one of the most imposing industrial buildings in this part of the country. Another manufactures wallpaper, giving its name to the 4th hole, one of three on a steep slope facing the moors to the east. It is a treacherous little hole and I have no doubt each member has his own pet theory on how to protect the card at this point. That might be a 7-iron for safety followed by a *spoon* or *cleek* through a gap in the vestigial hedge before curling down to the right with the slope. Those who believe that the longer shot must always be played before the shorter one will need local knowledge, expert guidance, or a stiff brandy boldly to strike out over the shoulder of the hill on the left and its grasping rough and scrubby trees. The drive at the 5th is steeply uphill (threatened by a fence on the right, too) and makes a nonsense of the nominal yardage.

If I were a local I would expect the 7th to be one of the (several) holes on which I should see off any visitor. Characterful, you might call the hole, perhaps even downright eccentric, or (in an earlier age) sporting. From a teeing ground shared with the 9th the drive is downhill, encouragingly so, towards a distant marker post. About 40 yards short of the green the fairway turns abruptly left running in over bumpy ground to the putting surface. A glance at the map might suggest the use of a short-cut via the 8th or 16th fairways. A glance at the rules informs that this is *off-limits*.

Life is then uncomplicated for a few holes until, approaching the 10th green and its attendant *Valley of Sin*, we glance right to notice for the first time, and with foreboding, the two quarry holes to come. The earlier of them, the 11th, is not too alarming perhaps, being a manageable carry over an abyss to a none too level green perched in a wilderness of gorse and scrub high up on the far side. Down below, on the floor of the quarry, snakes the narrowest of fairways, which, in former times, would have qualified for the cartographer's description, *Here be dragons*. There is no escape: you have to know to the inch how far it is to the relative haven of a little patch of flat fairway just below the cliff on top of which the green is to be found. From the forward yellow tee I needed a kindly bounce from a gorse bush to nudge my 5-iron into *Position A*. From the back tee, high up behind, it might need a 2-iron. Either way, the pitch must be made almost vertically. Those who, on a first visit, play through these two holes unscathed ought to qualify for a commemorative medal!

The next three holes take play back to the summit of the hill to stand on the aforementioned 16th tee. From it the fairway sweeps gently downhill all the way to the green, bearing first left and later right. Hidden in a little dip shortly before the green is an open ditch, and how remarkable it seems that so small a target is so frequently hit when the very much larger fairway of the 12th hole proves elusive!

The 17th is the last curiosity, a short par-3 up a valley so narrow as to be almost a tunnel to a ledge green atop a punchbowl. The 18th is simpler, but if your drive fails to clear the gully alongside the 17th green you are unlikely to agree.

Card of the course:

1.	329 yards	par 4	10.	401 yards	par 4
2.	163	3	11.	175	3
3.	162	3	12.	276	4
4.	371	4	13.	178	3
5.	256	4	14.	376	4
6.	143	3	15.	324	4
7.	419	4	16.	592	5
8.	354	4	17.	155	3
9.	336	4	18.	293	4
Out:	2533 yards	par 33			
In:	2770 yards	par 34			
Total:	5303 yards	par 67		s.s.s. 66	

Dunham Forest

6636 yards; par 72; s.s.s. 72

is hard to imagine that the immaculate ribbons of fairway and
majestic trees which frame them, the abiding memory of
nham Forest, were not all that long ago both a U.S. Army and
Italian prisoner of war camp. The land owner, Lord Stamford,
nted the place tidied up at the same time as a group of golfers
o had previously travelled across Manchester to a course on the
rth of the city had begun to tire of their journeys. In this unlikely
nner one of the most attractive courses in Cheshire came into
ing, first with 9-holes back in 1961, then with 15 holes four years
er, and only as recently as 1977 extending to 18 holes.

"I can't stand Dunham. It's a ladies' course," remarked one of
golfing acquaintances recently. What I think he meant was that
fairways are too unforgiving for his erratic driving. Some of
m seem indeed very narrow, or perhaps, more properly, the
rways are wide enough, it is just that there is no rough or
ni-rough beyond them. On most holes at Dunham the trees *are*
rough. In addition, many fairways curve or dog-leg signifi-
ntly and only if the drive is perfectly placed is there any hope of
hot to the green at all. It is on this penal element that Dunham's
tics dwell. If it was good enough to attract Alex Hay and Dave
omas to be the club's first two professionals then perhaps the
tics would be better advised to take a lesson or two from them
fore next writing off the course. (Thomas, incidentally, came
ond in the 1966 Open at Muirfield during this tenure of office).

One of the conditions to be met by the first course architect was
conservation of a little wooded hill, apparently a burial mound
ancient British or Roman provenance, and the course begins
m a tee right beside it. There is nothing intimidating about this
rticular tree-lined fairway – it is wide enough for anyone –
ding gradually uphill to a green just over the crest and therefore
ghtly blind, but not ridiculously so, attended by a stately tree.

As early as the 2nd tee the course tightens up, demanding a
ghtly drawn drive to open up the green at the bottom of a slope,

well defended by a deep bunker on the left. Then, after the
attractive short 3rd, a big drive is called for. The 4th is downhill
and handsome, but unless the drive clears a slight rise in the
fairway (and does so on the right line) there is no downhill
advantage to be gained.

Resuming now on the other side of the ancient monument, the
5th runs up a narrow, slightly curved valley and only the most
accurately placed drive gives any prospect of a viable second shot,
the green being a table-top raised up above a bunker on the side of
a tree-clad hill. From there the 6th takes play to the end of the
wooded section for the time being. It is short as par-5s go, downhill
at that, and easily reached in two shots by many, but only if they
split the fairway precisely with their drives. Go just slightly right
and there is no view of the green past the next stretch of trees. Go
further right and bunkers or the greenkeeper's stores of sand and
peat await. Miss the target area by only a small amount on the left
and further trees intrude on that side too.

Play then moves to the open air, to the most recent holes which
were designed by David Thomas and laid out over former farmland
giving fine views over the surrounding countryside and, less
happily, over the considerable industry of South-West Manchester.
Probably the demands made on the good player are no less than
those on the wooded section but for the less competent these holes
offer some relief. They will not agree if they are faced with a long
putt on the 8th green, a very tricky affair, nor if the flag on the 11th
is positioned on the right of the green right behind a bunker.

After these *al fresco* holes suddenly to be plunged into the trees
again on the 12th tee induces a moment's claustrophobia, though
the hole can be reached with two iron shots and the 13th has the
grace to be downhill, if narrow.

I always look forward to playing the homeward stretch from
the 14th, five very individual holes. The first three of them are part
of the middle phase of Dunham's development crossing an under-

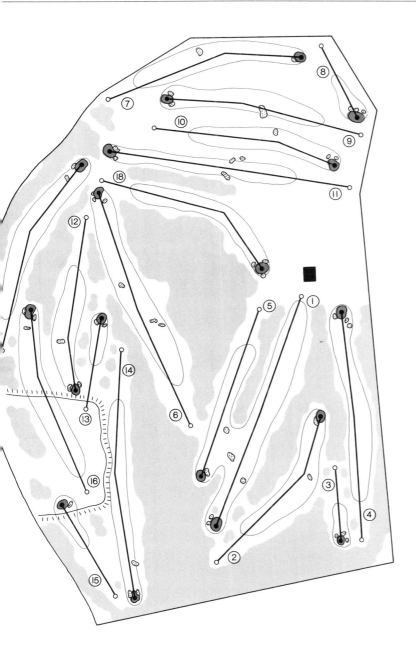

ground reservoir. On the 14th this means driving uphill (ideally with a little draw) to a narrow landing area right by the doors to this subterranean mystery. The view from there is inspiring, inviting a long second shot down into a slight valley and, on a red letter day, up the other side between trees and bunkers onto a tiny, elevated and tricky putting surface. When the rhododendrons are in bloom bring the camera.

When driving in to Altrincham from the direction of Northwich you come to a bend in the road right by Dunham's 15th green. From outside the course looks particularly enticing at this point but it can be a perilous spot! Quite a mild hook from the tee is all that is required to put a dent in the bonnet of a passing car. The green itself is a shelf halfway up the side of the reservoir and you are either on it putting for a birdie or floundering about far below it hoping for a miraculous pitch. There are no near misses here. There is also a fine par-3 spare hole which can be brought into play when another needs attendion.

The 16th runs away across the flat top of the reservoir, gorse bushes aplenty giving it a heathland feel, and a reasonable drive clears the far end by the marker post and rolls a good way down towards the green. Before playing the 17th, though, take a look at the grand house overlooking the tee and the spread of fairway beyond. One of its owners in the past on the occasion of club competitions opened his garden gate, set out a table of drinks and invited players in to keep their spirits up. No doubt this was temporarily deemed to be within the course boundaries. The hole itself is first class, another of these long, slow, curving fairways on which only a drive to the left half of the fairway rewards the golfer with a view of the green. That, naturally enough, is the harder drive.

Opposite: the 6th hole

And so to the 18th, enough of a dog-leg to the right to call for a drive down the left but, with a hollow and falling ground on the left, not too far left. The trees are a little thinner here, the fairway undulating, and for this one hole one could be in Berkshire.

Dunham Forest is a busy course with a large and active membership and full diary of society and company reservations, and yet I remember one lunchtime, sitting on the terrace outside the bar enjoying a post-round refresher, watching matches teeing off in the slot reserved for members. There were social fourballs — one fiveball even! — and several family groups. There are not many courses in this part of the country where they would not have been pushed out of the way by bustling men with "prior claims".

Card of the course:

1.	517 yards	par 5	10.	370 yards	par 4
2.	371	4	11.	484	5
3.	150	3	12.	351	4
4.	465	4	13.	188	3
5.	387	4	14.	506	5
6.	493	5	15.	216	3
7.	389	4	16.	388	4
8.	165	3	17.	422	4
9.	384	4	18.	390	4
Out:	3321 yards	par 36			
In:	3315 yards	par 36			
Total:	6636 yards	par 72		s.s.s. 72	

Eastham Lodge

5864 yards; par 69; s.s.s. 68

Oddities and eccentricities frequently capture my imagination and the thought of playing a 15-hole golf course might be thought sufficient to satisfy me. Perusal of the score card, however, reveals that golf at Eastham Lodge is played round a *tank farm*. What a picture! Collie dogs rounding up frisky turrets for market, newly cast gun-barrels tentatively spitting forth howitzer shells for the first time in their nursery, and so on.

Enough whimsy, for Eastham Lodge could well be held up as a model for aspiring golf course architects, so much being obtained from so little so easily. The site is far from promising, a tiny patch of flattish land with a handful of mature trees desperately acquired in the mid-1970s when the Port Sunlight Golf Club found its grounds about to be devastated under the twin indignities of proposed motorways and office blocks. Hawtrees laid out nine holes, and over the next few years six further holes were added so that with a little loop of three holes played twice a full 18-hole card is possible. There are hopes of obtaining a further 17 acres enabling Eastham Lodge to be completed.

From the picture windows of the comfortable clubhouse there are splendid views out over the Mersey, Manchester Ship Canal and Speke Airport and one might imagine the golf to be expansive, windswept and maritime. It is not. Allotments, houses, a main road and the drive to an educational establishment form the principal boundaries, and electricity pylons and their dependent wires loom over several holes. This is the prospect those passing on the main New Chester Road will see, and how easy it would be to dismiss the golf on such a sighting.

The 2nd hole is immediately attractive, only a short par-4 but a strategic gem, needing a drive of considerable accuracy to open up the green lurking round to the right behind a stand of pine trees.

The 5th, too, dog-legs to the right, this time round a big tree within driving range. Get behind or under that and there is no shot to the green handsomely set off against the gorse-clad hillock beyond. It is very tempting to take the drive on this hole immediately after leaving the 4th tee – one of the inevitable consequences of compressing a course into such a compact space.

Again swinging late to the right, the 7th curls round trees into a picture-postcard green, raised above white-sanded bunkers, framed in further trees. Interestingly there are two quite separate tees for the 8th/13th the first of the shared holes and the strategy is marginally different from each. In both cases, though, it is a vicious little pot bunker quite worthy of the Ayrshire coast which is likely to snatch the drive which merely attempts to skirt the big mound on the right.

A bunker on the right forces many a drive to the left on the 9th/14th hole only to be blocked out by the big tree some way further down that side – there is a second tree on the same line to make doubly sure. On the occasion of my visit a woodpecker in the trees beyond the green assisted the illusion of being right out in the country. Four trees then form the crux of the dog-leg 10th/15th, this hole for me being distinguished by the particularly threatening company of a low-flying kestrel.

A single bunker, properly placed, completely dominates the short 16th (a hole totally different from the separate white and yellow tees, almost at 45-degrees to each other). The 17th is fairly routine but there is plenty of golf left in the 18th, even at 287 yards. The stars might drive the green with an iron. The rest of us have to clear a dip, go round or over a tree, and avoid a pair of cross bunkers *en route* to the tricky green. Would there were more holes of this length on more golf courses!

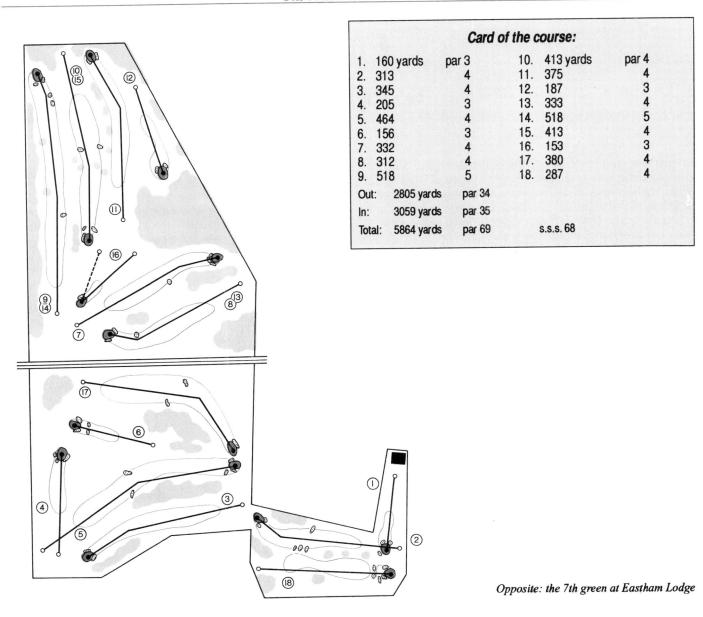

Card of the course:

1.	160 yards	par 3	10.	413 yards	par 4
2.	313	4	11.	375	4
3.	345	4	12.	187	3
4.	205	3	13.	333	4
5.	464	4	14.	518	5
6.	156	3	15.	413	4
7.	332	4	16.	153	3
8.	312	4	17.	380	4
9.	518	5	18.	287	4

Out:	2805 yards	par 34
In:	3059 yards	par 35
Total:	5864 yards	par 69	s.s.s. 68

Opposite: the 7th green at Eastham Lodge

Eaton

6562 yards; par 72; s.s.s. 71

It must have been heartbreaking for the members of Eaton to leave their original course in the grounds of the Duke of Westminster's home. The trees had grown, the fairways become established and the greens taken on a mischief of their own over twenty-five years, the course in the process acquiring quite a reputation as an all-round examination of the amateur's technique. From mid-summer 1993 they have been forced to begin anew.

The club procured a site just beyond Waverton, only a mile o two from their former home, and engaged Donald Steel as archi tect. I have to say that if I were given such a site, wide open wit a few mature trees and a stream at the bottom of a shallov depression, I would be inclined to litter the place with hundreds c bunkers, artificial mounds and a host of ponds. That is why Stee is an architect and I am not. He has confined himself to fewer tha 30 bunkers, the most conservative moundwork, and the extractio of the maximum strategic value from the few natural features

The 12th hole

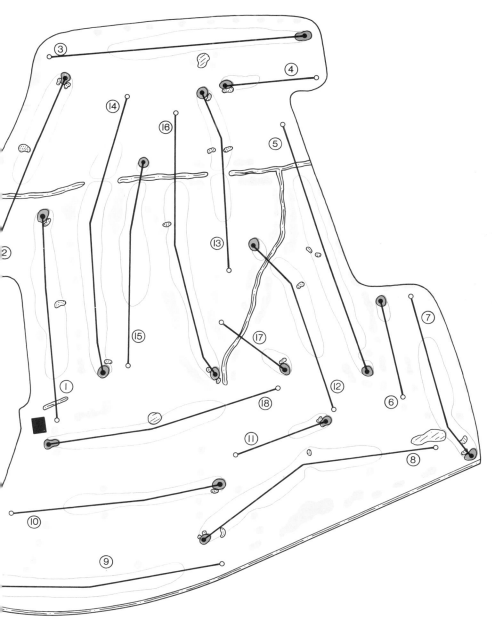

confident in his knowledge of the modern game and its protagonists' abilities. How many architects could, on the final hole, deny themselves the use of any bunkers at all, restricting themselves only to one tiny pond and a couple of long-established trees?

Steel *has* planted trees and in a quarter of a century golf at Eaton will be altogether tighter, more in the character of the stretch of the 3rd to 5th holes at Portal, and, to my mind, not unlike those holes at Bromborough which run back and forth across a little stream. What few bunkers he has created are of a vast acreage — broad expanses of the whitest sand expertly positioned — and there is a fine example forcing play out to the right after crossing the stream for the first time on the 2nd.

No bunker is required on the 3rd, its drive tight between a farm on the left (out-of-bounds, of course) and a soggy pit on the right. The green is long, thin, domed and running away to the right. Interestingly enough there are two bunkers as you plod up the 5th fairway but none around the green. This time a sort of double pit to the front and left of the green is hazard enough from afar, a diagonal ridge and trough running through the putting surface to trouble those who got thus far unhindered.

The 7th is also appealing right from its earliest days, swinging left round a couple of old trees before climbing over a pair of bunkers to a tumbling green becomingly backed by a bridge and distressingly close to the canal beneath. The 8th runs in a wide arc alongside the canal but does not involve it in play, utilising instead three trees to narrow the fairway, a small pit on the left, and as many as four bunkers.

For the moment the three following holes offer rest so that when the 12th is encountered it comes as something of a shock to the system. Only 347 yards long the hole is, never the less, rated 2nd in the Stroke Index. It is all about position from the tee to give a clear hit between the trees and over the stream simply to reach the green on the far side. Steel recognised the ideal spot from which to play that second shot and stuck a bunker there. He also compounded the problem by angling and canting the green to such an extent that, once again, no bunker was deemed necessary.

Position on the drive is again the key to clearing the stream and reaching the green on the 15th, a hole totally devoid of sand it should be said. There is a bunker to threaten the drive on the par-5 16th involving, yet again, a substantial carry over the stream. The more devious bunker, though, is the one at the front right of the green, forcing many a long approach shot off to the left, down the hill, and into the ditch close by. Those who know of the ditch's existence may, by the opposite inference, be forced into the sand. After a short par-3, protected at present principally by the wind, the 18th brings play home, as I said earlier, without the need for a bunker of any kind.

Card of the course:

1.	384 yards	par 4	10.	396 yards	par 4
2.	378	4	11.	178	3
3.	423	4	12.	347	4
4.	175	3	13.	348	4
5.	490	5	14.	527	5
6.	185	3	15.	386	4
7.	326	4	16.	509	5
8.	481	5	17.	152	3
9.	437	4	18.	440	4
Out:	3279 yards	par 36			
In:	3283 yards	par 36			
Total:	6414 yards	par 72		s.s.s. 71	

Opposite page: Ellesmere Port, 18th hole

Ellesmere Port

6432 yards; par 71; s.s.s. 71

The partnership of Cotton, Pennink, and Lawrie laid out this municipal course back in the early 1970s. It has matured into a lively test of golf, not significantly easier from the yellow tees when par is reduced by 2 strokes and standard scratch by as many as 3. I am sure I would rather play the final hole, for instance, as a 496 yard par-5 than a 445 yard par-4.

When you leave the A41 you may be forgiven for believing you have made the wrong turn and are entering a crematorium or mausoleum, the club house being through a church yard at once imposing or awesome. On my most recent visit golfers in sweaty T-shirts and muddy Jeans mingled incongruously with the frilly froo-froos and gaudy cravats of a wedding party sharing the same overflow car park. There is also a designated footpath through the course which ensures a goodly variety of canine visitations as you wait, let us say, on the 17th tee – and provides a decent, legal, and potentially profitable training ground for the youthful ball-hunters of the neighbourhood.

Ponds, ditches and copses are the principal hazards, but there are plenty of long par-4s, particularly on the back nine, to test the genuine strikers. Fall foul of the trees surrounding the green on the 15th or off the tee on the 16th and a big score will follow. On the 17th a ditch crosses diagonally making serious demands, and there is plenty of chance of finding a pond or another ditch on the 18th, a hole tightened also by the presence of deep woodland on the right.

Card of the course:

1.	425 yards	par 4	10.	412 yards	par 4
2.	484	5	11.	510	5
3.	378	4	12.	210	3
4.	367	4	13.	303	4
5.	188	3	14.	195	3
6.	179	3	15.	410	4
7.	285	4	16.	432	4
8.	438	4	17.	200	3
9.	520	5	18.	496	5
Out:	3264 yards	par 36			
In:	3168 yards	par 35			
Total:	6432 yards	par 71		s.s.s. 71	

Frodsham

6289 yards; par 70; s.s.s. 70

seems there was a golf course in Frodsham back in the 1870s, ich would make it one of the oldest in the country and second dest (after Royal Liverpool) in the county. In 1924 it closed and vas not until the summer of 1990 that a replacement appeared, st over the road from the original course. No course is mature in ee years, but this John Day layout has many natural advantages ich make it already an attractive place. When a few of the

recently planted trees have begun to catch the eye and influence the strategy this will be sterling for a day's golf, with a good balance between the penal and the strategic, welcome variety in hole length, and sufficient movement in the land to be stimulating without being daunting.

The 11th hole

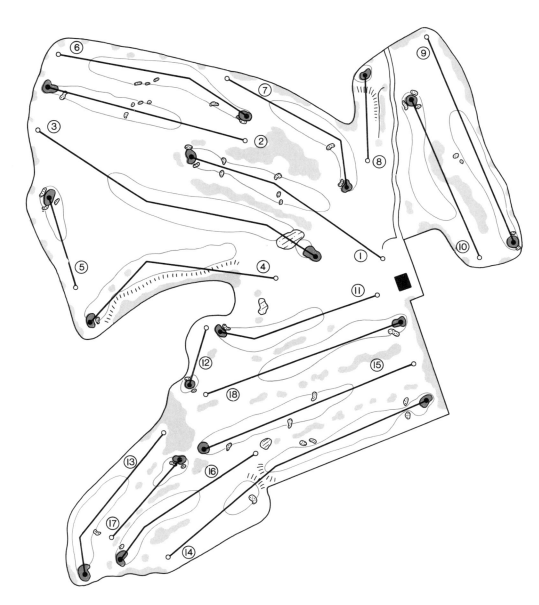

The start is magnificent, impo[s]ing or downright vindictive depend[ing] on your initial success, the 1[st] hole sweeping majestically in a wid[e] left-handed arc through five fairwa[y] bunkers as it climbs towards th[e] green. The 2nd, too, is a climb an[d] therefore plays longer than its nom[i]nal 388 yards, particularly as the ap[p]roach has to be made on the fly ov[er] a big cross-bunker.

The white tee for the 3rd stand[s] proudly aloof, 75 yards behind th[e] yellow tee, and from it the fairwa[y] snakes in a sinuous path downhi[ll] until, about 150 yards short of th[e] green, it bottoms out in a deep de[pression. From there the pitch [is] made steeply uphill, over a pond, [to] the pear-shaped green. For the m[o]ment there is room out to the side[s] but when the saplings have becom[e] bushes and trees this will be a toug[h] proposition.

Capable of holding its head up i[n] any company, the 4th is a real test [of] resolve, the archetypal *cape* hole. [It] is not all that long and can be playe[d] conservatively in part, but from an[y] tee the drive to the fairway is cha[l]lenging for a golfer, whatever hi[s] standard. A deep ravine runs acros[s] the line, at ten o'clock, as it were. [It] is present all the way to the green an[d] preys on the mind constantly, but th[e] architect, by leaving a couple of tree[s] growing in the fairway, has ensure[d] that the challenge cannot be ducke[d] on every shot. When the hole is c[ut] on the rear left of the green, up be[-] hind a deep bunker and implying [a] long carry over the ever-curving ra[vine] ıe, this is the place for a *balata* ball and the technique to match.

If by now your card is still intact you ought to be able to nurse ˙rom here in. Nothing will be quite so demanding and you may free to give a little more attention to the splendid views afforded ım this hilly site, notably those of the full sweep of the Mersey ᵗuary, handsomely framed between the sandstone escarpments Frodsham and Helsby. Further afield, in good weather, the ntrasting towers of the two Cathedrals stand out from the general ˙yscape of Liverpool, the higher ground of the Wirral completing : picture on the left. Keep out of the hedges on the left and there ɔuld be few problems over the remainder of the half, though it ll need stout hitting to make the putting surface at the uphill 9th two shots.

Few drives are as invigorating as that at the 11th, out over a ling fairway towards the Mersey itself. The prudent play for a ʾel lie short of the final ridge down which the fairway plunges st a stunted tree towards the very narrow green, angled to the ht, inhospitably domed and unwelcoming to all but the most phatic of pitches. The ground here is hilly and the 12th plays oss the slope, an all-or-nothing shot to a pimple green.

I should need more experience of the 14th to know whether it ɪ fine challenge or merely mildly eccentric, but I will vouch for distinctive character. Is there a genuine corner-cutter's route out ʰhe right, taking huge risks carrying a field with the the second ɔt? Is the long, straight hitter penalised when his drive dies in valley 300 yards out (this is noticeably downhill and that tance is not quite so fanciful as it might otherwise seem)? ʿeryday golfers will find their second and third shots falling short their targets as the fairway climbs relentlessly for its latter half.

Having climbed, there is another enticing view from the 15th tee, once again out towards the Mersey. Staggered bunkers tighten the drive and the approach may be semi-blind to the green over a rolling fairway. The 16th will not tax, but there is a premium on accuracy on the 17th, a hedge on the left balanced by deep rough on the right, and a cross-bunker protecting the left front of the green seriously enough to remind the author (if only momentarily) of the *Hill* bunker on the Old Course at St Andrews. The round ends with yet another hole which, because of its hill-climbing, plays much longer than it should, the green rising sharply, too. Full marks to John Day for taking maximum advantage of the given land without trying disadvantageously to push the course towards the magic 7,000 yard figure.

Card of the course:

1.	419 yards	par 4	10.	328 yards	par 4
2.	388	4	11.	315	4
3.	588	5	12.	121	3
4.	404	4	13.	328	4
5.	183	3	14.	571	5
6.	383	4	15.	428	4
7.	333	4	16.	334	4
8.	165	3	17.	196	3
9.	429	4	18.	376	4
Out:	3292 yards	par 35			
In:	2997 yards	par 35			
Total:	6289 yards	par 70		s.s.s. 70	

Gatley

5934 yards; par 68; s.s.s. 68

All seat backs are in an upright position, seat belts fastened, and cabin crew themselves strapped in their seats by the time aeroplanes pass over Gatley on their way into Manchester Airport. The railway line from Manchester to Crewe via Styal divides the course. And yet this is a splendidly secluded course, far from a road of any kind, hidden away from the relentless rush of everyday life.

Either side of that railway line the course assumes differen characters, rather flat and gentle over the first five holes, o somewhat greater individuality for the final stretch. Nobody tam gling with either of the craters interrupting the 1st fairway, o failing to get past the corner of the trees on the 2nd would agre with the description "gentle", but everything is comparative. Th 6th breaks us in amiably with a simple enough drive for positior

The 7th hole

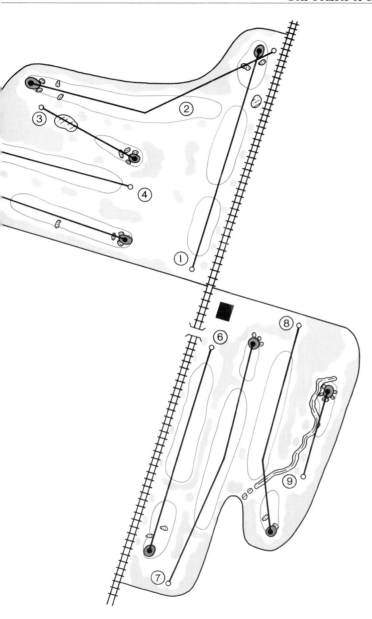

on a flat meadow, but the second shot must be played over a hedge and gully, a couple of bunkers too, to find the green.

Sepia tints of The Apple Tree Gang and Butcher Shotts's Cow Pasture were brought to mind as I essayed for the first time the extraordinary 7th. (The said cow pasture was where the first golf was played in the United States back in the late 1880s, in and out round the orchard from which the early players acquired their nickname). First there are hedges everywhere – to the left and right of the drive, and straight ahead, too. One of those hedges segregates the women's tee (and their fairway, if it comes to that) from the men's. Later the hedge on the left encroaches just where another depression worthy of the title gully splits the fairway. For good measure, the green is in a pit of its own, bunkered thrice on the far side. No one would be allowed to build a hole like this today. No one should be allowed to take it away.

The 8th is a glorious hole, alarmingly tight from the competition tee built on a gun platform in the depths of a wood. The fairway is again sundered by a gully, all the time sloping down to the stream on the left. Eventually the stream crosses the fairway and the approach shot must be hit far over this to reach the high ground on which the green is set. A couple of bunkers catch the mildly errant, steep slopes depositing the weak and feeble in the trees or stream. The course ends with a charming downhill par-3, well-wooded, well-bunkered, and well-watered on the left.

Card of the course:			
1.	406 yards	par 4	
2.	456	4	
3.	182	3	
4.	298	4	
5.	275	4	
6.	380	4	
7.	438	4	
8.	372	4	
9.	160	3	
Out:	2967 yards	par 34	
Total (18 holes):	5934 yards	par 68	s.s.s. 68

Hale

5780 yards; par 70; s.s.s. 68

9-hole courses, if they are good, can be exceptionally agreeable places with the anticipation and thrill of enjoying the best holes, not once, but twice in the course of a round. By the same token, it goes without saying, a poor 9-hole course can be purgatorial. Cheshire is fortunate to have a number of fine 9-hole courses, and Hale is prominent in that company.

It is locked away between Altrincham Priory and the M56 motorway, with taxiing aircraft at Manchester Airport almost within *brassie* range, and yet, miraculously, it is a spot of the utmost privacy enjoying the close company of the River Bollin, a panoply of centuries-old trees completing the task of cutting it o[ff] from the outside world. The trees are occasionally a golfing hazar[d] but it is likely to be the four skirmishes with the Bollin which wi[ll] determine the ultimate success of the full round. The continue[d] efforts of conservationists have returned the river to its former sta[te] of welcoming host to an abundance of wildlife. Arachnologists ar[d] lepidopterists playing golf at Hale will find themselves frequent[ly] calling their mundane brethren through as they stop to examin[e] their latest finding.

The double green of the 4th and 7th hol[es]

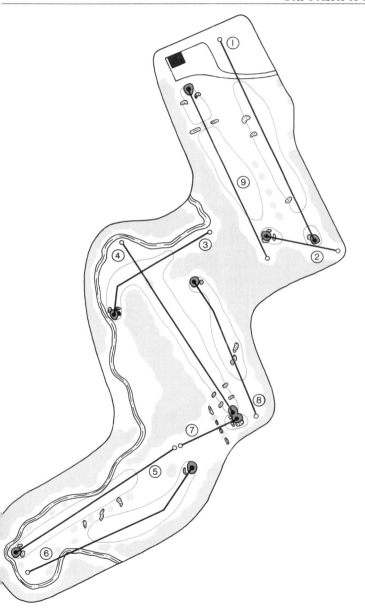

Serious golfers will not be disappointed, either, with a number of lively holes, such as the 1st, a none too taxing par-5 but a teasing birdie hole with the second shot having to carry a depression before the green, and a hedge encroaching down the left for all of the latter part of the hole. A little pitch over bunkers disposes of the 2nd, and then a short excursion down a woodland path leads to the first encounter with the Bollin.

The 3rd tee stands immediately above the waters and the fairway describes a long arc, swinging all the time to the left, round past a tree-covered hill and in to an ungenerous green again close to the river. With a steep drive uphill over a tree the 4th plays long with a second shot over grassy mounds and in to the green past four bunkers. This is one of the few holes on which the separate tees for the first and second time round differ significantly.

The 5th and 6th are the star holes, running along a tongue of land down towards the motorway, though few golfers will notice it, their minds fully occupied with the more immediate tasks. That 5th tee is up on high ground from which the hole sweeps down agonisingly close to the Bollin on the right and with three bunkers and a row of young trees defining the left of the fairway. There is little room for error with the pitch. The next drive is at least as intimidating with a narrow corridor through which to aim the drive. A few yards in front of the tee the river meanders across the line, waterside bushes adding to its impact, while further on those bushes become deep woods lining the right of the fairway. There is no escape route on the left, for as the fairway begins to climb back up the hill, swinging left in to the green, the ground leans ever more wickedly to the left and 350 yards can suddenly seem very much longer.

The 7th shares its tee with the 5th, playing in the opposite direction, and there must be some excitement here on busy days, but the hole itself offers a moment's breather. *Punch Bowl* is the name of the 8th, and my archaic interest in antiquated holes is immediately stirred, the far side of the punch bowl being lined with two cavernous bunkers. To clear them is not arduous, but there is a grassy ridge covering the front left of the green which tests the approach work with absolutely no margin for error behind the green, the ground racing away into the deep woods through which a winding path takes us to the final tee.

A big tree was allowed to remain when the 9th fairway was constructed and it dominates the drive, though well out of reach of most of us. It demands that we place our drive to one side or the other, and as the woods grow very close on the left there is almost no room that side. Given the luck of a good line in to the green we should note that the fairway rises between the two prominent bunkers giving the false impression that the green is much nearer than it really is. We set out on the second circuit eagerly and, hopefully, wiser.

Card of the course:

1.	476 yards	par 5	10.	476 yards	par 5
2.	167	3	11.	161	3
3.	304	4	12.	304	4
4.	417	4	13.	400	4
5.	382	4	14.	382	4
6.	357	4	15.	357	4
7.	125	3	16.	125	3
8.	298	4	17.	298	4
9.	370	4	18.	381	4
Out:	2896 yards	par 35			
In:	2884 yards	par 35			
Total:	5780 yards	par 70		s.s.s. 68	

Hazel Grove

6310 yards; par 71; s.s.s. 71

After a number of very temporary residencies shortly after its
formation in 1912, Hazel Grove settled at a home just off the A6
High Lane, engaged Alister Mackenzie as course architect and
back to enjoy three-quarters of a century's Doctor's examina-
ns. Had it not been for the threat of a new road I would now be
iting about the virtues of a typically cunning Mackenzie layout,
d the roguery of the infamous 17th, *Spion Kop*, a villainous short
le across a dark and dangerous gully.

"The King is dead. Long live the King!" There being no point
lamenting what is deceased we may as well celebrate the assets
its successor. To be fair, Mackenzie's work is not completely
literated. After all, why alter something perfectly good if it can
main intact? The present 4th, 5th, 7th, 8th, 10th, and 11th are still
entially Mackenzie but with greens brought into line with the
ds of modern play. Tom Macauley, the Irish architect already
niliar to Cheshire golfers through his work at Birchwood, is too
se a campaigner to ignore his heritage. What he has done is to
apt the best of the old course over the railway, restraining it
thin new boundaries, and lay out the rest as a totally new course
rolling open ground radiating from the clubhouse. My experi-
ce of it is limited to a visit shortly after the new course opened
May 1993 and, while the strategy is abundantly clear, the real
pact of the layout will not be felt until the grass and trees have
come rather more firmly established in a year or two's time. In
months between my visit and proofreading, the sward is
eady maturing handsomely, tree planting proceeding apace.

Macauley's new 1st hole is a courteous introduction, an allur-
g drive over, or round, a big oak tree to a flowing fairway, but
re is a sting in the tail, for unless the drive finishes adequately
ced there will be no sight of the green on the far side of a stream
d three well hidden bunkers. There are suppressed bunkers, too,
the long par-3 2nd, two of them just visible to the front of the
en, but two more lurking unannounced through the back.

On most courses the first stroke hole will be a long two-shotter,
many par-5s being reckoned to offer sufficient of a chance of
recovery not to be too savage. Hazel Grove's 3rd hole is one of the
exceptions, a real handful from the white marker, calling for a huge
drive if it is to clear a stream and reach the sanctuary of the further
bank. The second shot, past a pond, is not so demanding, but the
pitch is unforgiving, over a foreshortening gully to a narrow ledge
green above bunkers.

Over the railway the course is more established, existing holes
modified perhaps, but retaining most of the features developed
over the last half century. The 4th runs parallel to the railway to a
domed green, the 5th over rolling ground to a billowing green, and
then the 6th, from a panoramic tee, runs down a hedge, as close
as we are ever to get to the incessant roar of lorries pounding up
the A6. The hole itself is tricky, the fairway cut narrow, the flag
very likely only just over a neatly revetted bunker right on the
approach line. After an uphill par-5, the parallel 8th is a charmer,
not long, gently downhill besides, but the green is narrow and lies
on the far side of a bothersome little gully. A refreshment hut is
available at this point to assuage the thirst of vigorous golfers or
provide adequate cover for those who would prefer to spy on the
tribulations of others.

It is sad to see vestiges of the battle grounds of old lying fallow
beyond, awaiting meekly the butchery of road building, but Macauley has contrived to utilise as much of Mackenzie as is reasonable, and the final stages of the 10th are vintage stuff. In the last
150 yards of the hole you will be confronted by first a gully, then
a hulking mound topped off with a lunar bunker. The diffident who
try to go round by the left-hand route find themselves confronted
with further bunkers.

For the moment the golf is of the heathland, and the 11th is very
much in keeping, a narrow little green (wobbly, too) raised up
beyond a host of bunkers. The 12th, into the bargain, would be

equally at home at Liphook or Beau Desert. Like the 7th it is a gentle par-5 from the white tee and a stern two-shotter off the yellow markers. Either way, two king-sized bunkers guard the entrance to the green most effectively. Those who draw the ball will be only too fully aware of the railway running down the left of the 13th. Those who do not will be equally mindful of the plentiful bunkers on the safer routes.

Back over the railway, the remainder of the course is brand new, beginning with two par-4s up and down a hill past a pond, pretty to the eye but disquieting to the golfer. The second of them is an apprehensive drive for the muscular attacker or a pair of gentle 7-irons for the humble. The 16th drive is fun, moreover, once again over, or round, a tree and for serious golfers there is the challenge of landing between a pond on the left and an encroaching hedge on the right. From the front tees there may be some anxiety on the 17th, the fairway running out just short of a deep and grasping gully, and, for once, the hole may actually be easier from the ve back. Walking onto this green on a misty autumnal morning, t views of distant St George's Church conjured an image, albe momentary, of "That sweet city with her dreaming spires".

As if to redress the balance the final hole is a pleasant str from the front tees and a fiendish monster from the white mark with a final gargantuan carry over Ochreley Brook, trees on eith side demanding the utmost accuracy. Thereafter the fairwa sweeps down and up, past bunkers, to a (Macauley aware of h distinguished predecessor) Mackenzie green close to the impre sive new club house.

The 11th ho

Card of the course:

1.	366 yards	par 4	10.	545 yards	par 5
2.	217	3	11.	183	3
3.	537	5	12.	496	5
4.	388	4	13.	215	3
5.	175	3	14.	381	4
6.	378	4	15.	285	4
7.	492	5	16.	341	4
8.	343	4	17.	376	4
9.	190	3	18.	402	4

Out:	3086 yards	par 35
In:	3224 yards	par 36
Total:	6310 yards	par 71

s.s.s. 71

Heaton Moor

5887 yards; par 70; s.s.s. 68

The story of Heaton Moor Golf Club is long, the club being founded in 1892, and complicated, the course having been changed substantially some eight or nine times in those hundred years. Yet all those changes took place in the first thirty years, as land was lost and gained, leases expired and renegotiated, and plans made in the First World War for an aeroplane factory on the site, subsequently scrapped. With a couple of alterations what is played today is that which was laid out in 1924 in some hurry when part of the 1920 course was lost to a major council housing scheme.

Play on the two halves of the present course could hardly more different. Winding its way, tightly, round the old hosp (itself a considerable participant in the complex tale) the first n has a great deal more character than the remainder of the cour which may be longer but cannot hide the fact that it runs back a forth in parallel strips across a flattish field with plentiful remi ers of industry's proximity. It is hard to envisage that this rea was rural moorland back at the time of the club's conception.

The 1

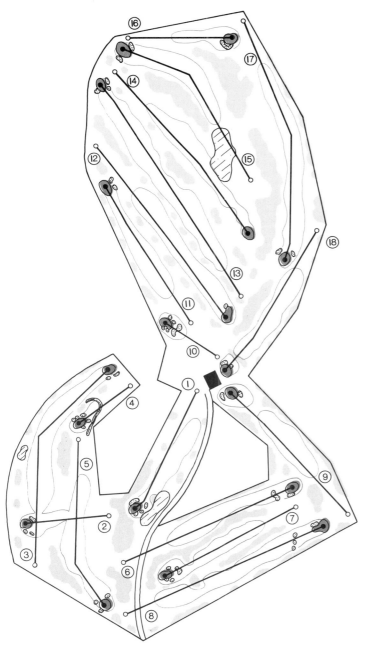

The holes with more personality on that back nine are the short 10th, played across a gully from a very public tee right outside the clubhouse door; the 14th with a demanding second shot across a dip in the fairway just short of the steeply raised green; and the sharply dog-legged 15th with a drive over a pit and a pitch right down to the factory gate, as it were. The 18th, though, is an extraordinary hole involving a devilish and nerve-wracking pitch to the green, very probably from a hanging lie, over a hedge and up the steep bank on the other side to a markedly domed green intimidatingly close to the clubhouse windows and 10th tee.

A plaque inside the clubhouse door just by this green commemorates the remarkable feats of one C.T. "Charlie" Chevalier who was for many years club professional and holds a world record for the number of holes-in-one achieved in a long career, 31 between 1918 and 1970. Several were on the 1st at Heaton Moor, an impish start to the round. Presumably the green can no longer be driven since the intervening trees on this sharp dog-leg will have grown a bit since Chevalier's days. Nowadays it is a prudent iron for position on the corner followed by a gentle pitch to an angled green well guarded by four bunkers, its raised position, and a pond for those who overshoot on the left.

Demands on placing of the drive are made on both the 3rd and 5th, the former seemingly much longer than its official yardage, the latter with a cunningly placed green at the top of a slope. The 6th is very appealing with a fine approach to the green over a dip and a vast bunker on the right, but the real skill is in getting the ball somewhere near (preferably below) the flag on this very sloping green.

The interestingly shaped 8th green is

hard to find with a long approach – a local rule prohibits the use of wooden clubs from the tee, for safety reasons, and 400 yards is on the very limit for a couple of iron club shots for most of us. On the bank beyond this green is the 9th tee, an intriguing hole with some possibility of the drive's colliding with trees on the direct line or finishing in a hedge further on, and then a pitch which must clear a minor chasm to reach the green which slopes down towards trouble on the right.

Card of the course:

1.	265 yards	par 4	10.	127 yards	par 3
2.	167	3	11.	327	4
3.	438	4	12.	417	4
4.	134	3	13.	509	5
5.	347	4	14.	415	4
6.	362	4	15.	352	4
7.	288	4	16.	208	3
8.	402	4	17.	497	5
9.	309	4	18.	323	4
Out:	2712 yards	par 34			
In:	3175 yards	par 36			
Total:	5887 yards	par 70		s.s.s. 68	

Helsby

6229 yards; par 70; s.s.s. 70

he Golf Club at Helsby has been in existence since 1902,
king it one of the older clubs in the county. The distant skyline
changed somewhat since then, dominated as it now is by the
ming chimney stacks of the petro-chemical industry. James
id is credited with the design of the course, but his hand was
on only lightly. For the record he laid out the original nine
es, and his work is pretty well untouched still on six of those.
ere is no disguising the fact, let it be said, that this is a meadow-
d course and the architect had little in the way of natural ground
vement of which to take advantage. Farmland all over Cheshire
distinguished by the multitudinous marl pits which once pro-
ed cattle with refreshment. Good use has been made of them at
sby and deep and treacherous they are, too. There is one right
the gate leading to the 1st tee as if to give ample warning of
at is to come.

Conservation has its place within the club and tree planting
ntinues apace, not just to give greater separation to the fairways
I to add strategic problems to the existing layout but also to
ance the environment in which play takes place. Lavish dis-
ys of daffodils in early spring can only be an inspiration to all.

A catalogue of each hole, shot by shot, is not necessary. It is
r to say that the general flatness of the site gives many of the
es a similarity, perhaps even uniformity, and that, provided the
fer is hitting the ball straight, most problems will be of his own
king. Judgement of distance on flat ground can be tricky, and it
ossible to be out-of-bounds on a great many holes.

The first really interesting hole is the 3rd with a tight drive
ween a prominent pit on the left some 200 yards out and a ditch
I out-of-bounds on the right. A drive of exemplary straightness
alled for here, and length, too, for the approach is far from easy.
e fairway curves to the right descending into one of the few
ressions on the course. At the bottom is a ditch and just beyond
aised up like a hog's back, is the green. Three bunkers protect
front and a hedge the back.

Then comes a splendid par-5, long enough to be a three-shotter
Ill but the giants. A notice by the tee warns of potholes into which

a ball (or foot) may unexpectedly disappear (a result of the under-
lying peat's drying out in a hot summer some years ago). After a
drive down a valley the hole suddenly narrows where the out-of-
bounds hedge curves in from the left and a line of trees on a ridge
closes from the right. At something like 350 yards out from the tee
this constriction and the slope of the fairway will give food for
thought to most players. Thereafter the approach to the green is on
the flat.

Over the road the back nine opens with a teaser, a very short
par-4 which could be played with a couple of 7-irons. We are all
too vain for that! Those who must attempt to drive the green will
be very aware as they stand on the tee of the proximity of the hedge
running down the left all the way to the green. What is more it
seems to encroach more as the fairway moves gently to the left.

The 13th is a serious hole calling for a long drive to avoid a
tree directly in line and yet another pond on the left. Trees guard
the approaches to the green in such a way as to close out the
approach shots of those who ducked the challenge of the pond —
ducked may not be an entirely appropriate word for moorhens
scuttled from its waters when my drive almost came to grief in its
murky depths.

The 14th is a teasing right-hand dog-leg made the more interesting by a newish plantation. It goes without saying that there are
ponds to the right which add to the fun.

It is the 17th, however, that will give most cause for concern
in this homeward stretch of decently long par-4s. The drive is not
too difficult, though trees to the right and a hedge to the left are
plainly visible. The second shot is the tester. The green is tucked
away at the bottom of a gentle hill in a corner with a lane on two
sides, so there are no marks for erring to the left or too far. A couple
of trees stand sentinel over the right front. Pin-point accuracy with
a long iron, maybe even wood, is essential.

There is something appealing about a par-3 to end the round.
That at Helsby is not without appeal, the green on the far side of a
substantial cross-bunker.

opposite: the 17th green

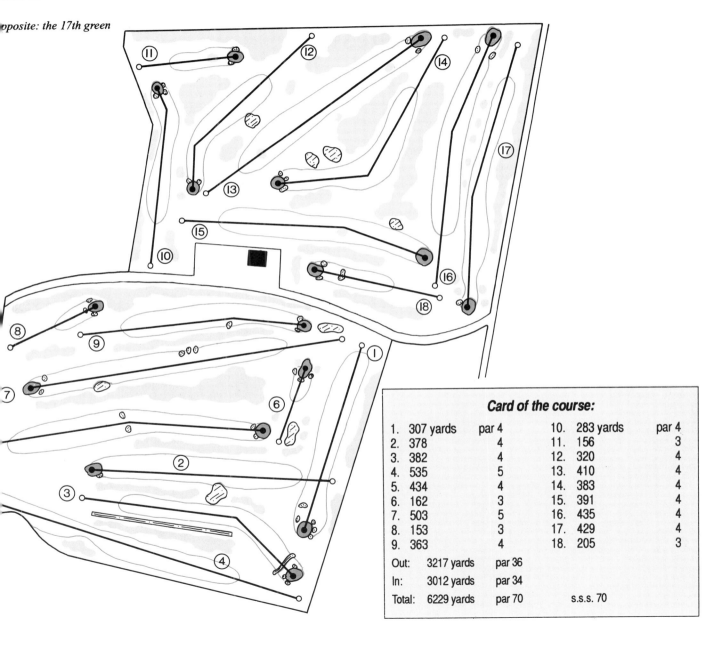

Card of the course:

1.	307 yards	par 4	10.	283 yards	par 4
2.	378	4	11.	156	3
3.	382	4	12.	320	4
4.	535	5	13.	410	4
5.	434	4	14.	383	4
6.	162	3	15.	391	4
7.	503	5	16.	435	4
8.	153	3	17.	429	4
9.	363	4	18.	205	3

Out:	3217 yards	par 36	
In:	3012 yards	par 34	
Total:	6229 yards	par 70	s.s.s. 70

Heswall

6472 yards; par 72; s.s.s. 72

I have never aspired to the solitary existence of the wildfowler, yet an early morning round at Heswall with a haar (to use the term well-known to the golfing inhabitants of the East coast of Scotland) cutting off all contact with the mundane and the constant bubbling of innumerable waders in the salt-marshes of the Dee Estuary is almost sufficient to extol the virtues of this extraordinary activity. How often, when speeding along the recently improved A55 along the North Wales coast on the way to my beloved links at Conwy, I glance down to wonder at the thick protective layers of mist rolling along the estuary, once the main shipping thoroughfare of the North-West (a vision of Roman galleys escaping from t predatory raids of *Asterix* and his band of *Indomitable Gauls* ente my warped mind), now silted up impossibly and only rarely full the brim with the sort of waves to rouse the enthusiasms of yachtsman. Were *"Oh, whistle, and I'll come to you, my lad"* n so immediately identifiable with Brancaster one could easily ima ine that M.R. James had spent a night or two at Heswall gatheri actuality before next terrifying his charges at Eton.

The 3rd ho

For all that, Heswall is no links. It is straightforward parkland lf, despite its proximity to the salt-marshes, stunted and leaning es providing ample reminder of the ferocity of the winds more ally encountered here. On the occasion of my visit (late April) t only was I treated to the cries of innumerable waders but also first hearing of the calls of cuckoo and yellowhammer of the ar. Heswall enjoys the best of both worlds.

It also enjoys a cracking good opening hole, sweeping first wnhill then up to a well bunkered green, all the time curving left und a hedge which keeps the equine inhabitants of the paddocks a manageable distance. They are company again on the 2nd, the rway this time running to two marker posts, the first on a hillock ly really breached with a powerful drive, the second overlooking green, sunken in its private hollow.

After a short walk down a woodland path everything suddenly anges. Whereas formerly we had taken only distant sideways nces at the salt-marshes now there is the most inspiring vista, short par-4 3rd separated from it, it would seem, only by a lge. We are merely required to hit an iron for position from the but, even so, the pitch is a matter of some concern, over bunkers an angled green more than adequately protected by a pond on right. Behind that hedge is the track-bed of the long defunct lway now in its second youth as part of the Wirral Country Park.

Impressions from the 3rd tee were slightly misleading: there is ther life beyond the hedge. From the tee the par-3 4th could be ost the 7th at Pebble Beach, so close does it seem to be to the ter's edge. Again impressions are false: there is plenty of room overshoot and remain dry, but a glorious prospect it remains. en we are introduced to one of Heswall's more extraordinary tures: on a number of holes the yellow tee is so far in front of white as to change the play out of all recognition. On one hole, 12th, the tee is a long, thin runway of at least 100 yards' length, ile on the 5th the yellow tee turns a short par-5 into a mere ve-and-pitch par-4, shorter by more than 130 yards! There can few courses on which the yellow course is 600 yards shorter n the white.

This 5th hole would be a long, flat, featureless beat if it were for the marsh which lurks all along the left of the fairway ning the hole into a hooker's nightmare. What is more, a stream sses the fairway 350 yards out from the tee, in theory easily ared in still weather but quite a problem when the wind is up.

The little green by the shore is our first reminder of that old axiom of seaside golf, that all greens lean towards the sea.

The 6th is utterly flat, apart from two artificial mounds guarding the green, and fairly innocuous, and so, it would seem, is the 7th. Someone noticed this and excavated a pond 200 yards away on the right of the fairway, turning a very ordinary hole into quite a handful in any sort of wind off the sea. A short hole, fairly harmless despite a pond to the left, ends this brief skirmish with the salty sea.

Over the track-bed of the railway, once again, the 9th reverts to pure parkland golf, a long, slow, drag curving right up a hill with a hedge to the left and another of those devastatingly accurately placed ponds on the right to confound the second shot which has been held up too well against the slope. A sea mist may imply no wind, but its humid air holds up the airborne shot and the dew-covered fairways grant little roll, and suddenly the golf seems unusually long. Even downhill on the 10th I found myself banging away with a wooden club for the second shot and failing to clear the cross-bunkers severing the fairway in a gully and preventing all but the aerial route in to the green. Mist, too, can have a remarkably foreshortening effect, inducing chronic underclubbing on hole after hole.

After a tricky short hole to a two-level green comes the 12th which, as I said before, begins on the runway of one of the longest continuous tees in Cheshire. From the back the hole is possibly more approachable in the form of a short par-5. From the front few will drive far enough round the corner, against the slope and dangerously close to wind-blown trees, to be able to reach the green in comfort. A rather simple short par-4, the 13th, is transformed by a little spinney planted on the direct line, forcing play out to the right. The pitch has to be accomplished over a deep ditch, almost a canal.

Crossing the track once more, the 14th gives us a last taster of the flat ground by the salt marsh, and the best has been kept for last. This is a fine hole, demanding a huge drive of immaculate straightness to reach the corner of the dog-leg without perishing in either the coppice to the left or the ditch to the right. The green, too, is a gem, secretively cradled in the arms of the hedge, sheltered from the wind but jealously guarded.

Not all the trumps have been played, for the 15th is a good hole, openly inviting and dangerously punishing when too many liberties are taken. The fairway climbs steadily upwards, bending to the

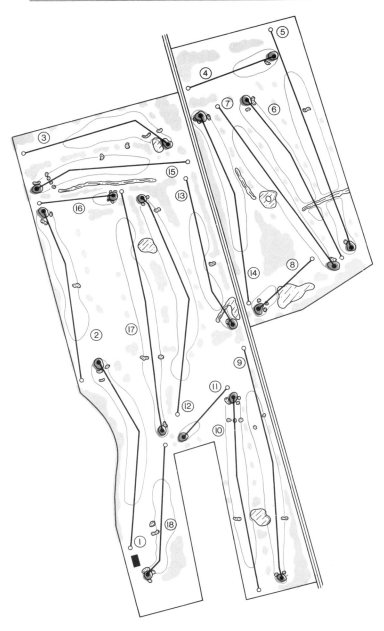

left as it climbs, a ditch threatening on the left all the way. The green appears to be just over the back of a row of cross bunkers. When our pitches finish just there we are made all too aware that another two clubs might have been taken safely.

After a deeply bunkered short hole, the 17th involves a big uphill drive to clear a punchbowl on the left. If that is accomplished successfully there is some hope of the second shot clearing the next hump and its two lots of dead ground to reach the green whose position is apparent only from the marker post standing at the back of the last tee. Then it is a stout uphill climb past a couple of fairway bunkers on the right and a pitch over distinctly serious greenside bunkers to reach the safety of that final green. We may be sad to have left the wildness of the salt-marsh holes behind, but the golf is at least as testing here on the open parkland below the clubhouse windows.

Heswall's story would not be complete without the tale of the first British *Caterpillar*. This is a club whose members have earned inclusion by their having saved their lives using a parachute (silk threads, larvae, caterpillars — you see the connection). It was not until 1925 that the Air Ministry decided to issue parachutes to the Royal Air Force and it took until May 1926 for the first to be issued. No sooner than 17th June of that year one Pilot Officer Pentland, practising half-rolls over the Dee Estuary, went out of control and used his parachute in earnest. He landed on Heswall Golf Course, lucky man, and thus became the first British member of the Caterpillar Club.

Card of the course:				
1.	421 yards	par 4	10. 435 yards	par 4
2.	393	4	11. 148	3
3.	337	4	12. 490	5
4.	209	3	13. 330	4
5.	494	5	14. 431	4
6.	396	4	15. 327	4
7.	434	4	16. 151	3
8.	160	3	17. 520	5
9.	509	5	18. 287	4
Out:	3353 yards	par 36		
In:	3119 yards	par 36		
Total:	6472 yards	par 72	s.s.s. 72	

Heyrose

6449 yards; par 73; s.s.s. 71

have often wandered over my uncle's farm land laying out imaginary golf holes. His farm ends at a brook and all my best holes crossed that brook onto a neighbouring farmer's land. It came something of a shock one day to find first that the neighbouring farmer had himself begun the construction of a golf course and secondly that his holes did not run at all in the same direction as mine! In his wisdom he had built a hole (now the 16th) parallel to that brook and many of the early members clearly had some difficulty keeping on the right side of the water. I did not need to buy any golf balls for ages. Now the players are more expert and the local lads more adept at finding stray balls and I am back to buying them by the dozen.

The 17th hole

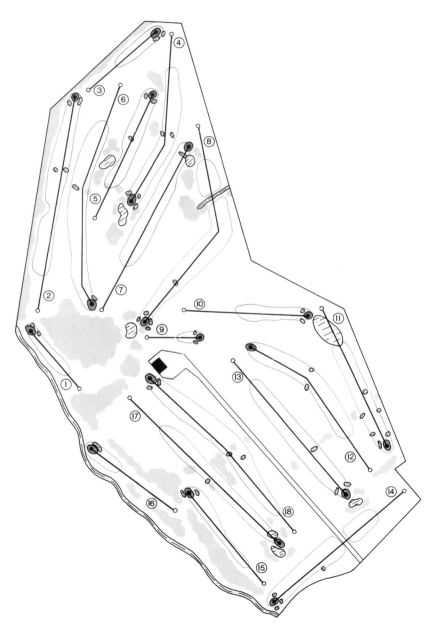

In this part of the county the soil is heavy with good deal of clay in its make up, the land itself rath flat and featureless. Those intent on golf course co struction can either spend a fortune on earth movin soil conditioning and importation of mature forestry, they can set their sights on something more modes charge rather less for membership and green fees, ar wait twenty-five years for things to grow. The latt seems to be the line taken at Heyrose.

It would not be unfair to say that the course is in a interim form. It has only recently expanded to 18-hol and tree planting is the order of the day. For such young course the fairways (or at least those on th higher ground, the majority of them) are impressivel lush though that means little roll on the drive and on or two clubs more to be taken on approach shots. Th flatness of the land is made the more apparent by th shallowness of so many of the bunkers and the lack elevation of the greens. While this means that it possible to trundle the ball onto the putting surface wit a scuffed shot it is equally possible to roll off the bac unhindered and into all manner of evil.

The pick of the holes on the way out are the 1st (fc its setting rather than its architecture), 4th (a tightis dog-leg to the right around a hedge at the corner) an the sequence of three holes, the 6th, 7th, and 8th. It the drive at the 6th which most particularly tests, wit a pond on the left and a bunker on the right just wher the fairway turns sharply left and a tree or two behin which it is possible to be stuck simply by not thinkin sufficiently on the tee. On the 7th it is the second sho which makes this very much a bogey-5 rather than par-4, for there is a deep cross-bunker just in front o the green and a pond close in on the right to make th approach decidedly tricky. And then it is the drive agai at the 8th which provides the fun, for even playe conservatively the drive must clear a little stream wit no room to opt out to either side. The adventurous ca attempt to shorten the dog-leg by driving out over hedge on the right and crossing the fingers.

There is plenty of space here, and no feeling o trying to cram too much into the available land, an ver the next few holes everything is wide open, waiting for the ees to grow to give it character. Only at the 14th is there a change, n extraordinary hole that seems to come from an earlier golfing ge. You see, the second shot, the long approach to the green, is layed blind, downhill, to a flat green just in front of the brook ith no lip at the back to stop the ball. The great players of the 9th-century would have thought it a sporting hole. I am not sure hat those of the late 20th-century would make of it!

Surely all who stand on the back tee at the 16th must experience ome concern for the problem is not that the green is almost out of each, nor that there is a stream running all down the left, but that ees either side of the line give just the narrowest corridor of ninterrupted flight and a hedge down the right is almost as unitive as the stream. It all looks so benign from the other side of e stream!

The 17th is a good hole, not too hard as a genuine three-shotter, ut quite lively when a birdie is sought, with a little pond just in ont of the green to the left and another on the right almost level ith the putting surface. Returning to the clubhouse is less hazard-ous, provided the drive does not finish behind either of the big trees left growing in the fairway.

Card of the course:

1.	171 yards	par 3	10.	284 yards	par 4
2.	529	5	11.	347	4
3.	180	3	12.	394	4
4.	385	4	13.	380	4
5.	319	4	14.	390	4
6.	522	5	15.	274	4
7.	457	4	16.	237	3
8.	495	5	17.	478	5
9.	123	3	18.	484	5

Out: 3181 yards par 36

In: 3268 yards par 37

Total: 6449 yards par 73 s.s.s. 71

Houldsworth

(course being rebuilt)

The(temporary) 12th hole

T*here is something a little melancholy in drinking wine from a vineyard no longer in existence*: Edmund Penning-Rowsell describing his only acquaintance, the 1929 vintage, with Château Laburthe-Brivazac, a Pessac vineyard of some repute swallowed up all too many years ago by the Bordelais bulldozer. Houldsworth is not extinct and by 1994 is being reconstituted, replanted, as it were. Never the less there was something grievous in 1993 about the sight of a building contractor's vehicles churning up historic turf, surely the closest to central Manchester, for the sake of a few new houses.

Houldsworth began life in 1910, taking its name from A.J. Balfour's one-time adversary, Sir William Houldsworth, M.P. for North-West Manchester. In those days it lay in farm land, but World Wars and property speculation led to its gradual transformation to parkland, in which form it is now surrounded by houses and the defunct remains of a railway, providing a very necessary retreat for golfers and wildlife alike in an otherwise urban environment. Even in reformation, its rolling greens and sporadic ponds are no sinecure.

Hoylake

6313 yards; par 70; s.s.s. 70

would be surprising if at least one innocent tourist had not paid to play here in the mistaken belief that it was over this very turf t the great golfers of the past did battle for such trophies as the en Championship. No, this is the public course welcoming all ners as long as there is space for them on the course, they have lub or two, and they can find the modest green fee. However appointed the tourists might be that they are playing the wrong urse, the rest of us need feel no shame: this is a decent enough t for us.

James Braid is reputed to have waved his magic wand over the ce when it was founded in 1933. He could do nothing about the y flatness of the site but he was able to raise his greens above

some very serious pot bunkers of the most vicious traditional kind, and to ensure a good variety to the hole lengths and their disposition. Unlike its big brother across the road, Hoylake Municipal enjoys the strategic advantages of a number of ditches and ponds punctuating play from time to time and causing, incidentally, many a card to be shredded prematurely. Frequently taking a line on a distant church spire the golfer is constantly watched over by the hilltop monument down to the south.

Card of the course:

1.	342 yards	par 4	10.	178 yards	par 3
2.	418	4	11.	399	4
3.	175	3	12.	477	5
4.	334	4	13.	324	4
5.	447	4	14.	360	4
6.	371	4	15.	479	5
7.	167	3	16.	203	3
8.	429	4	17.	463	4
9.	390	4	18.	357	4
Out:	3073 yards	par 34			
In:	3240 yards	par 36			
Total:	6313 yards	par 70	s.s.s. 70		

The 12th hole

Knight's Grange

5720 yards; par 70; s.s.s. 68

How often our first impression of a golf course is the most lasting! At Knight's Grange, for instance, golf begins with a walk down a tunnel (or so it would seem, being no more sinister than a passageway through the converted farm buildings doing duty as the professional's shop) during which the green fee is paid. Already there is a sense of privacy, of having the mundane shut off, for the time being at least. As it happens the impression will not endure — new housing developments alongside the course will see to that — but ponds and ditches, neighbouring woodland and gently rolling fairways keep up the illusion for most of the round. Bunkers here are filled with a notably pale sand giving a somewhat luxurious air uncommon on municipal courses and, unusually, on only two holes (6th and 9th) are the women's medal tees in front of the men's, though their par for the round is appropriately four strokes higher. The 1st and 9th holes cross a patch of level ground by the clubhouse. The other holes — the more characterful — lie on the far side of a lane. Their order of play may be altered before this book is in print.

The 8th hole

Card of the course:

1.	161 yards	par 3
2.	359	4
3.	256	4
4.	511	5
5.	273	4
6.	320	4
7.	379	4
8.	431	4
9.	171	3
Out:	2860 yards	par 35
Total (18 holes):	5720 yards	par 70 s.s.s. 68

Knutsford

6288 yards; par 70; s.s.s. 70

Jnquestionably Knutsford is the most beautiful 10-hole course Cheshire (probably in the world, for that matter)! Had it been ly 9-holes I doubt if there would be much competition either. id out on the edge of the Tatton Estate, just behind that brick wall running the length of the back road out of Knutsford in the direction of Mere and Ashley, the golf club enjoys the luxury of a generous assortment of trees, deciduous and coniferous, the company of deer and sheep roaming just over the fence in Tatton Park,

distant views of the lakes, and an ornithologist's dream: on reflection I realise that I had encountered over twenty easily recognisable species during the course of a round – someone who could identify the "little brown jobs" flitting about in the trees would very likely double that number.

The character of the course is entirely in keeping with its surroundings: stately, far from brash, in fact rather noble. There was a course laid out in Tatton as early as 1891, by George Lowe who was Professional at Lytham and had much to do with the establishment of that course in the very top flight. But a family death at the Hall caused the removal of the club in 1909 to a slightly more distant site, where the course is to this day. It remains for the most part the work of talented and visionary amateurs by the name of Speakman and Taylor.

A pair of decently long par-4s begin proceedings, the 1st made by a couple of depressions crossing the fairway, one in driving range, the other shortly before the green. A flat, well bunkered par-3 takes play to the far end of the course and the attractive 4th hole, dog-legging to the right around trees and then slightly downhill, if the angles have been correctly calculated, to a well protected green. While the short 5th ought not to be more than a little prod with a short iron the green is almost an oasis in a wasteland of bunkers, the hole by no means a push-over.

The 8th hole

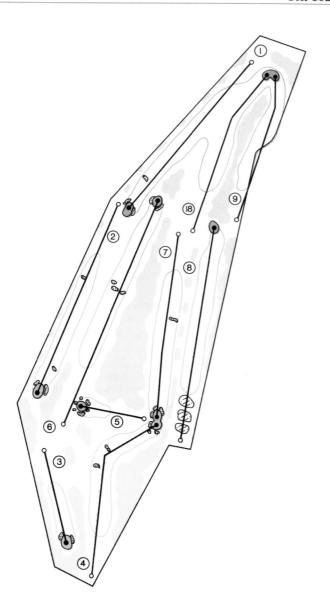

Comparison is bound to be made with Royal Worlington loyally said by all Cambridge golfers to be the finest 9-hole course on earth. There is a feel of "Mildenhall" (as it is known) about Knutsford's 6th with a drive out over a row of grassy mounds, first defining the hole on the right. Cross-bunkers threaten most players' second shots, or the drives of the really long hitter, and then is a deft pitch down to a sunken green, hidden just beyond the gull encountered just in front of the 1st green. The 7th is a straightforward short par-4 to a green beside a pond.

In fact there are three ponds here, separated by the various teeing grounds for the 8th hole, a long par-4 from the very back and a fine hole, too. Not only is there the ever present threat of out-of-bounds on the right in the form of the boundary wall but the trees which line the left of the fairway may be nearly as punitive particularly as the green is canted up above a little hollow on the left.

Knutsford gains its 10 holes through having separate equally attractive finishing holes for each nine. The 9th is a death defying skirmish with the ubiquitous brick wall, and there is little point in ducking the challenge for there is no shot to the green if you finish in or behind the trees on the left. The 18th is a right-handed dog-leg around those same trees making full use of the depression over (or into) which we drove from the 1st tee.

Card of the course:					
1.	401 yards	par 4	10.	401 yards	par 4
2.	426	4	11.	426	4
3.	200	3	12.	200	3
4.	383	4	13.	383	4
5.	139	3	14.	139	3
6.	492	5	15.	492	5
7.	317	4	16.	317	4
8.	448	4	17.	448	4
9.	311	4	18.	365	4
Out:	3117 yards	par 35			
In:	3171 yards	par 35			
Total:	6288 yards	par 70		s.s.s. 70	

Leasowe

6204 yards; par 71; s.s.s. 70

Like its neighbours, Wallasey and Royal Liverpool, Leasowe is already past its century. It began life a little to the west of its present home by the lighthouse, soon moving to the site which, I suppose, you would describe as being "round the back of Leasowe Castle" in its day, about the end of the 16th-Century, a sporting lodge for the Derby family, stage for early troupes of travelling Shakespearian actors, later the scene of horse racing when it was known locally as Mockbeggar Hall, and eventually a convalescent home for railway workers. As the course was first laid out here it enjoyed the challenge of a number of links holes in and out of the dunes but coastal erosion has destroyed that part, more's the pity, because what is left is undeniably flat. Indeed, it reminds me of the level inland stretch at Wallasey not a million miles away.

It was necessary to acquire new land at the rear of the Castle in more recent times and the course begins in this stretch with what, to me, are the most interesting holes. The 1st itself is certainly full of entertainment, almost driveable you might think, but those last 0 yards are the exciting bit with a tricky pitch in over bunkers to a sunken, angled green set in the midst of mock battlements and arrow slits!

Through a chink in the armour, as it were, on the second tee you are faced with a blind drive over a ridge or cop. Someone had the wisdom to leave the stump of the Moreton Lighthouse intact to act as a distant marker post. A ditch crosses the fairway just in front of the green to prevent the use of the traditional seaside low pitch shot. The 3rd should not cause problems, but the 4th is a tough hole over its last couple of hundred yards. The drive should take advantage of the wide, unfettered early fairway because the cop here encountered on the 2nd interrupts the route around the 300-yard mark, obscuring the many big humps and hollows waiting to deflect the ball from its intended path to the green, itself rather a lively angled affair just in front of the castle wall. About this hole there is something of the arbitrary nature of the *Star Chamber*,

entirely appropriate as the said chamber was apparently reconstructed in Leasowe Castle on its removal from Westminster in 1634.

There is only one sea view to be had at Leasowe (as with so many seaside courses) and that is from the 5th tee high up on the sea wall itself. Bunkers out to the right of this left-handed dog-leg limit freedom on the drive and the pitch is again interesting, over a little ridge and down to another slightly sunken green.

The 6th is a seriously long par-5, the narrow fairway dominated by the high sea wall running the length of the hole on the left, but it is not nearly so much fun as the 7th, the last really characterful hole. Here the drive is out to the right, away from the sea wall, with a bunker to restrain the ambitions of the mighty. At this point the hole swings through a right angle to the left and in over a minefield of bunkers to a rectangular green surrounded by a ridge.

The drive at the 9th is to be enjoyed, from a tee down in a corner by the neat rows of appetising vegetables in a market garden. Naturally enough, the drive has to clear a substantial acreage of greengrocery, cutting off the angle of the dog-leg, to ensure the green is in reach of the second shot, especially into the prevailing wind.

The rest of the course lacks the physical advantages of these earlier holes, and while the wind will almost certainly increase its challenge, the very nature of its location is unavoidably flat. Perhaps the most memorable features are the drive at the 13th out of gorse bushes to an angled fairway, the drive at the 15th with a ditch in the angle of the right-hand dog-leg, the pitch at the 16th over a long line of bunkers, and the final stages of the 17th with two really vicious bunkers halfway down the fairway and a charming two-level green set in a ring of grassy mounds. That is not to say that the golf is any easier for lack of undulation: ditches abound, ponds and boggy patches, too.

Card of the course:

	252 yards	par 4	10.	446 yards	par 4
	318	4	11.	299	4
	141	3	12.	151	3
	436	4	13.	314	4
	315	4	14.	406	4
	562	5	15.	402	4
	414	4	16.	369	4
	278	4	17.	478	5
	436	4	18.	187	3

ut:	3152 yards	par 36
:	3052 yards	par 35
tal:	6204 yards	par 71

s.s.s. 70

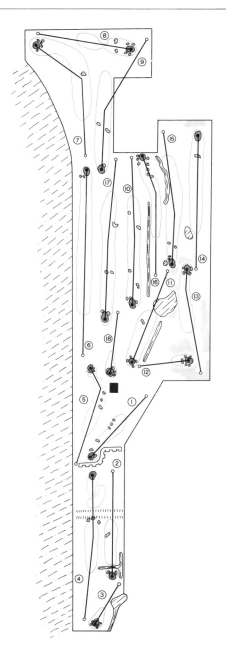

posite: Leasowe 1st green

Lymm

6304 yards; par 71; s.s.s. 70

As a village, or small town, Lymm keeps a remarkably low profile despite the attractions of its lakeside setting. It is close to Warrington, Altrincham, and Manchester, clearly commuter territory, yet retains its own quiet character. The only railway to serve it was a sleepy little L.N.W.R. branch line. In recent times the M6 and M56 have come awfully close to affecting the village but the real upheaval was the construction of the Manchester Ship Canal back in the 1880s and '90s. A huge quantity of earth had to be excavated and a tiny fraction of this forms the higher part of the golf course at Lymm.

Just as the village is quiet, so too is the golf course, down below. Approaching it along a causeway over a marsh I am always reminded of that most atmospheric of causeways over the reed beds and salt marshes between Brancaster and the Royal West Norfolk links. A good half of the course is down on the flat ground alongside these marshes, the rest of the holes enjoying rather mor movement on the higher ground alongside the Ship Canal on tha excavated earth.

Though the 1st sets the tone with its tree-lined level fairwa and the 2nd runs to a nicely shaped green in the trees, it is the 3r hole, on higher ground, that stands out amongst the early hole Here it is necessary to flirt with a substantial drop on the left (the 11th green) before swinging right and slightly uphill to well-bunkered green in the trees. The 5th gives a grand opportunit to view the log-jam of pantechnicons and articulated tankers a stationary, they decorate the skyline on Thelwall Viaduct. The hol itself, on slightly bumpy ground above the Ship Canal, is reminis cent of some of the golf to be found on the shores of the Rive Clyde, such as the admirable course at Erskine.

The 6th hol

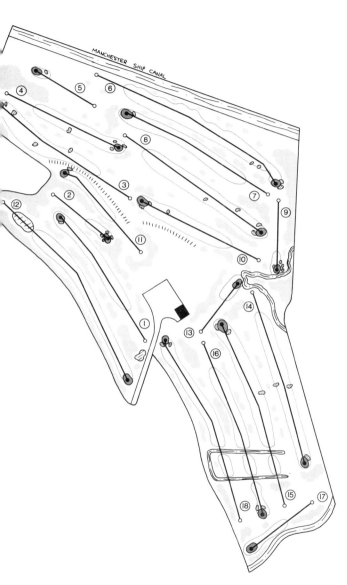

The 6th provides at least two opportunities of hitting into the murky waters and a little way beyond its slightly hidden green is the tee for the testing 9th. It is really nothing much as long as you do not pull the shot off the tee. Do it slightly and you are likely to find yourself in one of several imaginatively shaped bunkers. Do it a little more and your ball will be lost for ever in trees and a stream down a steep bank.

There is character aplenty on the 11th, almost driveable if you can keep out of the bunker set into the bank on the right, and, rather more importantly, out of the trees on the left. On the far side of a pond is the 12th tee and from it the drive is lined on a distant church spire, back over the pond. The 13th may be short and bunkerless, but when the pin is at the back of the green it is only a matter of feet from the waters of a brook.

You are asked for a bit of muscle over the rest of the round, particularly so on the 16th with its double water carry and a hill to be surmounted on the second shot. Those who cannot guarantee to make that sort of distance need to know to the inch where their second will land in order to avoid a wetting. Round the back of the green, the 17th utilises a hidden corner rather effectively before, from the elevated final tee, a fair old carry is required to clear both ditches crossing the 18th fairway.

Card of the course:

1.	371 yards	par 4	10.	345 yards	par 4
2.	173	3	11.	275	4
3.	400	4	12.	542	5
4.	308	4	13.	155	3
5.	175	3	14.	439	4
6.	527	5	15.	476	5
7.	403	4	16.	450	4
8.	420	4	17.	185	3
9.	176	3	18.	484	5
Out:	2953 yards	par 34			
In:	3351 yards	par 37			
Total:	6304 yards	par 71		s.s.s. 70	

Macclesfield

5625 yards; par 70; s.s.s. 67

Macclesfield is one of that select band which has almost forgotten the celebrations in honour of its centenary. It ran, until very recently, to 12 holes, made up of 9 genuine holes one or two of which had very distinct alternatives, described by the old *A.A. Guide* as a "very hilly heathland course situated on the edge of the Pennines. Excellent views." Apart from the number of holes the description remains intact.

The star holes, too, remain intact, and it says much for Messrs Hawtree that they have not sought to out-gun the best of th originals in extending the course to a full 18-hole circuit utilisin land made available down below, nearer the town. Interestingl enough these new holes do not attempt to push the yardage up nea 7,000 but, rather, decrease the 18-hole total to a mere 5,625 yard If my description of the course lingers on one or two of the olde holes it seems to me that it merely confirms my own feeling about the best golf architects, that if someone has already go the best out of a piece of land you leave it well alone!

Macclesfield begins remorselessly with a couple of brut ish uphill holes, and equally spiteful matters would still seer to be as you strike out blindly over a marker post on the 3rd As it happens, if you make sufficiently precise contact wit the ball, the drive should run on almost for ever to leave bu a chip over a wide and long gully to the raised green. To hol the green from further afield, very probably from a hangin; lie, is a matter for prayer.

One of the new holes, the 6th, would be no more than par-3 on a flat course, but up here it is a full par-4 to gorgeously sited green in the folds of the hillside with view of its own private valley beyond. Just above the green, th outstandingly sited 7th tee is the place to try out your *Fish-Ey lens*. Leave a snap or two in your camera for the newl renumbered 8th, in its way not unlike the 3rd and in its late stages over the same gully, but this time involving a darin; drive over a ravine and as many of the trees on the left as yo dare. The 9th winds its way back up the hill in parallel, excep that as a par-5 it is just a little longer and the final shot i: played blind over the hill to the green, really rather a matte of guesswork unless you know the course precisely.

Left: Macclesfield, 3rd hole

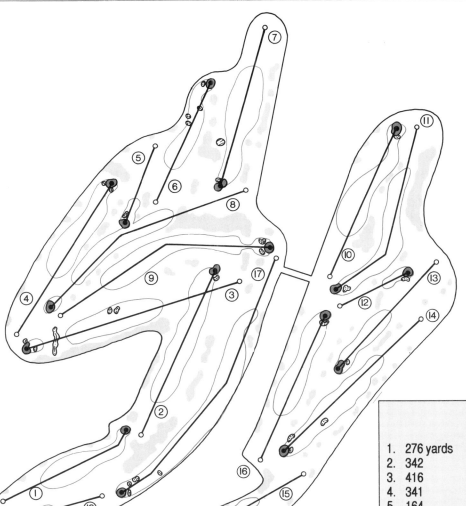

As I suggested earlier, it is one of Hawtree's strengths that they leave good holes well alone, and so they have done with the 17th, which as the former 8th could be played as a short par-4 to an elevated green on the right or as a long par-5 downhill almost into Water Green itself. Now the shorter option is removed, but the challenge of going for the green remains as tantalising as ever, for the hole is not outrageously long played down the hill. The second shot must avoid a tree-clad hillock on the right yet still hold the right side sufficiently to slip past a number of bunkers on that side and avoid excessive deviation in the various humps and bumps left in place by earlier architects. And, after that, all that is left is a mere flip down the hill, but, of course, it must be an accurate flip....

Card of the course:

1.	276 yards	par 4	10.	308 yards	par 4
2.	342	4	11.	359	4
3.	416	4	12.	143	3
4.	341	4	13.	271	4
5.	164	3	14.	355	4
6.	231	4	15.	184	3
7.	322	4	16.	297	4
8.	439	4	17.	542	5
9.	468	5	18.	167	3
Out:	2999 yards	par 36			
In:	2626 yards	par 34			
Total:	5625 yards	par 70		s.s.s. 67	

Malkins Bank

5977 yards; par 70; s.s.s. 69

As one of the very few (pitifully few) municipal courses in Cheshire, Malkins Bank has an important rôle to play despite its humble origins (built it is said on top of a rubbish tip!). For the most part it enables golfers from the absolute beginner to the quite expert to coexist without too much mutual danger, with reasonable encouragement for the player as yet unable to get the ball airborne and a degree of challenge to the vanity of those who would fee[l] they ought to be capable of tearing the place apart. Many of th[e] holes move in a straightforward manner over flat ground wit[h] bunkers confined only to the sides of the greens, enabling play t[o] flow as reasonably as four-ball play and overcrowding permit.

The 13th ho[le]

There are, however, one or two holes which present rather ~~eater~~ difficulties – holes which would not be out of place on a ~~embers'~~ course. The 4th, for instance, with its teasing drive over ~~stream,~~ the green hidden round to the right. Big-hitters will be ~~mpted~~ to cut off most or all of the dog-leg but in doing so they ~~ust~~ take on a great deal more of the stream. The same stream also ~~ns~~ the length of the 7th hole presenting a very finite boundary ~~down~~ the left of the fairway and a disincentive to draw the ball. ~~it~~ these are mere trifles compared with the 13th:

It is usual on a course of this type to provide alternative and ~~ntler~~ strategies for those of modest ability. On the 13th there is ~~alternative~~ to a perfectly lined tee shot of generous length to ~~ld~~ the top left side of a narrow fairway. An inch or two to the left ~~d~~ a thick hedge ensures that it is "three off the tee". An inch or ~~o~~ to the right and the ball plunges down a steep slope very ~~ssibly~~ perishing in the thick undergrowth or impenetrable forest ~~ing~~ off to the right. Even the pitch is notably tricky, across a ~~cond~~ depression to a ledge green.

There can be similar trials on the 14th with a stream in play and ~~avily~~ overhanging trees. Some tees call for shots of the utmost ~~licacy~~ to avoid the overhead branches yet still bite sharply on the minuscule green. If these obstacles are overcome successfully the remaining holes will make few demands.

Card of the course:

1.	359 yards	par 4	10.	171 yards	par 3
2.	516	5	11.	359	4
3.	164	3	12.	388	4
4.	329	4	13.	355	4
5.	197	3	14.	145	3
6.	312	4	15.	368	4
7.	495	5	16.	364	4
8.	343	4	17.	369	4
9.	366	4	18.	377	4
Out:	3081 yards	par 36			
In:	2896 yards	par 34			
Total:	5977 yards	par 70		s.s.s. 69	

Marple

5565 yards; par 68; s.s.s. 67

It is quite extraordinary how many of the oldest Cheshire clubs are upland, if not highland, courses. Many of them are hard work, and I do not duck the issue when writing about them in this book. The one exception is Marple, to which you might be directed if you fancy a day's golf looking down on the expanse of Cheshire plain without too much strenuous effort. It is not spectacularly long, there are crossing holes, and the turf is more akin to meadowland than moorland, but there are sufficient characterful holes not only to test golfers of all abilities but to remain in the memory when the rest (assisted by post-match drinks, no doubt) have blurred into one.

The back nine is perhaps the key to a good score, but it will take good play to reach the 3rd green in two shots, uphill, with the need to fade a long second round trees on the right. Those who fail career on into a pond over which the 4th is played to a double green with the 18th. Take time, too, to enjoy the view from the 5th tee, looking up towards a hillside village, the drive lined up on its church tower. A cross-bunker short of the green easily deceives the eye and many a pitch falls short.

Local knowledge is an advantage, too, in pitching (blind) to the 7th green down in a hollow below a masterpiece of red-brick industrial architecture. The other excitement going out is a twin-pronged attack from trees on the left of the drive on the 9th, but those trees and their watery contents are a greater factor as the round progresses. First you pitch into them over a host of bunkers on the 265-yard 10th—seemingly nothing from the tee, but naughty at closer range. The trees are irrelevant to the 11th, but played uphill to a green in a punchbowl, some of which is hidden round the corner to the left, it is not an insignificant hole.

The major encounter with the said trees is on the 12th, a roguis[h] hole! A gap in the trees is plainly visible and the visitor has n[o] alternative than to aim for it. The trees close in to narrow th[e] fairway and give way to a ditch on the far side of which the fairwa[y] turns abruptly right, the green being hidden from view until th[e] ditch is crossed. I have no doubt locals know precisely where tha[t] green is wherever they put their drives!

Pond life may be examined on the 13th, but the next rea[l] excitement comes with the drive on the 14th. In front of the tee i[s] a gap in the hedge, but if you try to go through that you are likel[y] to plunge into the depths of a pond lurking in bushes on the righ[t.] It may be better to ensure that you clear the trees slightly left o[f] that gap, and also that you do not plough on into the bunkers whic[h] interrupt the fairway alongside the pond. The rest of the hole i[s] clear-cut, and so, in its way, is the 15th. Quite simply if you canno[t] guarantee to clear the ditch on the direct route to the green mak[e] sure you drop short and hope for a close enough pitch to set up [a] single putt.

Fiendish is the word which comes to mind as you stand on th[e] 16th tee and wonder whether you can clear the ditch and it[s] attendant hedge more or less directly over the 1st green. In the bes[t] traditions of *cape* holes the more risk you take the more chanc[e] there is of a decent shot to the green, and the more liability if yo[u] should fail. A similar drive, back-to-front, as it were, opens pro[-] ceedings on the 18th.

Opposite: Marple, 5th hol[e]

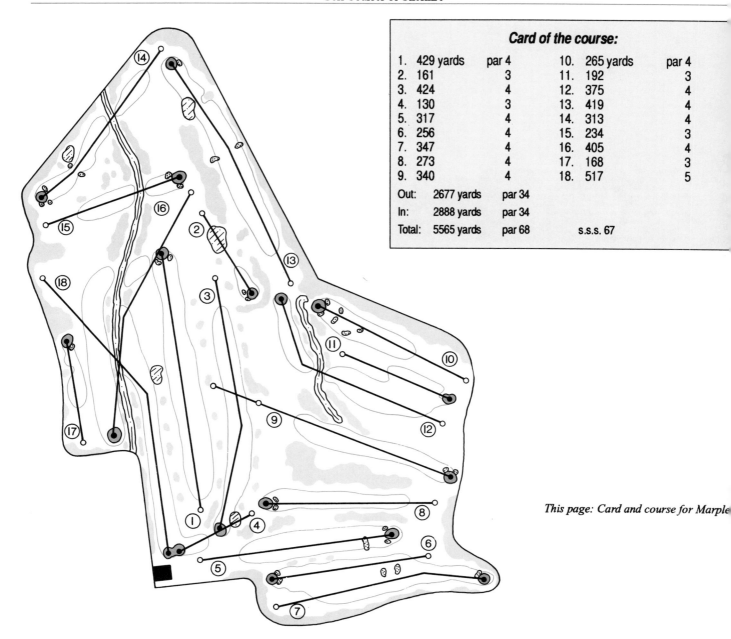

Card of the course:

1.	429 yards	par 4	10.	265 yards	par 4
2.	161	3	11.	192	3
3.	424	4	12.	375	4
4.	130	3	13.	419	4
5.	317	4	14.	313	4
6.	256	4	15.	234	3
7.	347	4	16.	405	4
8.	273	4	17.	168	3
9.	340	4	18.	517	5

Out:	2677 yards	par 34
In:	2888 yards	par 34
Total:	5565 yards	par 68

s.s.s. 67

This page: Card and course for Marple

Mellor and Townscliffe

5925 yards; par 70; s.s.s. 69

Mellor is one of the oldest clubs in the county, founded almost 100 years ago in 1894, though golf was fairly certainly played there in the previous decade. It has also one of the hilliest courses in the county, marvellously scenic in good weather and tremendous physical exercise. A mixture of parkland and moorland, the course is laid out on a mountainous site and while not every hole requires crampons and ice axe this might be the place to send our golfers to train before the next Ryder Cup – we have seen the benefits of altitude training on Kenyan athletes. Mellor claims to have the highest tee in Cheshire, 850 feet above sea level, which is at least half way to rivalling the engaging little 9-hole course at Leadhills in Lanarkshire, reckoned by those who collect statistics to be the highest course in Britain.

The 9th hole

Mellor expanded to 18 holes in 1925 when it opened its doors to members of the recently dissolved Townscliffe Golf Club. It lost some of its holes during the war, but a recent land purchase opens up the prospect of extending the course further. Geographically Mellor seems currently to be in Greater Manchester, but having previously graced both Derbyshire and Cheshire, and being a long-standing member of the Cheshire Union, there is no gainsaying its inclusion in these pages.

Hills are splendid things to play down and can be invigorating to play up, but they are a sure test of true striking when the golf is along the hillside and there will be many sidehill lies during the course of the round. A good number of the greens on the downhill holes are simply the end of the descent and a very confident touch is required to land a long approach shot some way short of the green, just short enough to let the ball trickle onto the putting surface with sufficient vigour to reach the flag but not so much that it bounds off the far end of the green. That is not a criticism any more than it would be of unwatered greens on a seaside links, merely a statement of one of the more frequent problems this course poses.

It does it straight away with an invigorating downhill drive to a wide open fairway but a pitch over a little brook to a characteristically unreceptive green (only two greens are more than 30 yards in depth). The 2nd, too, makes the same demands, though this time the water is encountered on the drive in the form of a little pond in front of the tee, the fairway dog-legging sharply to the right and downhill, it hardly need be added.

There is a goodly number of quaint holes, old-fashioned if you like (and I do like), and the next three qualify easily. The 3rd, *Punchbowl*, involves a drop-shot into a leafy glade with any number of overhanging branches to deflect the less than perfectly lined shot into severe trouble. The first hill-climb is gentle but it is sufficient to deter any thoughts the average golfer might have had of reaching the 4th green from the tee. A hedge on the left and a row of bushes on the right just short of the green confirm the wisdom of sticking to the pragmatic approach. The 5th, *Windybottom*, is theoretically no more than a short pitch over a deep gully, but the bluebell wood has grown since the hole was created and there is even a birch tree to be cleared on the direct line.

The 6th is called *Longhurst*, referring to the locality and not, so far as I am aware, the great golf writer. This is certainly a hole on which he might have been tempted to quote the Irishism of,

"It'll take four good shots to get up in three" – the hill climbing has begun. It sets in in earnest on the 7th, a brutal method of climbing back to the 1st tee. But relief is not at hand.

The 8th continues the slog, not quite so steeply and angled across the slope of the hill, never the less wickedly punishing the slice or pushed shot. The green, in such mountainous surroundings, looks perfectly flat but instincts, intentions and results rarely coincide. It is a mere preface to the immensely demanding 9th. The problem it sets is exactly that of *Calamity Corner*, that memorable 14th hole at Royal Portrush: a big hit is needed but the slightest fade and perdition awaits. At Mellor there is room on the left, but little chance of recovery on the right. The 10th provides a breather before the *Quarry* hole, the 11th, poses many of the same questions set on the 9th, only this time there is no escape route on the left, stone cliff being almost as damaging as the huge drop on the right. At least it is only half the length.

One magical hole remains, the 12th – magical only if you get your drive airborne and straight. Then it will run for ever down the ski-slope of a fairway and it may very well be that your second shot is played with a putter! Get the angle just a little wrong and will be "three off the tee" if the error is on the left. Admiring the splendid view from the tee on my visit was a man walking his three dogs and a cat (white with a tortoiseshell tail) and he responded to my unnecessary chit-chat about the need to be fit to play here by recalling the remark of a friend of his who was a member of a lowland club, "Mellor? Isn't that the place where there's a long waiting list – to leave." As I lumbered down the fairway I was reminded also of the comment of a friend who used to command the Brigade of Gurkhas in Hong Kong. Annually he was required to visit Nepal to look up old members of the Brigade, recruit new members and so on. This involved going from village to village on foot, often only 3 or 4 miles apart but separated by a valley 6,000 feet down (and 6,000 feet up). He always reckoned it was harder work going down.

The golf is hardly flat from here on but it is of a comparatively lowland kind, a pond and stream to catch the second shot on the 15th and another stream likely to thwart the birdie seeker on the 16th perhaps the most strategic features until the final hole, that is. The drive is not demanding but must make good progress to give the second shot any chance of clearing a road and its attendant stone wall 100 yards short of the armchair green nestling in comfort in front of the clubhouse.

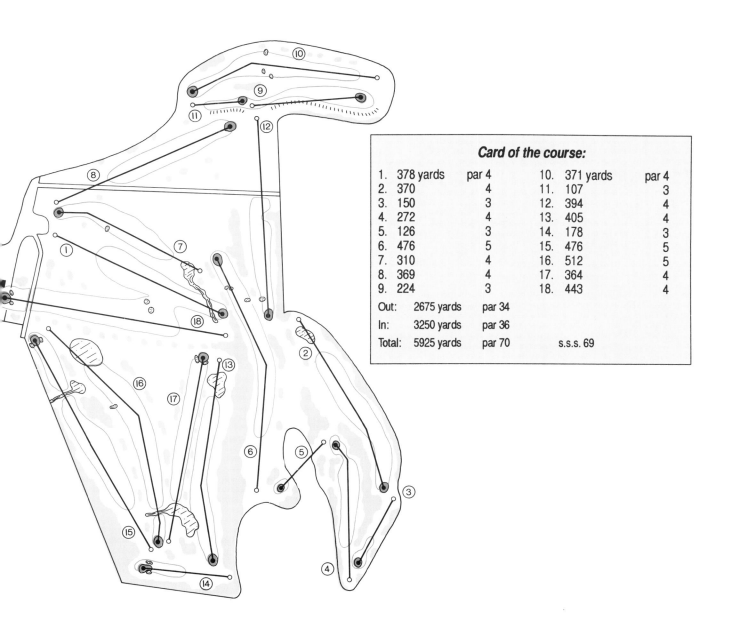

Card of the course:

1.	378 yards	par 4	10.	371 yards	par 4
2.	370	4	11.	107	3
3.	150	3	12.	394	4
4.	272	4	13.	405	4
5.	126	3	14.	178	3
6.	476	5	15.	476	5
7.	310	4	16.	512	5
8.	369	4	17.	364	4
9.	224	3	18.	443	4

Out:	2675 yards	par 34
In:	3250 yards	par 36
Total:	5925 yards	par 70

s.s.s. 69

Mere

6817 yards; par 71; s.s.s. 73

As a member of Conwy Golf Club I have a conscience about George Duncan. After all, we sacked him! He went on to win the Open Championship in 1920 and subsequently settled at Mere as its first Professional back in the mid 1930s. (For the record he was sacked from Conwy for playing football on a Saturday afternoon).

There is a timelessness about Mere suggesting that it has been in existence in this form ever since its creation in the Old Testament age of Adam and Eve, but that is far from the case. There *is* mention of Mere in the Domesday Book and Mere Manor had passed from the Venables family to the de la Meres to the Brooks family before the *Book of Common Prayer* had emerged in 1662, but the New Hall around which the estate revolved was not built until 1834, just three years before Queen Victoria's accession. Rather more pertinent to this book is the fact that the golf club did not open until September 1934 (with a swimming gala at that!). The course itself was opened officially in May 1935, making it a relative junior by Cheshire standards.

Duncan clearly had a major rôle to play in the construction of the course, as did Harry Quick (chairman of the construction committee) and the head greenkeeper, Harold Jackson. The layout, though, is essentially the work of one of Duncan's great friends and sporting adversaries, James Braid. His rapidly sketched plans have formed the kernel of the layout ever since. Very little has changed, though a thorough examination of the club's excellent Golden Jubilee booklet reveals the constant tinkering that has gone on in the intervening years, on more than one occasion lengthening and subsequently shortening the very same hole.

Road access is hazardous (anyone who has tried to turn across the A 556 will have immediately joined the lobby for the construction of a motorway-standard M6-M56 link) and it is entirely reasonable that some visitors should arrive by helicopter. There is an undeniable opulence about the place and in its modern guise it plays host to all manner of conferences and conventions, social occasions and promotional activities only some of which are related to golf. Despite appearances few of the buildings are old - the New Hall was burned to the ground in 1973 – but the atmosphere is entirely that of a well-to-do country estate and fortunate indeed are those able to play their golf in such an environment.

It will be apparent from many of the illustrations in this book that most of my recent visits to these golf courses have been made at the crack of dawn. At Mere, teeing off at sunrise, I was met on the 1st fairway by a fox trotting past totally unconcerned, no more than twenty feet from me, his mind bent on a good day's rest and from the look on his face, with a deviously acquired full stomach. The hole itself is long, but not forbidding. At once the purpose of the course is declared. Fairways must be wide enough, carries easy enough, and bunkers far enough out of reach not to interfere with the progress of four-balls of occasional golfers playing from forward tees. By the same token good players, professionals even, must be challenged seriously when playing from their back tees. Over the front nine holes the subtlety of the architecture and its adaptation to modern play is a fascinating study in itself.

Play at Mere is not confined to the summer months and it is expected to be in the sort of condition its visitors' fees warrant all the year round. Clearly the brief of the greenkeeping staff is very demanding, but the quality of fairways and greens at all times of the year is testament to their very considerable efforts and skills. True, the course is laid out on a sandy base, but even this does not guarantee tip-top condition 365 days of the year: craft and expertise are essential.

The visitor may be slightly disappointed on first seeing the course driving in across the 13th fairway. Everything looks flat and wide open, and for those first thirteen holes, fourteen even, golf seems to be simply a matter of avoiding trees, bunkers or the new ponds put in on the 7th and 8th. On the fifteenth tee, however, begins one of the best finishing stretches in the county, up hill and own dale, over water and around trees, taking risks on every shot there is to be any chance of matching par.

Perhaps I *am* being slightly dismissive of the opening holes, at least the 1st which runs down the shores of The Mere, a slicer's nightmare. A really decent drive (directly in line with a white disc erected on a tree as a marker) gives a distant view of (and the prospect of reaching) the green lower down to the right, girt about with sand. The 2nd is a handsome specimen, dog-legging late to the right. Attempts to shorten the hole leave the second shot cut out by trees (in which lurks a sinister little pond) while the bigger hitters can run out of fairway in the trees on the left.

There is a feeling that the fairways gradually narrow one by one until driving back towards the main buildings on the 7th there an impression of the tiniest ribbon of fairway punctuated at frequent intervals down both sides with uncountable bunkers. A badly pond in front of the green takes what advantage there is to be gained from what had been, in the past, an area of doubtful drainage. Into the wind it is a devilish hole.

One of the hazards of a course's evolution by lengthening is abundantly clear on the next hole where the route from the tee to the green passes the 9th tee. It is very tempting to break the Rules of Golf immediately and simply tee off at the 9th on the way past before sauntering over to the 8th green to putt. That 8th green lies on the far side of another recently added pond, while the 9th green lies a little way the other side of cross bunkers making it a splendid two-shot hole.

That same temptation to play out of sequence exists *en route* the 10th green when any lazy golfer (or work study expert) could take a detour to the 11th tee to drive off before coping with the approach shot to the 10th with its pond (shared with the 8th) down to the left. That 11th is the first hole in which there is a significant change of level and the second shot has not only to climb the hill in front but also to clear bunkers in front of the green. From this point on the trees are more strategically employed and many holes might qualify for the title of forest.

The 12th takes my fancy with its humpy green on the far side of a dip and no fewer than five big, deep bunkers generously filled with a quick draining sand from which there can be no excuse for failure to escape, and escape here is made towards the picture windows of the bungalow situated just beyond the green, a potentially shattering experience. Broken windows, too, have been the principal reason for alterations to the 13th, variously a short par-5

and long par-4. At present it is the latter, and unreachable into the wind for most weekenders but, according to the booklet, "a comparatively easy four for a low handicap player". The green, on a ledge above a big drop, is not one to overshoot.

James Braid returned to Mere in the early 1950s to design the new short 14th hole, well bunkered and decidedly tricky. The position of its green has allowed much experimentation with the 15th hole, the start of the outstanding closing stretch. As it stands at the moment (and not dissimilar to its original form) the hole is a mid-length par-4 with a swooping downhill drive towards a stream. That stream is very much in range for most players and it can be an agonising decision over whether or not to attempt the carry. A big fir tree on the right halves the width of the fairway which then sweeps uphill to an elevated green from which there are pleasant glimpses of The Mere.

A big drive is called for on the 16th to clear the corner of the trees around which the hole bends sharply to the left. Unfortunately the gardens of the big houses lining the right of the fairway form an all too obvious out-of-bounds on that side and unerring straightness is called for also. Even after a perfect drive problems remain for the second shot is long, possibly played from a hanging lie, and must clear a minefield of cavernous, steep-faced bunkers of which Muirfield would be proud. What is more the green is raised up and on two levels.

The 17th is not unduly long, but no less trying to the nerves when attempting to protect a good score. There is a long carry over a grassy gully to a fairway leaning down to the right from which the second shot is played to a pimple green. Unfortunately that green lies downhill from the player, slopes down from front to back, is well guarded by bunkers and is approached via a little tongue of raised ground which throws the weak shot off into one or other of the bunkers. Stopping the shot on this putting surface is a job for the professional with a *balata* ball!

Mere has not finished playing trump cards, keeping up its sleeve a hole which is both strikingly attractive and disturbingly treacherous with which to end. This has been played as a par-4 and a very difficult proposition it must have been, as indeed it still is for those with the strength and nerve to attempt to reach the putting surface in two shots. Accepted as a genuine par-5, however, the hole can be played slightly more conservatively, with a pleasant drive across the gully in front of the tee to reach the summit of the hill opposite, preferably avoiding the prominent bunker on the

ight of the hill. Then progress is made downhill, past further unkers, to stop short of the ridge on the far side of which there is steep drop to the green on its promontory above the waters of he Mere. Birdie seekers must go round the corner of the first hill n a line dangerously close to the trees along the water's edge, angerously close to the water itself for that matter. Their second hots must then fly all the way to the green over boggy rough, again gnoring the higher ground to the left and running the risk of olliding with a Spanish oak around which the final stretch of airway twists. Whatever golfers' fate on the course their relaxation fterwards will be no disappointment, for sure, with all the facilities of the best country clubs available, the fit perhaps indulging n tennis, squash or swimming, the exhausted enjoying the lavish osseting of its bars and restaurants before leaving (once again by elicopter?).

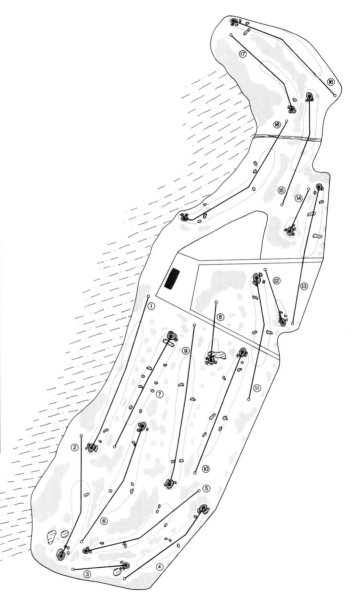

Card of the course:

1.	530 yards	par 5	10.	427 yards	par 4
2.	409	4	11.	401	4
3.	174	3	12.	188	3
4.	357	4	13.	467	4
5.	428	4	14.	169	3
6.	437	4	15.	393	4
7.	402	4	16.	441	4
8.	195	3	17.	371	4
9.	531	5	18.	497	5

Out:	3463 yards	par 36	
In:	3354 yards	par 35	
Total:	6817 yards	par 71	s.s.s. 73

Opposite: the 18th hole

Mottram Hall

7006 yards; par 72; s.s.s. 74

Since the war Mottram Hall has been a hotel, originally a modest affair occupying the early 18th-century country house, more recently a 100-plus bedroom luxury retreat with all the trappings of the conference and functions business. Owned by the same group responsible for The Belfry it was almost inevitable that a golf course would become part of the considerable leisure facilities at Mottram and, hardly surprisingly, the same architect, David Thomas, was engaged to make what he could of a none too promising patch of flat meadowland and a rather more inviting part on the higher ground towards Prestbury.

Essentially the front nine holes occupy the uninteresting bi Thomas has created a number of mounds, both for golfing interes and for the convenience of spectators, but those initial holes nee not detain us. There are, of course, mature trees including, it i reputed, the oldest known oak tree in the county, but it will be ou children and grandchildren who will gain the benefit of these hole when present saplings are fine trees themselves.

Mottram Hall, 15th hol

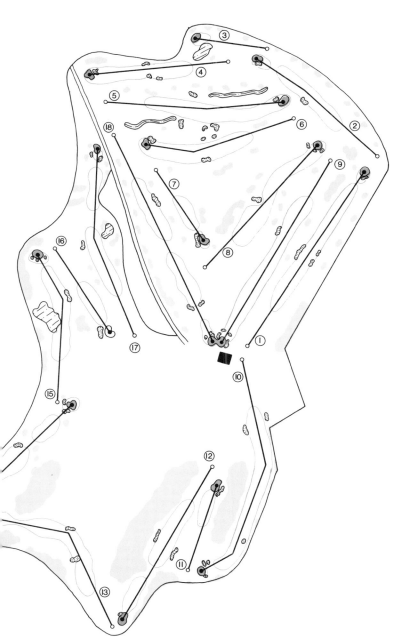

300 yards longer and altogether hillier, the second half makes up for any shortcomings in the earlier holes with a vengeance. Starting off still on flat ground the 10th curves remorselessly to the right eventually climbing to a green raised up behind bunkers. Then heading more or less due West back towards the formal gardens of the old house the 11th plays very long indeed, the fading shot liable to run off into sand or an unfriendly coppice.

Going out there was only one substantial par-4, the 5th, but the 12th is the first of three big two-shot holes on this half. The drive is not too demanding if conservative golf is being played, but the professionals who come here on the Northern circuit will need to ensure their drives do not perish in the gully which splits the fairway 250-yards out. Trees here leave a narrow gap through which the second shot is threaded over a rolling fairway. I presume players of this calibre would expect to reach the 13th green in two shots but how they might do it is beyond my comprehension. For a start the fairway climbs two hills, one to the designated landing zone beyond one bunker and before a second, the other hill grinding up directly into the prevailing wind to a green set behind mounds in which the architect saw fit to confront the weary with a pair of deep traps almost hidden from view.

There is a breather of a kind on the rather charming 14th with a characteristic gully to carry *en route* to the ledge green protected by a couple of serious bunkers, and then it is time for another difficult decision. From the 15th tee it is the simplest of tasks to drive straight into the pond around which the fairway bends. To clear it from the very back is a carry of 225 yards, and there is a long bunker set into a mound on the right. Chickening out on the tee and taking a modest iron implies a very long second shot uphill to a handsome green sheltering under tall, remarkably shapely, pines, evoking, if only momentarily, Gleneagles.

A feature of Mottram is the substantial nature of its par-3s and the longest of them is the 16th. It has the grace to run downhill, but a *Valley of Sin* before the putting surface disposes of the running approach, while a mound eating into the green on the left and a wickedly raised back portion can transform putting into a nightmare. The screw is turning slowly but resolutely.

The 17th is at least as forbidding as the 13th but it is so attractive that one can almost forgive it for mauling the faltering golfer who has run out of reserves on which to draw. From the tee it is not too intimidating, trees screening a predatory pond on the right from view. If you can drive as far as the pond you will be able to see round the corner and what you see may alarm you unless you can also carry at least 200 yards with your second shot, over a couple of depressions and up a tidy hill to the stepped green. Bunkers, low down either side, and mature firs add to the extensive fortifications. And, sad to say, the excitement ends there. Cross the road to the last tee and it is a return to the flat parkland of the opening holes. Incidentally, it is an unusual disposition of holes here with par-5s on level ground to open and close each half.

Card of the course:

1.	502 yards	par 5	10.	561 yards	par 5
2.	381	4	11.	220	3
3.	176	3	12.	422	4
4.	394	4	13.	470	4
5.	430	4	14.	377	4
6.	364	4	15.	368	4
7.	209	3	16.	229	3
8.	395	4	17.	463	4
9.	506	5	18.	539	5
Out:	3357 yards	par 36			
In:	3649 yards	par 36			
Total:	7006 yards	par 72		s.s.s. 74	

Northenden

6469 yards; par 72; s.s.s. 71

have had a soft spot for Northenden since, many years ago, I
.nd myself with a free morning in February, an inauspicious
onth for golf in Cheshire. Having tried a number of extremely
:ll-known courses and found them water-logged, I was wel-
med at Northenden and I duly responded by playing exactly to
/ handicap. Hardly surprisingly I still have the card and it (the
rd, not my play) makes an interesting comparison with that of
day. The course is essentially the same, but the odd tee has been
oved, the 13th substantially lengthened, the 6th and 14th short-
ed. That 6th used to measure 596 yards and I am happy to see
it the marker is still in place even if the card suggests the hole is
w 20 yards shorter.

Being one of that group of courses clustered around the River
ersey and the M63, resemblance is inevitable. Northenden,
ppily, is favoured with a markedly meandering stretch of the
er and is, therefore, a nightmare for the persistent slicer. The
st six holes run along the banks of the river bestowing on
orthenden one of the wickedest starts in Cheshire golf, the 1st
le to be ranked almost alongside the famous *Course* at Royal
verpool. It is not the worst likeness, for the bunkering over these
st few holes is beautifully constructed to create deep, devouring
verns of a kind more usually found within earshot of breaking
ves.

That 1st hole is not too horrifying from the yellow tee, but, if
u are allowed, try it from the very back, pretty well on the
onwork of the Palatine Road bridge. With trees on either side the
ve is fearsomely narrow, and the bunkering around the green
ıkes enormous demands on what, for most of us, will be a very
ıg approach shot. Even we, though, would fancy our chances of
eaking one back on the 2nd, not long as par-5s go and just that
le bit gentler from the tee. Again we may tangle with the trees
ound which the fairway bears markedly right and even from short
ıge we might, all too easily, pop our pitches into one or other of
the stout bunkers on the front left of the green. Lavish bunkers
adorn the 3rd hole, too, which continues the journey out to where
the river suddenly swings round in a semi-circle, the short 4th
being as much as can be accommodated inside the arc.

I still remember the perplexity with which I essayed the drive
on the 5th on my first visit. It seems as if you ought to strike out
over a reach of the Mersey to find the fairway, except that the direct
line is very luxuriantly occupied by a row of enormous willows.
So out to the left you go, tentatively, as there seems little room out
there either, but room there is and, in fact, there is little point in
trying to cut the corner because a stand of recently planted trees
blots out the right-hand half of the green from all but the far left of
the fairway. Fortunately it is not a long hole.

The aforementioned 6th continues the journey along the river
bank, and I am sure it has not been unknown for a ball to be
despatched into the water on each of the drive, second shot, and
approach, but, despite the length of the hole and its inexorable drive
into the prevailing wind, it is really the introduction to the rest of
the course, quieter and more forgiving.

Of the rest, I like the 7th with its tricky approach, a tree on the
front right of the green forcing a great many shots into the prominent bunker on the left, and the 10th, not a difficult drive, but a
subtle pitch in to a green angled across the line from left to right.
The 13th also appeals as it climbs gently over a bouncy fairway of
a kind more usually encountered at the seaside. It bends, too, first
left, then right, finishing eventually in a raised green up by the
motorway.

There is plenty of opportunity for bunker practice from here in
and, with five bunkers around the final green, it may be possible
to conduct that practice under the gaze of the members. That is
infinitely preferable, it must be said, to having to extricate yourself
from the neatly trimmed beech hedge which protects the practice
putting green and which creeps awfully close to that final green.

Northenden, 1st hole

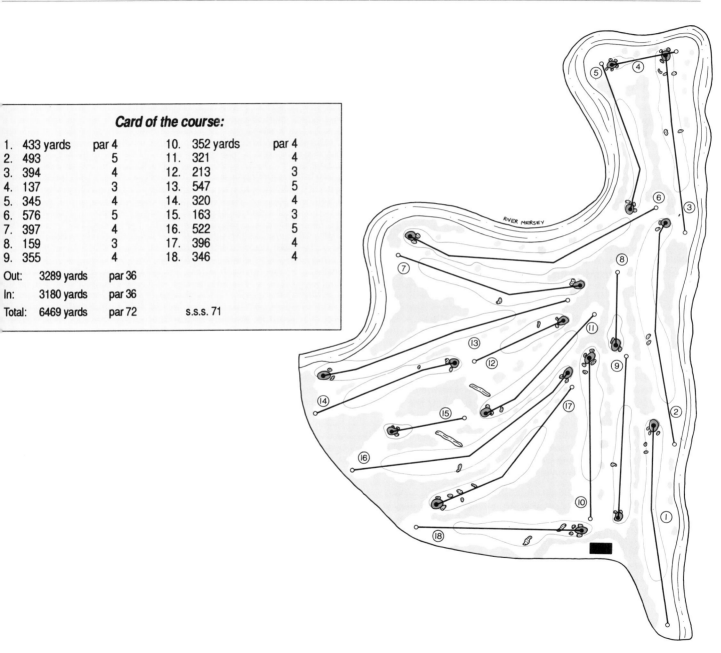

Card of the course:

1.	433 yards	par 4		10.	352 yards	par 4
2.	493	5		11.	321	4
3.	394	4		12.	213	3
4.	137	3		13.	547	5
5.	345	4		14.	320	4
6.	576	5		15.	163	3
7.	397	4		16.	522	5
8.	159	3		17.	396	4
9.	355	4		18.	346	4

Out: 3289 yards   par 36

In: 3180 yards   par 36

Total: 6469 yards par 72   s.s.s. 71

RIVER MERSEY

Oaklands

6508 yards; par 71; s.s.s. 72

Inevitably, comparison is bound to be made between Oaklands and Portal, overlooking each other and separated only by a single field. I am going to leave that debate to the locker room for they are about as similar as the blue and red Cheshire cheeses made on surrounding farms. Both courses have outstanding views and a number of outstanding holes, and at my level of incompetence there will always be a disastrous hole or two during the course of a round at either place.

Oaklands occupies three very different pieces of ground with much of the course laid out over a central ridge, the 4th to the 8th tumbling about on one side of it, the final four holes down below on the other side. These are the more characterful holes, though as early as the 2nd one is made to work hard with a hugely long par-5 running uphill alongside a hedge until plunging down over the last 150 yards or so to a handsome green.

Bunkers litter the tempting 3rd, but it is at the 4th that the devilry really begins. The fairway is narrow, steeply downhill and tipping away towards rough and young trees on the right. The views are magnificent but the golf is tricky with the fairway turning abruptly left to run uphill again over a dry moat to a ledge green in the trees. The 5th, too, is not a green to miss with out-of-bounds on the left and through the back and wicked slopes down which anything less than inch-perfect is likely to race.

The 7th green is unusual in being set into a little quarry with rocky cliffs providing a serious hazard on the left and beyond. There is a good deal of trouble down the hill to the right, too. Sufficiently wide open to offer a breather, the 8th gives a last view of the plains of central Cheshire.

One has to admire the marvellous signs by the 9th tee warning golfers to keep out of the neighbouring field protected, it would seem, not only with an electric fence but also by the presence of a bull. The hole is the first of a lengthy trio of which the star is undoubtedly the 10th beating a treacherous downhill path back to the clubhouse. The drive must, naturally enough, avoid finishing in a pond halfway down the hill. But that is only part of the business for it is all too easy to end up totally blocked out by the big trees which surround it or running off into deep rough as the fairway slopes away to the left. It is astonishing just how much that pond and those trees cut off the green from any kind of approach shot.

Two tall trees constrict the drive at the uphill 11th, well out of my reach but I have seen it played with a drive and towering 6-iron high over the big tree which guards the left front of the green. It is tempting to take the drive at the 13th before completing the 12th to avoid a route march, and also in eager anticipation of the fine view of South Cheshire, North Shropshire and North Staffordshire (not to mention the infamous bull) to be obtained on the armchair green at the 13th. The difficulties of stopping the ball on the ledge green precariously perched above a big drop on the 14th mean that there is no safe option on the tee. A hedge threatens on the left, but there may be no sort of second shot at all from the safer pasture on the right.

It is down that big drop that the tee shot is played at the 15th, from the yellow tee a splendid drop shot, from the white a rather more troublesome carry over young trees, bracken and brambles. The trefoil green is raised above three bunkers and a fence on the left adds to the dangers. Down here in a damp corner the 16th begins its sinuous path curving first left then right as it winds past a pond on the right with a ditch ever present on the left. A ridge in the fairway adds to the problems of attacking the flag on a shallow but wide green.

The term "Signature Hole" seems to have crept into the vocabulary of golf course architecture in recent years, most frequently applied to some extraordinary concoction with an island green entirely surrounded by snapping crocodiles. There are (I presume) no crocodiles on the 17th at Oaklands but in most other respects it would qualify for the term, even to the big mounds on e far side on which spectators can indulge their loodthirsty tendencies. They may, however, be in ome danger from the 18th tee, at least if high-handi-appers are about. The fairway slopes severely to-ards the trees surrounding the ponds on the 17th, hile those who take the prudent right-hand route may nd their stance perilously hilly as they essay their econd shots. The green is a huge affair surrounded, nce again, by spectator mounds.

The 7th hole

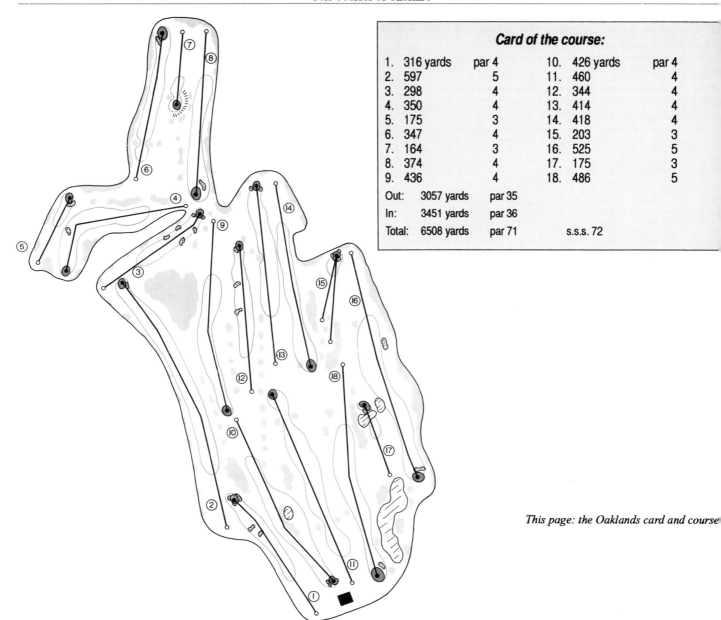

Card of the course:

1.	316 yards	par 4	10.	426 yards	par 4
2.	597	5	11.	460	4
3.	298	4	12.	344	4
4.	350	4	13.	414	4
5.	175	3	14.	418	4
6.	347	4	15.	203	3
7.	164	3	16.	525	5
8.	374	4	17.	175	3
9.	436	4	18.	486	5

Out:	3057 yards	par 35	
In:	3451 yards	par 36	
Total:	6508 yards	par 71	s.s.s. 72

This page: the Oaklands card and course

Portal

7145 yards; par 73; s.s.s. 74

Look, where he goes, even now, out at the portal." (*Exit Ghost*).

Portal makes much of its ancestry, individual holes given ppropriate names (which I will leave readers to discover for emselves as they peruse the course brochure in the Golf House ver a glass of something suitable – Sack, perhaps? – after the und), and, with commanding views of the fortress at Beeston and e epic scale of the golf, Shakespeare in the guise of *Hamlet* seems fitting preface.

The rarely performed *King John* runs to the lines:

"We tread In warlike march these greens". Having failed lamtably to get near the hole with anything longer than a 2-inch putt left the greens vanquished, a broken man!

The spot chosen for the golf club fell largely in Arderne Park, vast acreage of rolling land around the site of Arderne Hall, a ictorian house demolished in the 1950s. Arderne, in this context, ems an unfortunate name: only a few years earlier the Arderne hapel in Tarporley Parish Church lost its historic title, gave up its ecifically local connections and became associated with All ouls, undoubtedly universal and no doubt spiritually more uplifug. Donald Steel laid out the course generously. Not for him ould there be the slightest possibility of an errant shot gaining e advantage of landing on an adjacent fairway. As it is the course well over 7,000 yards in length. It could just as easily have been ,000.

Because of the nature of the hilly ground over which the course as built the greens are impossible to read, at least to those of us ho have no experience of playing at Augusta. No green is flat or vel and many of them seem to have at least three different orrows conspiring at any one time. Played in early May the irfaces were already quite fast in comparison with neighbouring urses. My account of this course must be confined, therefore, to at part of the play which takes place before the green is reached.

It was the quality of the greens which persuaded tour stars David Gilford and Andrew Murray to become members here – which in small part explains why they are tour stars and I am not! Motorised buggies are the convention at Portal. Normally I prefer to walk, even to carry my own bag on my back, but the distances from green to tee on many holes at Portal are so very considerable, the grass on (and off) the fairways so lush, and the potential for slow play so great that my normal prejudices are willingly suppressed.

Agincourt has the right ring about it for an opening hole, and as you climb the hill there is a little ruined chapel on the left. It does not bear closer inspection. It is a folly built by the same Egerton who is commemorated by the 7th hole and who, one gathers, liked to sip his lemonade in its shade. Its green is right up at the highest part of the course, exposed and windswept.

It was intended originally to build a hotel on this high ground and what is now the 2nd hole was to have been the fine opener, not too long, downhill and with big trees to either side. The odd gap opens in them to reveal the first glimpses of Beeston Castle standing proudly, even in decay, on its rocky outcrop. The green is angled slightly from the left, the side where the trees are most likely to interfere with your tee shot. Thought must be allied to brawn here.

To reach the next three holes it is necessary to drive over a footbridge into an area reputed once to have been a battle site. These holes, a benign par-3 and a pair of parallel par-4s, are in something more akin to meadowland and should not ruin the scorecard, provided, that is, the pond and rock garden just to the front left of the 5th green are avoided.

There has been no great insistence on length so far, but when play moves round behind the Golf House all the stops are pulled out. Even from the yellow tees the 6th is over 550 yards long, and from the very back it is just over 600. Teeing off amidst garden shrubs the hole runs down a magnificent avenue of trees with early

strategy dictated by a big tree on the right around which the fairway bends. Taking its model, perhaps, is the famous 16th at Firestone there is a pond guarding the front left of the green.

Egerton's Oaks is the name of the 7th hole, commemorating the general of that name who saved the trees around which this hole bends. From the golfer's point of view the trees are not so much of a problem as the steep rise over the last 100 yards or so up to the green. The 8th is straightforward, as short holes go here, and the 9th a matter of avoiding a tree on the right in easy driving range, the 10th blind uphill. There are plenty of bunkers, too, for the big hitters, and even by Portal standards this is a difficult green to read.

The 11th, again uphill, is named *Done* but does not refer, as one might suspect, to the debilitating effects of consecutive uphill holes. In fact the Done family (pronounced, I believe, *Doune*) lived at nearby Utkinton Hall and were described by Fletcher Moss as "necessarily a rough and quarelsome breed. They had power of life and death in the forest, or if they had not legally full power, they were not within taking it....". In fairness to the family name they were also, later, considerable church benefactors.

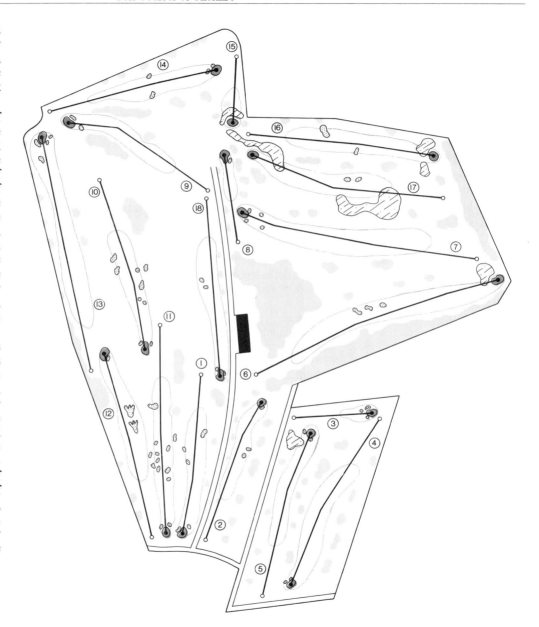

Left: the 15th hole

From what had been golf of a parkland nature the character has gradually changed as the hill has been climbed and the 12th, *The Temple*, threads a narrow path first downhill and then up to a domed green perched on the top of another hill. Splendid views out over miles of unspoiled countryside reward the eye. How many golfers, I wonder, spot the humour in the two bunkers threatening the drive? They are shaped like a pair of giant footprints, representing the pre-historic pterodactyl whose bones were discovered on this site.

The 13th runs down to lower ground, but it does so over a fairway which leans steeply to the left, giving a left-hander like me an awkward hanging lie. The 14th, not over long, is all about position, the green angled and raised up above a bunker. The drive here is slightly deceptive and semi-blind over a mound.

All is abundantly clear, though, on *The Horn*, the only par-3 on this half (which explains the exceptional length). It may be picture postcard stuff but the green is very shallow and guarded not only by the pond running completely across the front but also by several tall trees which effectively block out the direct line when the pin is some way off-centre.

Water is significant, too, on the 16th and 17th as the screw is turned gradually tighter, the former a handsome downhill hole falling steeply at the end to yet another pond immediately in front of the green. The 17th is called *Waterloo*, appropriately enough, and for the average player is a very testing hole. A round pond or well on the left about 180 yards out is easily driven into by most of us. Those who land short will be unlikely to clear the next stretch of water, on the right this time, about 100 yards short of the green. (A pair of Canada Geese and six furry goslings inhabited this lake at the time of my visit). Mightier players will still have difficulty reaching this green in two, for it is uphill throughout its length very steeply so on the final approach to the putting surface.

After this life is easier, the 18th a none too taxing finishing hole. True, there are trees up the left of the fairway and bunkers on the right in driving range. The green is on two levels and the prudent will have taken note of the position of the flag on arrival as they drove into the car park right beside the green.

Every hole here, as I mentioned earlier, already has a history. When a few generations of golfers have fought their own battle over this fine turf there will be an equally large, if alternative, history.

Card of the course:					
1.	374 yards	par 4	10.	402 yards	par 4
2.	343	4	11.	489	5
3.	186	3	12.	433	4
4.	436	4	13.	525	5
5.	393	4	14.	395	4
6.	603	5	15.	135	3
7.	544	5	16.	423	4
8.	215	3	17.	439	4
9.	399	4	18.	411	4
Out:	3493 yards	par 36			
In:	3652 yards	par 37			
Total:	7145 yards	par 73		s.s.s. 74	

Poulton Park

5447 yards; par 68; s.s.s. 67

Some years ago I spent a week working in Valencia and each time I crossed the dried up river bed running through the middle of the city I thought what a splendid linear golf course could be laid out between its banks! I have similar thoughts when I look down from Thelwall Viaduct onto the vacant land alongside the Manchester Ship Canal. I had not until recently realised that a similar narrow patch of land only a mile or two further up the M6 has been put to just such a use, and very effectively, too.

Poulton Park is exactly that for which I have searched for some years: that is, a course mid-way between the overcrowded and lamentably funded municipal establishment and the long-established and rather exclusive private club a quantum leap further on. This is a flat, relatively unsophisticated layout running out-and-back between houses and the motorway embankment, but its condition is good, there are rakes in the bunkers, the greens are true and the tees beautifully mown. As you play you become aware gradually that the few available features of the site have been used

8th/17th hole

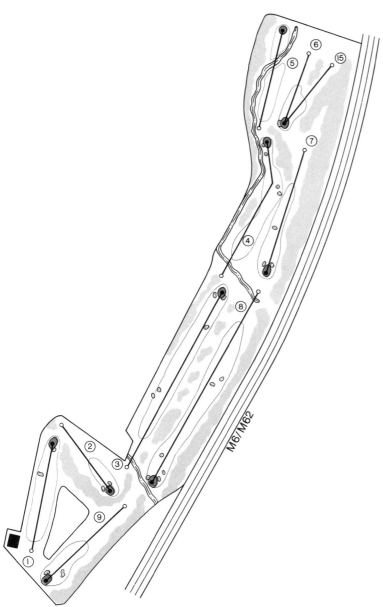

to maximum architectural effect, that trees grow in precisely the right places, that bunkering has been carefully positioned and that there is no point in attempting to tear the place apart unless you can hit unerringly straight. By the use of separate teeing grounds a considerable variety is introduced between the first and second circuits, even to the conversion of a par-4 into a par-5 and *vice versa*. Angles of approach, too, are significantly altered. It is all the more heartening, then, to learn that the members themselves designed and built the course back in 1978/9.

If I had to single out one hole as an example of the ingenuity that has gone into this course it would be the 4th/13th. The fairway curves to the left beyond a stand of recently planted trees. Some might drive over the top, but most will be content if they can curl the ball round the end. A pair of bunkers out to the right spoil that option, and a stream running the length of the hole on the left threatens every shot. A big bunker on the direct line dictates that the approach shot must be high flying, but a shallow dry moat around the green means it must land spot on the putting surface and stop immediately. Trees to the right and beyond add a touch of seclusion to the hole. Simple, but very effective.

Card of the course:

1.	251 yards	par 4	10.	251 yards	par 4
2.	147	3	11.	188	3
3.	432	4	12.	477	5
4.	340	4	13.	377	4
5.	288	4	14.	311	4
6.	195	3	15.	182	3
7.	377	4	16.	310	4
8.	509	5	17.	434	4
9.	176	3	18.	202	3
Out:	2715 yards	par 34			
In:	2732 yards	par 34			
Total:	5447 yards	par 68		s.s.s. 67	

Prenton

6411 yards; par 71; s.s.s. 71

Rapid contrast is almost as common on the Wirral as it is in London. Cross a London road and you leave Hampstead and enter Kilburn, or leave Dulwich and enter Brixton. In a matter of yards you can leave the terrace houses built for Birkenhead shipyard workers and enter the realm of the big villas of prosperous Merseyside businessmen and bank managers. The golf course at Prenton is almost as varied in its environment.

Starting off in the villa world of Golf Links Road the course winds downhill past farmland until at the very bottom of the site it is separated from the M53 only by a little coppice. Down there, in a damp corner, it is soon realised that it will be necessary to return to the clubhouse uphill and a glance at the card suggests that the back nine will be 300 yards longer than the front. Life is indeed somewhat more strenuous because the holes are generally longer and the fairway grass lusher. The character again changes with everyday housing on the left looking up the hill and something resembling heathland in the middle.

The 8th hole

The current layout owes a good deal to the same Dr. Mackenzie whose best work endures at Cypress Point, Augusta National, and Royal Melbourne. At Prenton his task was to restore the course to playing condition after the First World War, which he achieved by following much the same route as those who had laid out previous courses on the same site. Visitors expecting to find the sort of extravagantly contoured greens and mischievous moundwork for which Mackenzie became noted may be disappointed to find that only the 3rd, 5th and 8th greens are in any way wicked, and the final green, perhaps the most characterful of them all, is part of a hole reconstructed as recently as 1978 to a design by the Hawtree Company. The card displays an attractive anomaly: the half with the higher par is the shorter by those same 300 yards.

Do not be mislead! The 75th Anniversary Handbook produced in 1980 contains an account of play of the course by a leading amateur of the day. On almost every hole he indicates that a bogey is not to be sniffed at.

The club house is on high ground giving distant views of the Denbigh moors and sufficient of a glimpse of the course to make one aware that there will be precious little shelter from the winds which habitually race over this exposed land fresh from their first batterings on the coast at Royal Liverpool and Wallasey. The start here is markedly encouraging, six downhill holes in succession. In theory the 1st hole is a par-4. Most of us will be relieved to play it that way, but for those intent on an early killing copious bunkers must be avoided.

There is no great length in any of these early downhill holes and the only restraint on excessive enthusiasm on the 2nd hole is a hedge running down the left. The 3rd, however, is a little beauty standing up on a shoulder of land, surrounded by bunkers of all shapes, and borrowed in the most devious of manners. The gorse bushes and pine trees hereabouts complete a fleeting encounter with genuine heathland.

A ditch crossing the 4th fairway is very much in play for all standards of golfer: only 255 yards from the medal tee, downhill at that. Commanding greater attention than the track which also crosses the fairway (a Roman road no less), that ditch might be driven by the mighty but they have no margin for error with a hedge encroaching from the left just where the ditch interrupts and the fairway turns abruptly to the left. The hedge and ditch, running on down the left of the hole, remain a threat until the ball is safely on the putting surface.

The 5th green is a marvellous period piece sunken down i what used to be a little pond. If you think the walls of this cradl will caress your errant approach into the hole itself, just try it! On more hole will take us to the far end of the course and, dare I sa the end of the magic. This 6th is, for most of us, a genuine thre shot hole, involving a downhill drive for position, second sh across another ditch, and approach shot played across a ne plantation as the fairway bends late to the left. With the green s tight up against the hedge and trees just through the back this mus be an exciting business for the tiger bent on putting for three.

However imaginatively bunkered and sculptured, the short 7t is marred by the high tension cables through which the highest o tee shots must pass. The 8th, though, is charming, a long-iro followed by a gentle pitch to a green raised above bunkers and big depression. Those who feel that 284 uphill yards can be drive will need to send their tee shots blind over the corner of a hedg closing in from the left about 180 yards out.

Three rather plain holes follow, though the approach to the las of them, the 11th, is handsome, across a dip to a raised green. Th 12th then gives the only blind drive of the round, up to a marke post on the central heathland near the 3rd green, to be followed b two very solid par-4s. The latter, the 14th, is much more a "par four-and-a-half" with its second over a depression to a raise two-tier green.

It is not immediately apparent why the yellow tee for the 15t should be 5 yards behind the white, and on the same teeing groun at that. This, the first of back-to-back par-3s, enjoys a rathe sinuous green, while the 16th involves a tee shot across one of th few remaining ponds (and a goodly selection of bunkers). The 17t is wide open.

To end the round Prenton has, as mentioned earlier, onl recently acquired the current 18th hole. From a tee low down i front of half a dozen kitchen windows what fairway can be see rises over a ridge with gorse bushes and trees to the left and selection of bunkers on the right. Instincts suggest that an advan tage can be gained by risking a tight line on the left. It cannot. From that side the approach is blind over further gorse bushes to a gree whose vicious slopes run across the line. If the drive can b contrived to finish somewhere near one of the right-hand bunker life will be easier. The green is a raised, two-level, slippery slop contained within another cockpit, quite exasperating or thoroughl exhilarating depending on the outcome of the final shot, and al

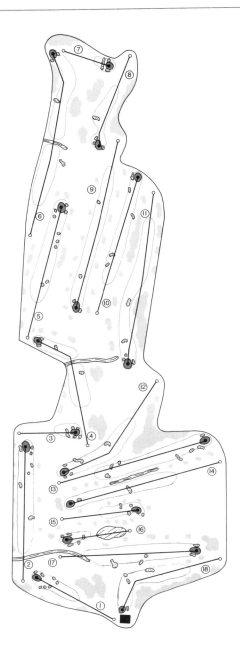

achieved under the noses of the members who were wise enough not to leave the comfortable surroundings of their white-washed clubhouse.

Card of the course:					
1.	256 yards	par 4	10.	418 yards	par 4
2.	396	4	11.	511	5
3.	161	3	12.	393	4
4.	368	4	13.	436	4
5.	396	4	14.	443	4
6.	548	5	15.	215	3
7.	141	3	16.	186	3
8.	284	4	17.	392	4
9.	506	5	18.	361	4
Out:	3056 yards	par 36			
In:	3355 yards	par 35			
Total:	6411 yards	par 71		s.s.s. 71	

Prestbury

6359 yards; par 71; s.s.s. 71

In this materialistic age we all too readily associate Prestbury with the rapidly gained wealth of football stars, currency speculators and property developers but there is another, worthier, and longer established, side to this handsome village with an important ecclesiastical history, many fine domestic buildings, a set of stocks, and as lovely a golf course as you could ever wish to play. The tone of the golf course is that of historic and traditional Prestbury, not that of the *nouveaux riches*, unostentatiously secreted away on hilly ground to the south-west of the village centre. If you are lucky enough to be treated to a round by a member, first take down your Thesaurus and mug up the various synonyms for "majestic, imposing, glorious and testing". You will need them all in plenty if you are to avoid repetition.

In conversation with the Head Green-keeper, at an idyllic spot overlooking the 16th green, I learned that this historic course, laid out by Harry Colt, did not happen overnight (*pace* those new generation designers who try to achieve just that). Certainly he laid it out, but as first built the greens were simply levelled off, their grass sown on whatever sub-soil happened to be exposed. It was only five years later that proper greens were constructed, and they remain to this day as exacting a test of approach work as is to be found in the county (almost to be mentioned in the same reverent tones as Ballybunion and Royal Dornoch), nearly every one of them raised up to repulse all but the surest of shots. Raised greens on hilly sites unfortunately mean few options on trolley routes and around these greens, as if to add to the examination of pitching, there are one or two very tight lies to be found. As someone with a spiritual affinity to traditional links golf I am hardly to complain about that.

When first I played at Prestbury the opening hole was an impossibly long par-4 from the yellow plates and a reasonable par-5 only from the medal tee. Happily that anomaly is now resolved so that those of us who fail to carry far enough down the

hill in front of us need not despair at having to try to climb the ensuing slope in a single blow. The green, it is hardly necessary say, resembles a pyramid whose top has been worn flat with the passing of two thousand years of desert storms. It is a noble setting though, looking onto the 2nd fairway running away below and the more distant panorama of the Cheshire plain.

That 2nd is impish in the generous leg-break it imparts to the drive as it lands, and to the approach, too, as it runs on to the green at the foot of the slope. At Prestbury it is a self-evident truth that feeble though it may be to finish short of the putting surface there is almost invariably something far worse through the back of the green. One of the exceptions is the 3rd with a green on a ledge on the far side of a cavernous depression. Hit the up-slope with your approach and it will almost certainly shoot off down the hill again veering drunkenly to one side or the other. Up behind the green, a ledge in the trees, is the 4th tee, the green only a drop-shot away as long as swirling winds do not carry the ball off into one of four surrounding bunkers.

It is fairly likely that the 5th drive, whatever the club taken, will finish in one of a number of hollows, some very much deeper than others, from which the pitch must be made uphill to a ledge green perched on the side of a steeply falling hill. It is an old-fashioned hole which remains largely untouched by advances in club and ball design, which is not the case on the 6th. Running back parallel with the 1st its fairway is gentler, a mere ocean swell, until passing the green-keeper's appealing white house it heaves upwards to a plateau green, his children's teddy-bears observing sagely the inadequacies of most visitors' efforts. For a moment or two this is golf of the heath, broom catching the eye from the 7th tee. Take note of the yardage here for there are no marks for falling short into the bear pit separating the bushes from the green, and little comfort to be found down the hill to the right.

Swinging uphill to the left the 8th can be played conservatively

ll to leave no more than a gentle iron to the narrow, bunker-beset
een on top of a hill. It is a charming hole but the mind is already
cupied with anticipation for the drive to come on the 9th,
hilarating or terrifying depending on the security of your driv-
g. The fairway is ordained to plunge down directly towards
nkers, the alternative being a contest with the shoulder of the
l interrupting the flight on the right. Given a happy outcome
ere is then a slight right turn and a stiff climb over the final 200
rds to the green. A necklace of bunkers stresses the ever narrow-
g nature of the fairway as it is squeezed between a wood on the
t and fence on the right. The final affront to our dignity is being
ade to putt on a green on three-levels, all of which appear to slope
wn with equal venom.

In comparison the 10th is a mere breather, as long as you do
t miss on the right, shoot through the back, or drop short in the
nker front-left. Then it is all-or-nothing time again, it being
perative to make the carry on the 11th as far as the marker post
the ridge in front. In that case there is every chance of the ball

rolling down the far side sufficiently to give only an iron shot in
to the green nestling in front of some of Prestbury's most desirable
houses. It is not all sweetness and light, however, with a big oak
tree on the right waiting to thwart the slice.

Down in a dark corner below that green the 12th tee looks out
on a clipped hedge, one of those hazards so beloved of the "Apple
Tree Gang". Beyond it the fairway breasts a rise from which it is
still a hefty clout to reach the sunken green just the other side of a
treacherous stream. Then, striking back alongside the 2nd, the 13th
is uphill all the way, a big hole to cover in just two shots. Its green,
adjoining the 17th, is something of a meeting place, the 14th and
18th tees also more or less abutting. From that 14th tee only the
cleanest of strikes will suffice to carry the abyss in front, and if you
make the carry the pitch is appropriately rewarding. You might,
after that, feel invigorated enough to attempt to drive the 15th
green, having dismissed the threat of the out-of-bounds road on
the left and plentiful green-front bunkers.

5th hole

The 16th is solemn stuff, there being no alternative to the drive's holding its own on a leftward leaning and curving fairway, the approach shot similarly having to pitch well right of the green if it is to run on to the green and not perish in the valley to the left. Here you might stop to admire the guile of Harry Colt and his skill in visualising the potential of such a place without the aid of helicopters, aerial photographs and satellite surveys. You might reflect, too, on the wisdom of a club which includes in its statutes a rule forbidding the altering of any aspect of the course architecture other than with the agreement of the consultant architect (currently Martin Hawtree), backing it up, so to speak, by the engagement of a Head Green-keeper who can appreciate Colt's finest work, having previously been employed at another of Colt's masterpieces, Wentworth.

Since last I visited Prestbury the bushes and briars which formerly lined the dingle over which the 17th is played, somewhat perilously, have been cleared out so that now you can see just how awful your tee shot is if it fails to make the carry to the green. The hole is, thankfully, not too long (nor is any par-3 here) neither will one be overstretched coming up the 18th, as humane a way as can be found expeditiously to gain the succour of the exceedingly comfortable clubhouse.

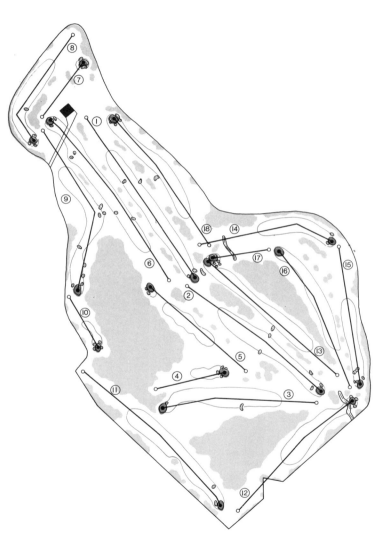

Card of the course:

1.	498 yards	par 5	10.	150 yards	par 3
2.	431	4	11.	487	5
3.	385	4	12.	357	4
4.	178	3	13.	438	4
5.	324	4	14.	345	4
6.	508	5	15.	354	4
7.	174	3	16.	397	4
8.	332	4	17.	143	3
9.	455	4	18.	403	4
Out:	3285 yards	par 36			
In:	3074 yards	par 35			
Total:	6359 yards	par 71		s.s.s. 71	

Queen's Park

4920 yards; par 68; s.s.s. 64

As a sporting centre Crewe's reputation has rested solely on the occasional cup exploits of its Crewe Alexandra footballers. In the not too distant future the new "stadium" golf courses at Weston may bring added lustre to the town's sporting image.

Beginners and those not fortunate enough to be able to play at a private club will have to confine themselves to the municipal course laid out in Queen's Park, and that is no hardship. The high proportion of short par-4s will encourage the beginner, though the odd internal out-of-bounds (imposed, I presume, in the interests of safety) might not flatter the card. The 1st is a charmer, having something of the feel of the more formal ornamental gardens just over the road. There is a temptation to try to drive the green, the hole running gently downhill to the bottom of the gully which runs right through the course, the green just on the farther side, but the aforementioned out-of-bounds lurks close at hand on either side to punish the foolhardy.

The 1st hole

Card of the course:			
1. 256 yards	par 4		
2. 264	4		
3. 252	4		
4. 275	4		
5. 139	3		
6. 344	4		
7. 452	4		
8. 139	3		
9. 340	4		
Out:	2460 yards	par 34	
Total (18 holes):	4920 yards	par 68	s.s.s. 64

Reaseheath

Until very recently there was an area of some 400 square miles or so around Nantwich devoid of golf of any kind. Yet it is to Nantwich that we may look to find the greenkeepers and course managers of the future, for at Reaseheath College four levels of study in the art and science of greenkeeping march with food science and fish farming amongst the widely varied courses on offer. Soil analysis, tractor maintenance, bunker revetting, the solving of drainage problems and budget projection for course managers, for instance, become subjects of academic and practical study rather than orders handed down from autocratic Chairmen of Greens Committees. The classroom, naturally enough, is a 9-hole golf course. It is also home to a small playing club, affiliated to the county and national unions, which welcomes small visiting parties by arrangement.

I shall not attempt a detailed description of the course because it is constantly changing, and for that reason, too, I give no course statistics. Everything here has to be relevant to study. No sooner is one piece of research completed than another one starts, hence the changes. It is sufficient to say that the nature of the rough and its proximity on this short course, currently playing to a par of 59 for 18 holes, mean that considerable accuracy will be required. The Course Development Manager, Dennis Mortram, is himself no mean golfer and clearly has a keen eye for the subtler aspects of strategic design.

Student greenkeepers need to learn how to cope with difficulties such as poor drainage, ill-chosen grass strains, constant shadow and so on, so there will always be problem areas. One green, for example, was constructed on a deep base of almost pure sand. There is never the slightest danger here of residual surface water after even the most torrential rain. The only problem is that it is the devil's own job to persuade the grass to grow on it at all. Another green, though no longer in regular use, was grassed with the fashionable American strain, *Penncross*. The growing season here is simply too short for it to thrive and the paler greens of indigenous grasses are gradually suppressing the import's bluer hues.

A Mackenzie green, unusually flooded after record overnight rain.

A two-level Mackenzie-type green set off against dark trees attracts the eye of the golfer, yet it attracts the eye of the agronomist even more. It was made by cut-and-fill: the soil removed from the lower level being used to create the raised part. Different depths of soil induce different growths of grass and, therefore, different speeds of putt. The greens at Reaseheath are a study in themselves.

Bunkers are there for study, too. Some kinds of sand take longer to rake than others and budding course managers will need to know how to relate the savings made by employing one particular sand to the larger wage bills incurred raking it over a number of years.

Individual bunkers vary considerably, not only in their sand content but also in their shape, ranging from the shallowest flash-traps to fully-fledged Scottish pot bunkers.

Perhaps the most salutary lesson, however, is to be learned in an area across the road in the arboretum. Here no weed-killers are allowed and nothing has been done to the grass for a quarter of a century other than mowing. The greens in this part, totally natural, with no artificial drainage or irrigation, are quite outstanding. Years of mowing have removed all the coarser strains leaving only the finest heathland grasses to make the truest of putting surfaces.

Reddish Vale

6086 yards; par 69; s.s.s. 69

Reddish Vale presents me with a dilemma: is it my duty to share my findings with others, or should I underplay its merits and keep the place to myself? The plain fact is that it is a very fine test of golf indeed which would be very much better known if it were not in the least fashionable part of south-east Manchester. Its pedigree is impressive, a design by Alister Mackenzie, no less, making the best use of a splendid site full of natural ravines and gullies, not to mention the River Tame which is a considerable part of the architecture of several holes. One tends to think of Mackenzie working his own brand of magic at such spectacular natural sites as Cypress Point and Augusta National but he could make an authoritative and original contribution on any terrain, and those who play at courses from nearby Cavendish in Buxton to the Uruguay Golf Club at Montevideo have cause to be thankful for his originality, vision and wisdom.

So, what of Reddish Vale? The start is not auspicious, a tee at the back of a run of houses, the fairway nothing to speak of, or so it would seem until you come to play the second shot, a long, difficult carry over the first of the many gullies, *The Dip*, after which the hole is named, to a well-bunkered green. Immediately you are called upon to clear the gully again, with an all-or-nothing shot to the 2nd green. The gully makes its third appearance on the *Roadhole*, the 3rd, again just before the green and already the stern nature of the test is apparent.

There are those who would complain of four short holes in the first nine but anyone who plays them in 12 shots has done well. The 4th, as it happens, is the least of them, as long as you do not veer left. Its green is almost an extension of the 1st, and the 5th fairway runs back parallel to the 1st, a fair thump over that same gully and a blind second shot in to a green set just in front of a conservatory! So far these are good holes, if nothing spectacular, set on high ground overlooking the Tame Valley.

A gentle walk through a chestnut wood (archetypal wood-pecker country) gives no hint of what is to come until suddenly you are on the spectacular 6th tee, a platform far above a plunging abyss at the bottom of which is the green and its myriad attendant bunkers and, flowing only a little to the left, the River Tame making its first entry into play. There are conservative ways to play this hole, but who wants to duck challenges at this stage of the round? Save that for the 7th, the longest hole, but not the most difficult and the start of a six hole stretch over which good scoring ought to be practicable. Only the most wayward of golf brings the river into play (a dreadful hook off the tee or a prodigal pitch to the beautifully set green). The stroke index rates the next hole, the 8th, as the second most difficult on the course, but it is fairly straight-forward provided the pitch makes the climb up the hill to the green.

The climb continues steeply on the 9th, a short par-3 almost as high as it is long. The green is small and bunkered below and once you get there the view is well worth the climb. Up there, too, is the tee for the slightly perplexing 10th, almost driveable downhill if you are prepared to risk a close encounter with the out-of-bounds on the left, until quite recently the track of a working railway. A major landslip has, for the time being, taken Mackenzie's original green with its narrow entrance out of use.

From the white tee the 11th is almost a par-5, certainly out of reach of two shots to the longer handicap player, which is perhaps just as well with the green hidden from view on the far side of a low rise. The 12th runs back alongside and is the last of these less demanding holes, simply getting you to the 13th tee, as it were. This is another of those par-4/bogey-5 holes with a drive over bushes to an old-fashioned crinkly fairway. A marker post indicates that the green is on the far side of a sloping ridge far in the distance. Few can clear it. Even from close to the pitch is blind, revealing nothing of the horrors befalling the shot that does not quite hold its line, a cavernous pit awaiting on the right. The green is micro-scopic, deviously sloping, and situated in a secret dell surrounded by bluebell woods, a very siren.

The 16th hole

Strong nerves are needed on the 14th tee with the river describing an arc inside which the fairway curves right past a couple of prominent bunkers to another less than generous green, this time surrounded by sand and with the added threat of water just through the back. The drive, I need hardly add, must make good distance to clear the trees and a little stream immediately in front of the tee. The 15th provides a breather of a kind, particularly if the drive is long enough to breast the rise in front. Then there is a fair chance of making the putting surface with the second shot.

One of the most individual, and charming, holes in Cheshire golf follows. The 16th fairway is shaped like a 320-yard banana, curving steadily to the right along the banks of the River Tame. You are invited, provoked perhaps, to attempt to cut some, or even a good deal, of the corner, a watery grave awaiting the foolish or incompetent essay. The fairway narrows as it approaches the green, set at the far end of this tongue of land and therefore surrounded, on three sides at least, by the river. Tree-clad hills rolling down to the river complete an idyllic setting.

As you make the long trek to the 17th tee you will notice that there is room for a decent par-3 in the spare ground out to the right, something of a wilderness of heather and birches. Any sort of hole might be preferable to the existing 17th, a cruel hole. The drive is fiendish, the fairway an extremely narrow strip between a ridge on the right and the ubiquitous river on the left. If that can be negotiated successfully the second shot is simpler, but a new stream appeared recently on the approaches to the green and is not easily spotted from afar. I imagine it appeared at about the same time as the landslip by the 10th green.

All that remains is to return to the clubhouse, and this is done in the most energetic fashion up the same monstrously laborious hill that the 6th descended so dramatically. The hole is no longer as Mackenzie left it, one long, gradual slope replacing the Doctor's stepped fairway. You might just be wandering in an arboretum, the variety and beauty of the trees lining this slope worthy of more than a casual glance — adequate excuse, you hope, to give your heart and lungs time to recover.

Card of the course:

1.	421 yards	par 4	10.	343 yards	par 4
2.	179	3	11.	460	4
3.	390	4	12.	188	3
4.	166	3	13.	456	4
5.	306	4	14.	340	4
6.	240	3	15.	477	5
7.	538	5	16.	322	4
8.	393	4	17.	377	4
9.	137	3	18.	353	4

Out:	2770 yards	par 33	
In:	3316 yards	par 36	
Total:	6086 yards	par 69	s.s.s. 69

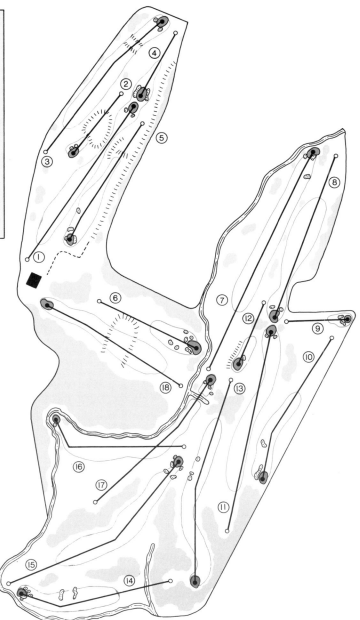

This page: Reddish Vale card and course map

Ringway

6494 yards; par 71; s.s.s. 71

To most of us Ringway is the familiar name for Manchester airport, growing in magnitude and importance almost daily. It was once, we are led to believe, no more than a village and Hale Barns does its best to maintain a similar image despite the volume of traffic constantly rumbling through on its way to and from the M56. Right in the middle of the village, opposite the Church of St Ambrose, is a striking, modern, red brick building, the clubhouse of Ringway Golf Club, its recent construction necessitated by a fire of such devastation that almost nothing remained of its predecessor. Its facilities, the comfort it provides and the atmosphere it lends are not out of keeping with the quality of golf to be enjoyed on its course.

the 15th hole

The clubhouse is an imposing and intimidating companion on the opening drive, right across its front, but the hole is not otherwise ferocious, the cunningly-angled green giving some indication of the kind of problems to be faced throughout the round. This is one of the holes which remains relatively unaltered from the original, 1909, layout of Harry Colt. He did further work in the early 1920s to expand the course, James Braid making further amendments and additions in 1952, and this hybrid course is still providing pleasure and challenge forty years later.

The first four holes are up by the main road and houses of the village but for the rest one could be right out in the country, the regular procession of *Jumbo Jets* and *Airbuses* excepted. The 2nd is a tricky par-5 with its fairway sloping down to the left, tempting the big-hitter to flirt with the gardens on the right, and a very long

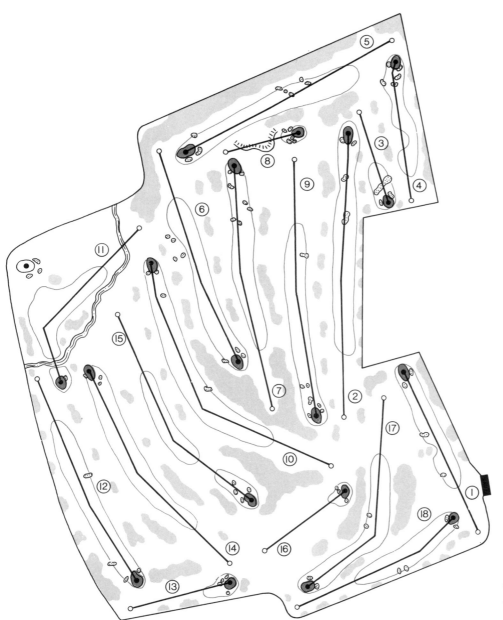

green – almost 60 yards – higher at the front than the back: the sort of period feature too hastily removed when a course is "modernised". The 4th, too, is a marvellous throwback to old-fashioned golf architecture, and, to my way of thinking, all the better for it. Played conservatively it only needs a mid-iron to clear a bit of a hollow on the left, but from any range the pitch is immensely tight, the narrow green surrounded by a horseshoe of steep-faced bunkers, grassy ridges and mounds, and all within inches of the main road.

The 5th may be the most attractive of Ringway's longer par-4s (there are seven of them over 400 yards in length), downhill all the way to the green. A hedge and five bunkers on the right tend to push the tee shot over to the left, but then trees further down the left can impede the second shot. The green itself is at the end of its own private valley hollowed out from the centre of the fairway.

The star hole on the outward nine, my considerable enthusiasm for the 4th notwithstanding, is the 7th, a tough hole to reach in two shots. The drive should not really come to grief but the problems start with the second shot. Can a number of bunkers and ridges interrupting the fairway for the last 100 yards or so on the direct route be carried and, if not, where on earth do you lay up? The 9th, slightly uphill, is out of reach of two of my shots but ought to raise the hopes of the low-handicap player who can hold his drive straight on a fairway which curves left but leans right.

The 10th takes play out towards the countryside again where the 11th waits to infuriate or delight. The hole is not long, but its 90-degree left hand bend does not take place until the 200 yard mark is passed, so a big drive is called for. This is made the more imperative by the height and width of the trees which lie between a shorter tee shot and the green and the presence of a stream crossing just in front of the putting surface. A very attractive spare green might be spotted out to the right by the practice ground and in the low sun of early morning its bunkers would not have looked out of place on the Old Course at St Andrews.

It is not always apparent to the first time visitor just why the Stroke Index is as it is. At Ringway the first stroke is gained at the 12th, a hole named *Hercules* (all the holes here have names, a happy practice provided it does not descend to affectation). There is a slight danger of driving out-of-bounds onto the road on the right and there are bunkers just short of the green but the hole is not otherwise appropriately laborious. With the rhododendrons in full flower the 13th is particularly handsome, a short hole playing uphill and therefore seeming somewhat longer than its yardage.

There are several parallel holes here and the trees which were planted in the early years of the century to separate them are now mature, not to be toyed with. The 14th is parallel to the 10th and similar in the demands it makes on the drive, with trees awaiting the slightest deviation from the line yet a need for a full shoulder turn if the green is to be reached in two. That is particularly true of the 15th, which has a grassy gully cutting through the fairway 100 yards short of the green and bunkers beyond. Just through the back of the green the gorse bushes rival the rhododendrons in vivid splendour in early May.

The last big drive is required on the 17th, preferably finishing beside the marker post which stands at the top of the hill where the fairway shoots off down to the right. Shorter hitters will be faced with a trying second shot played blind over bunkers and a stand of trees, very probably having to guess at the correct line. The line at the uphill 18th is no problem. Aim straight at the Tower of St Ambrose and seek his benediction.

Card of the course:

1.	329 yards	par 4		10.	516 yards	par 5
2.	531	5		11.	352	4
3.	175	3		12.	412	4
4.	288	4		13.	183	3
5.	430	4		14.	453	4
6.	409	4		15.	422	4
7.	457	4		16.	184	3
8.	139	3		17.	402	4
9.	476	5		18.	336	4
Out:	3234 yards	par 36				
In:	3260 yards	par 35				
Total:	6494 yards	par 71		s.s.s. 71		

Romiley

6421 yards; par 70; s.s.s. 71

On a summer morning with rabbits and squirrels as companions, watching the dew lift as the "red and roundy" sun rises above the horizon, Romiley is an agreeable place for golf. Benches are provided on most tees to facilitate that most amiable of pastimes, spectating as others toil. None is more perfectly sited than that on the 6th tee, on the edge of a wood at the very highest part of the course, the views splendid, the golf entertaining.

It is not mountainous golf, merely gently hilly, hardly enoug to puff even me, the fairways rolling benignly as they thread the sinuous trace through the woodlands. The turf is moorland, the so peaty, and with a good selection of par-4s of manageable propor tions the course is reasonably compact yet in no manner crampe

A couple of sturdy par-4s frame a delightfully crumpled shor hole *en route* to the far end of the course, the 4th climbin significantly, curving left round a stand of trees as it does so. Th

The 4th hole

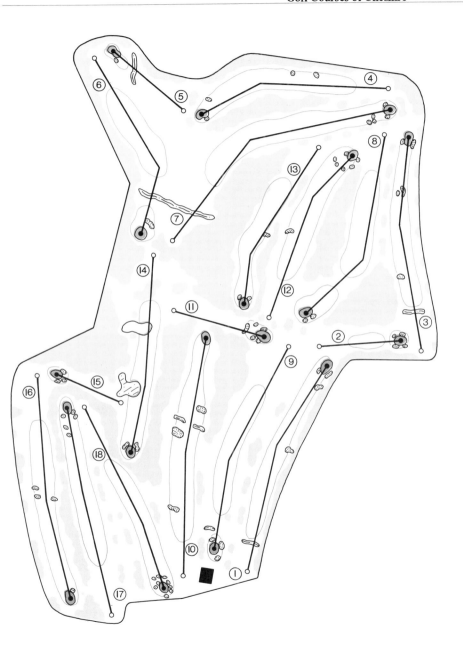

drive may need to flirt with the hedge on the right to yield a sight of the green round behind the trees. Climbing further, the 5th is played across a slight valley and up the far side onto a narrow two-level green angled to repulse all but the truest of tee shots. And then we are standing on the 6th tee I mentioned earlier.

The hole itself is quite special, too, first plunging downhill, corkscrewing to the right, and then turning sharply right across a damp gully, climbing to a green raised above an abundance of mounds and bunkers. Next to it is the 7th tee, the drive running out over the same damp gully before the fairway turns abruptly right, dropping at a leisurely pace to the green.

By now it is obvious that the course is set up to test the placing of your drives, there being few intimidating hazards in front of the tee, and unless your drive finishes in a particular part of the fairway you may have no shot at all to the green. That is so on the 8th, the drive needing to finish in the lower left part of the fairway, just where the trees close in, to give a chance of seeing the green round the corner behind the trees on the right. The lie of the land around a good number of these greens also asks that your angles are calculated with mathematical precision. The longer 9th, too, is very much a second shot hole with a handsomely positioned green on the far side of a coomb, framed prettily by tall trees.

I am much taken with the charm of the gentle dog-leg 13th, just sufficiently wooded to close out approaches from the wrong bit of fairway, the green once again nestling attractively in a ring of trees. So does the 14th green, but it may take some finding. The white tee is away on a remote platform offering precious little view of the fairway and its double trouble. From the yellow tee you can see everything, but that might be enough to overawe the bashful. The problem is ensuring that the drive clears a crater some distance in front, the carry made all the harder by the presence of a number of low trees growing on its walls. From the yellow tee it may just be possible to hit too good a drive and career on down into an expansive lily pond eating into the fairway further on. You simply have to know exactly how far you can drive on a particular day and heed the advice contained in the useful maps printed on the scorecard.

An uphill poke finds the little 15th green from which there is a majestic view of the long 16th fairway running away below almost as far as the distant clubhouse. Such a view can only inspire a masterly drive. Perhaps the 17th and 18th are less demanding, but the view up the 17th fairway, yet again towards a green nestling in the trees, is uplifting enough for me.

Card of the course:

1.	428 yards	par 4	10.	477 yards	par 5
2.	159	3	11.	182	3
3.	417	4	12.	360	4
4.	378	4	13.	350	4
5.	179	3	14.	381	4
6.	382	4	15.	142	3
7.	526	5	16.	445	4
8.	399	4	17.	407	4
9.	384	4	18.	384	4
Out:	3293 yards	par 35			
In:	3128 yards	par 35			
Total:	6421 yards	par 70		s.s.s. 71	

Royal Liverpool Golf Club, Hoylake

6821 yards; par 72; s.s.s. 74

It is at Hoylake that all golfing dentists should be forced to take their holidays. Hoylake probes relentlessly, finds the soft spot, and reaches for the drill. (Patric Dickinson)

This drear flat historic expanse of Hoylake, blown upon by mighty winds, has been a breeder of mighty champions. (Bernard Darwin)

The view from the smoking room at the Royal Liverpool Golf Club on the first floor of that supremely plain Victorian clubhouse in red Ruabon brick shows a vast flat space, apparently without character or guile, bounded by some uninspired examples of later Victorian and Edwardian domestic architecture. (Peter Allen)

There can be no debate, the above comments notwithstanding, about the standing of the Royal Liverpool Golf Club in the hierarchy of Cheshire clubs: it is the senior club, not only in age (being, incidentally, only the second seaside course in England) but also in the superiority of the challenge it has set to golfers of all abilities since its founding in 1864, and those golfers have included the illustrious fields of no fewer than ten Open Championships. Harold Hilton, Alex Herd, Arnaud Massy, J.H. Taylor, Walter Hagen, Bobby Jones, A.H. Padgham, Fred Daly, Peter Thompson, and Roberto de Vicenzo: a roll call of Champions to match any.

What, then, has happened to Hoylake that the Open has not returned since 1967? The answer, of course, is that nothing has happened to Hoylake, but plenty has happened to the Championship. There is no doubting that the course itself would continue to examine any field as thoroughly as it has always done but that test of golf is only a part of the modern Championship. Such is the enormity of the operation nowadays with its tented villages, towering stands, worldwide communications requirements and accommodation needs of players, officials, the press and hundreds of thousands of spectators that Hoylake's hallowed turf would simply sink into the sands of the Irish Sea under the strain. For the once we can only speculate on how it would stand up to an onslaught from the modern giants, and delight in its hosting of the

Amateur Championship in 1995. Perhaps its most treasured (and nerve wracking) recent memory, for those on this side of the Atlantic at least, is of the Curtis Cup regained in 1992 by the ladies of Great Britain and Ireland.

The first time visitor, though, may well be disappointed in the prospect before him (as indeed he might at St Andrews, Carnoustie, Royal Troon or Royal Lytham), an apparently flat meadow girt about by housing (of an admittedly imposing nature however "uninspired") and nothing in sight worth calling a sand hill. To be truthful there is a short stretch from the 9th to the 13th where the golf climbs onto the sea wall, strategy for once dictated by crinkly sand dunes, the distant views of the North Wales hills entrancing on a summer day, the wild roses and maritime grasses a botanist's delight (and erratic golfer's nightmare). That is not to say that the club is something of a period piece for it is thoroughly up to date in the matter of course management, fairway watering, for instance, still being very rare on English links courses.

The level ground on the landward side was once host to the Liverpool Hunt Club Racecourse and a couple of holes, *Stand* and *Course*, commemorate this . In the early days golf and racing had to co-exist but since 1876 the golfers have had their patch to themselves, the Royal Liverpool Club buying the ground for £30,000 back in 1911. It retains a forbidding relic of its earliest days in the central tract of land surrounded by a man-made mound, or cop, that acts as a practice ground and, being out-of-bounds, completely governs play on the 1st and 16th holes. In fact out-of-bounds is the dominant psychological threat throughout the round.

No golfer can stand on the 1st tee at Hoylake without experiencing something of the feelings of the doomed at Balaclava:

Out-of-bounds to right of them,
Out-of-bounds to left of them,
Into the jaws of Death,
Into the mouth of Hell.

What makes it all the worse for those not at peace with their conscience or their driver is that it is a very public opening hole, running the length of the clubhouse before turning right up a second side of the practice ground to a distant green hard up against the cop. As Patric Dickinson wrote, "It is unpardonable but horribly easy to put your second out of bounds, as well as your first".

Then it is up and down towards the main road and its attendant domesticity, taking in a new 4th hole put in for that last Open, and hopefully avoiding the arboreal perils of the 6th once described by J.H. Taylor as "one of the most difficult in the world of golf". All this acts as a kind of exposition of the subject matter (nearly all commentators make some sort of parallel with final examination papers) explaining simply but forcibly that there are no liberties to be taken and that scrambling is something better kept for some other time and place.

Before us, as we stand on the 7th tee, is one of the most famous of all short holes, *Dowie*. Much depends on whether or not the cop running all along the left side of the green is in play or not, and that seems to change periodically, or even according to the nature of the competition. The front of the green has been flattened and the back enlarged slightly to accept a greater proportion of decent tee shots but even so a great deal of control is needed to hit and hold the green. "Unless the green is soft, to aim at the flag is either heroic or stupid, depending on the state of the game". (*World Atlas of Golf*)

Relief comes in the form of an accessible short par-5, the 8th, with what the current Secretary, Group Captain Moore, describes as "the exquisitely shaped bunker to the right front of the green which collects inaccurate shots from a wide landing area". We may be chastened, too, if reminded of the difficulties into which Bobby Jones played himself on this very hole back in 1930, accumulating

The 17th hole

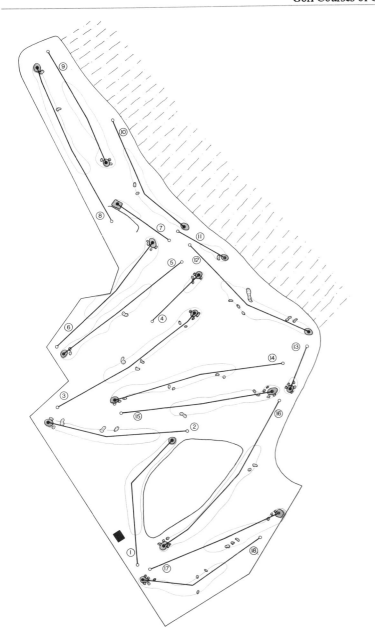

a seven. The crowd it seems, excited by this surprising turn of events, delayed play from the 9th tee and we can imagine the pressure on Jones as he faced the drive. His courage and technique were not found wanting. A public footpath crosses the course at this point, just behind the 9th green in its secretive dell, and it is a grand spot from which to watch play with a good view of the sweeping 10th and plenty of opportunity to share in the agonies of those losing their battle with the venomous 7th.

With its tee up on the dunes the 10th could just as easily be found in the seaside stretch at Turnberry, the fairway below curling gently to the left before rising again to the green. It is good practice for the 12th: much the same thing, but longer, more heavily bunkered, and with an even narrower entrance to the green. Take a moment, if you have it, to make the excursion to the championship tee here and thereafter be thankful you are playing from the front! The short hole in between crosses some very rough ground, appropriately entitled *Alps*. While these *Alps* may be mere foothills in comparison with some further up the west coast they are quite punitive enough to make recovery a very uncertain business. (In the interests of accuracy it should be added that this hole used to be played to a different green guarded in front by a high dune and the name was retained when the present hole was constructed in the 1920s). The last short hole, the 13th, returns us to the flat land exactingly, a tightly bunkered and lonely target.

And so the slog begins, five holes stretching over 2,350 yards as near as dammit from the professionals' tees. The 14th and 15th, long though they undoubtedly are, have the grace to be reasonably straightforward, but that wretched practice ground and its attendant cop totally dominates the sixteenth. We mortals who strive simply to keep our drives out of the left hand bunkers can only close our eyes and pray as our second leaves the club, hoping for a safe landing on the correct side of the cop, to be followed by a delicate pitch to the angled green. To us it is quite incomprehensible that Vicenzo in a moment of the highest tension in the closing moments of the 1967 Open could strike a fairway wood so sweetly that his second shot should defy the out-of-bounds for all its soaring flight, the ball coming to rest in the very heart of the green to assure him of a birdie and, in due course, victory.

Victory is not automatically assured, of course, even if we leave the 16th green with a lead, for the 17th is as treacherous as most here. As Patric Dickinson says, "You can get to the green in 2, or be in the road in 2", although it is not unknown for the ball to bounce back from a parked car leaving the lucky striker with a birdie putt and/or a potential insurance claim. Like so much at Hoylake it is a question of angles (and again the "examination paper" rears its ugly head). Relatively speaking the 18th is reasonably simple, a gentle dog-leg to the right, but there are three bunkers in driving range and a further five around the green. Only the British with their delight in match play would at this stage relish the prospect of returning to the 1st to settle a tie.

Card of the course:

No.	Yards	Par	No.	Yards	Par
1.	428 yards	par 4	10.	409 yards	par 4
2.	369	4	11.	200	3
3.	505	5	12.	395	4
4.	184	3	13.	157	3
5.	424	4	14.	516	5
6.	383	4	15.	460	4
7.	200	3	16.	533	5
8.	479	5	17.	391	4
9.	393	4	18.	395	4
Out:	3363 yards	par 36			
In:	3456 yards	par 36			
Total:	6821 yards	par 72		s.s.s. 74	

Runcorn

6035 yards; par 69; s.s.s. 69

Considering the might of Runcorn's industry and the length of time it has been established it seems remarkable that until quite recently Runcorn ran only to a 9-hole golf course. Given that a good few Scots must have been employed in the area it surprises me that they did not take possession of *The Heath* long before the coming of ICI offices and housing, mostly since the war. *The Heath*, or what is left of it, is something of a barren place or wilderness – a usage of the word in its Old English or German sense, rather than a place of heathers, in which manner golfers tend to understand it.

The 10th green, with the 17th fairway beyond

About a decade ago a little rearrangement of the old course took place and a new patch of land on the far side of a bridle-way was acquired enabling expansion to the full 18-holes. Inevitably the new holes have not yet taken on the depth of character of the older ones, but perched, as they are, on the end of the high ground overlooking the Mersey Estuary and Weaver Valley there is character enough when the wind gets up, as it does. The routing of the course has been arranged to include old and new holes in both nines, thus granting an alternative starting place at the 10th.

Of the newer holes, the 3rd, 4th and 5th run down the side of a hedge and the raised, domed green of that 5th hole is not one to miss. (Incidentally, as on the 1st, the yellow and white tees are

169

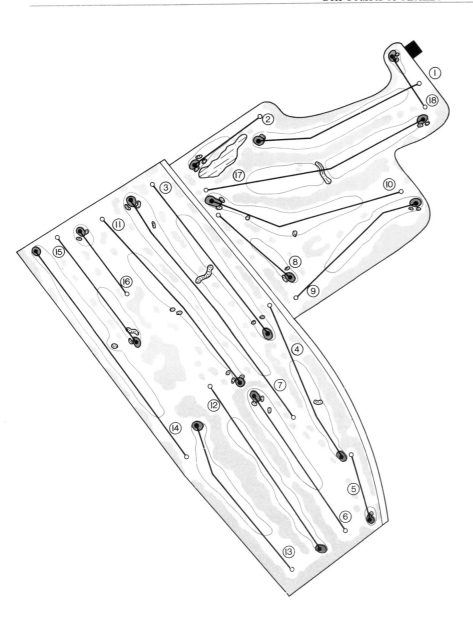

some way apart, giving completely different aspects to the hole and a different appreciation of the various hazards and their influence on play). The 7th is long, but the more interesting new holes appear later in the round. The 11th and 12th are strategic holes, the former curving right late on, two bunkers governing the long approach shot, while the 12th enjoys a leaning fairway and a circular raised green at the end of a slight rise.

There could not be a more prominent (or unfortunate) target on the 13th drive than an electricity pylon, the fairway turning sharply right at this point up to another plateau green. It might seem prudent, too, to drive in the direction of the next pylon on the long 14th, especially as the fairway tends to lean left towards the out-of-bounds hedge. Depending on your vigour you might, in that case, drive into a deep *beef tub* in the bottom of which is a liberal sprinkling of sand. Others of us might, just as easily, deposit our second shots there. Fingers could be crossed, profitably, on the approach to the green here, the ground falling away steeply on the left and through the back on this most exposed part of the course.

Turning now to the original tract, the 1st and 9th are gentle dog-legs, the 2nd a tight short hole with a fence on the right and pond on the left, while the 8th is a substantial par-3, slightly downhill, but also across the slope. At 128-yards the 18th ought not to trouble us, but it is a small target and must be attained in full view of the clubhouse.

Two holes remain unaccounted for on this side and they are real corkers. The 10th runs uphill, bearing right late in the day. There is to be no thought of cutting off the dog-leg: tall trees and white posts dispose of that. A bunker on the left provides a counter-threat. Even if the microscopic ideal landing zone is reached and, therefore, the green lies in range of two hots, there are further bunkers, while the green itself is a hugely ong, multi-level affair, rocking and rolling all over the place. The 7th runs home in parallel with the 10th but the two holes have little in common, apart from out-of-bounds markers. A ditch rosses the 17th and, according to the wind, might on occasion be leared, approached or, sad to say, reached precisely. Conditional n that is the answer to the question of whether or not the green is n reach of two shots. A couple of bunkers in addition to bushes nd trees help to distinguish between accurate, controlled hitting nd wild swiping.

Card of the course:

1.	382 yards	par 4	10.	404 yards	par 4
2.	169	3	11.	431	4
3.	399	4	12.	393	4
4.	356	4	13.	358	4
5.	142	3	14.	533	5
6.	336	4	15.	273	4
7.	548	5	16.	160	3
8.	207	3	17.	470	4
9.	346	4	18.	128	3

Out:	2885 yards	par 34
In:	3150 yards	par 35
Total:	6035 yards	par 69 s.s.s. 69

St Michael Jubilee

5638 yards; par 69; s.s.s. 67

Split by the main Speke Road, this municipal course rolls about a good deal more than its near neighbour, the private club at Widnes. Marker posts are necessary on a number of holes and lend an ancient Scottish air to the foreground, the backdrop being unmistakably industrial. In time, when the trees grow, the rate payers of Halton will be immensely grateful to those councillors with the foresight to establish the place back in the 1970s.

Card of the course:

1.	376 yards	par 4	10.	353 yards	par 4
2.	481	5	11.	127	3
3.	215	3	12.	300	4
4.	510	5	13.	302	4
5.	164	3	14.	295	4
6.	346	4	15.	357	4
7.	338	4	16.	322	4
8.	198	3	17.	127	3
9.	362	4	18.	436	4
Out:	2990 yards	par 35			
In:	2648 yards	par 34			
Total:	5638 yards	par 69		s.s.s. 67	

The 12th hole, a reminder that the wealth of industry is necessary to pay for golf.

Sale

6346 yards; par 71; s.s.s. 70

Tournament professionals nowadays sail under their own steam. They may commit themselves and their lives to the manufacturers of golf shoes or clothing, but they rarely have affiliations with particular golf clubs. I can still recall Tony Jacklin's link with Potters Bar or that of Dai Rees with South Herts. Very occasionally a club professional is able to keep his end up with the very best of them even today and Brian Waites has carried the illustrious name of the Notts club at Hollinwell amidst some very exalted company, David Huish that of North Berwick, too.

The 16th hole

The name of Sale Golf Club will never be expunged from the record books because its professional, Dick Burton, won the last Open Championship to be played before the Second World War, the 1939 event at St Andrews. Since Burton's day much has been changed at Sale, a great deal of it enforced by the advent of the M63. Yet crossing the bridge over the motorway somehow removes all contact with suburbia, giving the course a feeling of seclusion and privacy. The ground itself is flat, very much so, with the result that many of the raised bunkers assume a gigantic aspect, particularly when golf takes place in the low light of early morning

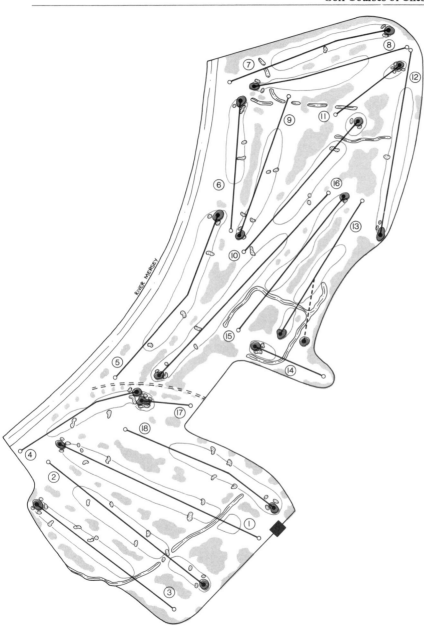

or late evening. The other main features are the tree which, happily, cut off the worst effects of the motor way and separate the fairways, and the ditches which must be crossed at strategic places on a number of fairways, not least the 1st.

There are those who disapprove of opening a golf course with a short par-5. It would seem that play is all too frequently held up while golfers who have no possible chance of reaching the green in two wait until the green is clear before themselves shooting for it. Place a ditch across the fairway about 100 yards out and already the sheep and goats are separated. Plentiful bunkers line the fairway. They are present in numbers on the 2nd, a longish par-4 to a ledge green, notably in the form of a pair of cross-bunkers 100 yards short of the putting surface but seemingly much closer. A short hole used to be played next, and it is much lamented by some members of long standing, but not by those who found it just too tight.

The next excitement occurs on the 4th, a tantalisingly short par-4 with a bridle path running down the left and an abundance of bunkers on the safer right-hand side. The green, as it should be for a hole of this length, is tricky, raised up behind deep bunkers, vigorously contoured, and dreadfully close to the fence on the left. It is almost a double green shared with the 17th.

The course then moves to a difficult par-4 separated from Chorlton Golf Course only by the River Mersey and its high containing banks. Those banks run in a long, slow curve to the left and so does the fairway putting considerable demands on both line and length. Such is the flatness of the environment that the bunker to the front right of the green, by no means the only one, is given a sinister, cavernous demeanour. A ditch on the 8th and exuberant bunkering on the 9th are perhaps the more memorable features of the outward half and, with no short hole currently in play, par is a sturdy 37 despite the modest length of most of the two-shot holes.

The tee on the 10th is the only tee in my experience to be bunkered! I know of bunkered greens, fairways, ditches, ponds, even a tree or two, but no other tee. The reason is that it is situated just off the 16th fairway in riving distance. The hole itself is handsome, the fairway running ver a ditch to a green which was, until recently, almost encircled y trees.

At last a short hole is encountered, very narrow, pleasantly vild, and adequately bunkered. Just beyond is the tee for the 12th, good hole if somewhat marred by the electricity pylons running own the left just beyond the out-of-bounds hedge. The green is aised at the back and surprisingly difficult to hold. On the left is teeing ground from which play was once taken across to the ummocks which now give their name to the 15th, but before we rrive there we must dispose of the challenges of the 13th. At the noment it is a straightforward hole with a ditch crossing the airway 75 yards in front of the lobed green. By the time this book ppears in print golfers will have accustomed themselves to the ather sterner demands of driving out to the right in order to open p a new green in amongst the trees on the left, with an out-of-ounds fence horribly close at hand on the left and a second ditch o boot. On a cursory glance the famous 11th at Merion was rought to the mind of the author.

The 15th is distinguished by the aforementioned hummocks vhich can give a testing lie in mid-fairway, the 16th by a green amed in trees. Sharing a big mound with the 4th green, the putting urface on the 17th is only attained after clearing a couple of deep unkers and avoiding another on the left. The 18th green, long and deep, sits atop a rise which at Sale certainly qualifies as a hill. The distant roar of the motorway is never inaudible as the round proceeds, but it is not until the bridge is once again crossed that we are reminded that, *pace* The Oldest Member, there is life beyond the links.

Card of the course:

1.	492 yards	par 5	10.	392 yards	par 4
2.	436	4	11.	182	3
3.	386	4	12.	427	4
4.	295	4	13.	351	4
5.	439	4	14.	168	3
6.	296	4	15.	386	4
7.	366	4	16.	556	5
8.	354	4	17.	115	3
9.	332	4	18.	373	4

Out:	3396 yards	par 37	
In:	2950 yards	par 34	
Total:	6346 yards	par 71	s.s.s. 70

Sandbach

5593 yards; par 68; s.s.s. 67

The golf course at Sandbach is within easy walking distance of the Saxon Crosses and bustle of town life, in the best traditions of Scottish golf. Driving into the car park one might just as easily be turning up for a game of tennis or cricket, the attractive clubhouse resembling many a pavilion.

A 9-hole course laid out in the mid-1920s, it has been altered here and there over the years and with two sets of tees for each hole some variety of tactics is provided for those playing a full 18-holes. The soil is clearly conducive to the growing of lush grass and many holes feel longer than the yardages credited to them on the card. That seems particularly true of the two full-length par-4s in the middle of the round, the 4th and 5th. The former involves a big hit if the drive is to carry a broad hollow. There is a gully just to the left front of the green and a big tree beyond, either or both of which can snare the fading approach. The 5th fairway, running back parallel, tips over to the left and from a sloping lie there may be some difficulty getting the length and straightness required to reach and hold the green up on a plateau in a corner of the course.

Earlier in the round a pond in trees just to the right of the 2nd green awaits the slice, and there is water, too, just in front of the 6th tee, but it would be a pretty awful shot which failed to carry it. The gentle (first time round) and challenging (for the second time) 7th hole returns play to the substantial houses built along the Middlewich Road whose value must be all the greater for their enticing views over the golf course. The final hole is unusually well bunkered and makes an attractive sight from the tee. A triangle gives those finishing at this point a chance to signal to anyone waiting on the first tee that they will not be asked to yield precedence as well as appealing to the budding percussionists amongst musician golfers.

The 2nd (winter) green

Card of the course:

1.	391 yards	par 4	10.	396 yards	par 4
2.	169	3	11.	147	3
3.	297	4	12.	297	4
4.	416	4	13.	414	4
5.	447	4	14.	439	4
6.	315	4	15.	315	4
7.	151	3	16.	191	3
8.	298	4	17.	294	4
9.	304	4	18.	312	4

Out:	2788 yards	par 34
In:	2805 yards	par 34
Total:	5593 yards	par 68	s.s.s. 67

Sandiway

6435 yards; par 70; s.s.s. 72

It is an intriguing, but unanswerable, question whether or not Sandiway would have achieved greater national or international recognition if the Open had returned to Hoylake. In 1967, the year of Roberto de Vicenzo's popular Open Championship victory at Hoylake, Sandiway was chosen along with neighbouring De-lamere Forest for the final qualifying rounds, and worthy of the honour both proved. Fields of good amateurs and satellite pros have taken Sandiway on since then but the tour stars have not had that opportunity.

On paper the course may seem short for one in the very top rank, but a Standard Scratch Score two over par gives some indication of the seriousness of the challenge. Birches, beeches, pines, gorse, bracken and heather make considerable demands on the golfer's straightness, but the real strength of the course is the strategic use made of the hilly ground over which it is laid out. Hilly ground can be damp and boggy but the soil here is mostly sandy implying good drainage even in winter and, given Sandi-way's high proportion of ICI staff amongst its membership, play here is a seven days a week activity all year round. In the mid-1980s the condition of the course began to show evidence of the weight of traffic over it, but a good deal of work has been put in recently to remedy that. One or two new tees have been built, too, to help control wear and to improve safety on a busy course, but for the most part the layout is that built just after the First World War by big-hitting Ted Ray and subsequently improved by Harry Colt. The exceptions are the 2nd, 3rd and 4th, constructed when the by-pass was widened.

There is no more welcoming invitation to a round of golf than that on the 1st tee at Sandiway. The ground tumbles away in front, rising gently on the far side of a valley to a distant green framed by trees. The feeblest of prods must surely make admirable progress. That, of course, is not the case with a couple of bunkers on the direct line to the green at the sort of range that most of us can

manage. Out to the left may appear safer, but then the shot to the green is longer and harder, angled across the line of the slope. From any lie the length of the approach is difficult to judge being sufficiently uphill to affect club selection but not so severe that it becomes a lottery. Already we are introduced to the subtleties of good golf course architecture.

The first of the newer holes, the 2nd, is in many ways the most featureless stretching out across a level field as far as the eye can see, but the drive, as so often here, is the key. It must defy the tall trees on the direct line and out to the right at the same time avoiding a perfectly placed bunker in line with another stand of trees on the left. A long, slow fade would be perfect. Thereafter it is mostly a matter of making adequate distance to allow a gentle pitch in to the slightly raised green. The short 3rd, though, is a cracker, handsomely framed by trees all round, and punishing to anything drifting off to either side.

On the 4th we encounter Sandiway's malevolence for the first time. From the tee, a spectacular high platform daring us to give our all, there is a marvellous aerial view of the hole before us but little indication of what will happen to our drive when it lands. A seemingly safe shot straight down the middle breaks sharply to the right and may end up blocked out by the fir trees on the right at the top of the hill. Only a daring drive hugging the trees on the left will leave big-hitters a clear shot to the green and any prospect of a birdie. Those of us who got our angles wrong will find that those trees on the right are followed by others on the left further on as we tack our way to the narrow green.

It takes courage to believe the marker post on the 5th, too, for the drive is blind out over a coppice. Our instincts tell us to aim safely to the left, but if we do we will run out of fairway, while those who take the advice offered will find their drives bounding on for ever down the hill towards the armchair green which is, none the less, very tricky to hold. The 6th is tight, as it should be for a hole of this length, prettily set off in front of magnificent beeches.

First time visitors will have little clue of the strategy of the 7th hole driving out from amongst the trees towards a distant ridge. All too frequently opting for the wide-open spaces to the left of the fairway we plough on unthinkingly with our second shot over the ridge and perish in a huge cross bunker embarrassingly short of the green. Even if our drive makes it to the top of the ridge on the right-hand side there is a long approach to be played gently drawing round behind a shoulder of the hill to reach the long, thin green.

It is then something of a route march to find the 8th tee newly built high above the first green. The drive from here is to a hog's back fairway running up a hill in front of us. Anything the least bit off line to the left will shoot away towards the 1st fairway from which there is little hope of recovery uphill over trees to make the green. From the regulation fairway the pitch needs perfect weighting to reach without overshooting. This is the turn for Sandiway, the 9th tee providing the alternative starting point.

I find it hard to believe that this hole is less than 400 yards in length. Even after a good drive the second shot, downhill at that, always seems impossibly long, thrilling though the shot may be. The green lies enticingly on the far side of a valley protected by cross bunkers in front (with more to either side, for added insult) and can only be reached by golfers of my ability with a fully flighted long-iron or wood carrying all the way to the putting surface. We will not be able to reach the next hole in two.

The 10th hole

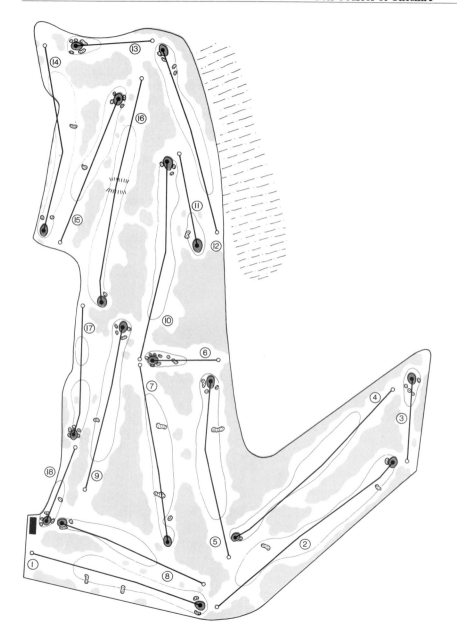

Again the drive is wicked, across a valley to a fairway sloping down sharply to the right. To hold the high ground on the left, though, means steering a perilous course as close as possible to the tall trees running all the way up the left of the hole. Failure at this stage is miserable. From the low ground to the right there is no prospect of making the distance uphill to the green and the best most of us can hope for is an accurate pitch and the chance of a single putt. Most members would readily accept the gift of a bogey-5 on the tee and march thankfully on to the next hole, a picturesque, if relatively straightforward, short hole down towards Pettypool.

Along its shores runs the fine 12th needing a big drive slightly to the left of centre to give a clear run in to the green which is well protected by bunkers and boggy ground down the hill to the right. The next hole, the short 13th, runs at right angles to it, similar in feel to the 6th, and, if anything, even tighter.

Substantial hitting is called for again on the 14th particularly from the back tees when the drive must carry over the corner of an out-of-bounds field. Then it is another big thump to reach the green perched on top of a sharp rise. Putting from above the hole here calls for a deft touch when the wind has dried this exposed green to a lightning pace. Alongside, the 15th tee looks out on a fine downhill drive angled slightly to the right followed by a gentle pitch, provided the drive has not finished behind the trees on either side of the landing zone.

Beating back up the hill again the next drive, at the 16th, is another of those malevolent Sandiway specialities, breaking this time sharply to the left on landing, not at all the outcome expected from a cursory forward glance as the ball is addressed. At worst the drive charges away down a cart-track into the depths of the forest but even the slightest deviation to either side might well eave a blocked second shot round trees and up over a steep bank. The green is still a long way distant at the end of a slow downhill curve to the left in its own private glade. Position on this hole is everything.

The round thus far has had just about every length of hole imaginable, calling for every shot in the bag. The only absentee has been a really short par-4, and the 17th corrects the omission, and a very good example it is, too. On the far side of a deep valley stands an oak tree, bang in the middle of the fairway. We simply have to pass it on one side or the other. Unfortunately that valley is not only deep but also pretty wide and all but the giants of the game will be firing away with their drivers in order to make the carry. It is exciting stuff, but to be left with no more than a wedge in to the tiny green surrounded by bunkers is a just reward.

Sandiway shares with Lindrick and Harlech (amongst others) a short hole to finish. It is not a hole memorable for its beauty, unlike so many here, but it is testing enough with a bunker to be cleared on the direct line and an artificial out-of-bounds all down the right. I have no doubt each successive greens committee has thought of rearranging the course to end with a longer hole, and I suspect there is enough spare land somewhere to slip in a short hole (there is already a spare hole up by the 2nd tee). I shall dream, then, of telescoping the 17th and 18th into a devilish par-5 with that same drive to the oak followed by an exacting second over a ridge down an avenue of trees with no room at all for error for the tiger who fancies getting on here in two.

Card of the course:

1.	405 yards	par 4	10.	467 yards	par 4
2.	523	5	11.	219	3
3.	193	3	12.	446	4
4.	502	5	13.	138	3
5.	416	4	14.	441	4
6.	151	3	15.	362	4
7.	413	4	16.	519	5
8.	357	4	17.	305	4
9.	396	4	18.	182	3
Out:	3356 yards	par 36			
In:	3079 yards	par 34			
Total:	6435 yards	par 70		s.s.s. 72	

Shrigley Hall

6305 yards; par 71; s.s.s. 70

When I first moved to Cheshire, back in 1979, Shrigley Hall had that cold, forbidding greyness of a religious establishment of the Salesian Order. Before they took it over, in 1929, it had been a private house, built to the designs of Thomas Emmett in 1825, though there had been an estate there since the 14th-Century. While the missionaries may blench at the thought of their chapel's being turned into a swimming pool I doubt if they would have many reservations about using the grounds for a golf course. Just look at the list of course record holders at a number of Irish clubs and prominent amongst them are several members of the priesthood. Standing on the terrace overlooking the course as the sun sets it is hard not to dredge up biblical or theological quotations about "Might, Majesty, Dominion, and Power", though you will have to work hard with ingenuity and *Cruden* if you are to turn the Psalmist into a golfer. I leave the Book of Job to experts in the field.

The 18th hole

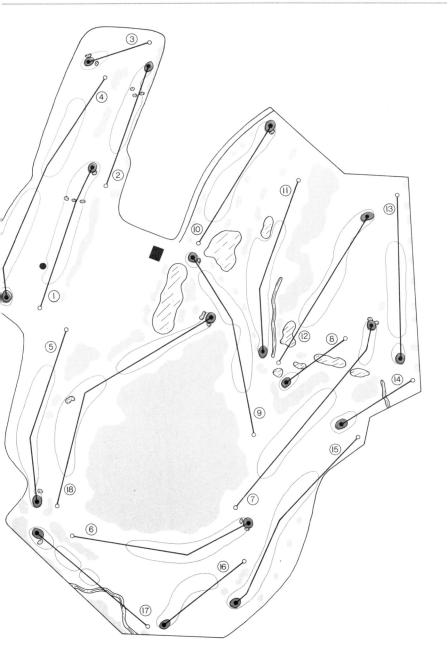

Though I have experienced magical sunsets when at the hotel for musical reasons I have been singularly unfortunate over golf here: it has always been a day of torrential rains, bitter winds and sodden fairways. If I have, therefore, missed some of the subtlety of the place I must hope for the reader's understanding. The house was built in a spectacular location on the side of a hill overlooking the whole of Cheshire and, inevitably, if there is any weather to be had, Shrigley will have it in full measure. I can imagine that in kind weather golf here is worthy of Eden.

The course, another creation demonstrating Donald Steel's vision and originality, is not long as the crow flies but there are hills everywhere giving all manner of problems and rendering yardage *per se* irrelevant. The *introit* is innocent enough, climbing slowly onto the high ground behind the hotel, a gully and stone walls compelling straightness on the 4th. While the 5th and 6th are attractive, leaning sideways around *The Oakridge*, a tree-clad hill described in the hotel brochure as a nature trail, they lull the golfer into a false sense of security. Stern resolve, however, is required to deal with the venom of the 7th, particularly if you drive well, but not brilliantly. Where do you put your second shot? A ravine severs the fairway and there is something of the order of 100 yards of *no man's land* in the 300-400 yard zone. Very few of us can avoid that on a par-5.

We are now on the most interesting part of the course, hilly in the extreme, and savagely punishing of only the slightest inaccuracy, the ground lying below the hotel. The 8th is not long but a tiny target at the bottom of the hill, while the 9th skirts a hillside before sweeping left, in over a gully, and past a pond to the green. By now it is apparent that these are some of the smallest greens in Cheshire. I am not going to measure them all to prove or disprove my point, but, from bitter experience, I can say that on this kind of terrain tiny greens leave no room for error.

The 10th green is eminently missable — you are bound to have noticed it, perched on its hillside, as you drove in. On the 11th the great art is in clearing the pond with your drive. And then comes a really murderous hole, the 12th. It is not too difficult to clear the pond far below the tee, but the fairway climbs steeply up the opposite bank and, being angled across the line, welcomes only the most accurate of drives. The climb becomes vertiginous towards the green and 371 yards suddenly seem like 471. It means, however, that you might well drive at least 300 yards on the downhill 13th, as long as you can keep out of the road on the left and away from the lone oak on the right.

Take enough club to climb the hill opposite on the 14th which runs across a severe depression and dreadfully close to the out-of-bounds wall, across a corner of which the ideal drive is made on the 15th, those ducking the challenge very likely threatening the lives of those on the 16th tee with their second shots.

Cheshire is well provided with 17th holes of a short, but very demanding, nature — Royal Liverpool, Sandiway, Mere, for instance. Shrigley's is in that league of severity, a vast carry over all manner of horrors — trees, water, steeply terraced grass banks — and sandwiched between inhibiting trees on both sides.

The longest hole is kept for last, an apparently never ending slog round *The Oakridge*, probably into the wind as well. Played as a genuine three-shotter it is a double dog-leg, first down a valley past a bunker on the left, then sharply right trying to hold the shot up against the slope and finally up over bunkers to a green overlooking the lake beneath the Hall. I suppose there are players capable of fading their prodigious drives round the corner of the wood, following this with a towering slow draw to reach this green in two shots, but I am thankful to say that I do not normally play with people of this calibre. Were I to I would give up now!

Card of the course:

1.	331 yards	par 4	10.	306 yards	par 4
2.	279	4	11.	383	4
3.	141	3	12.	371	4
4.	533	5	13.	383	4
5.	386	4	14.	177	3
6.	394	4	15.	467	4
7.	486	5	16.	223	3
8.	159	3	17.	314	4
9.	411	4	18.	561	5
Out:	3120 yards	par 36			
In:	3185 yards	par 35			
Total:	6305 yards	par 71	s.s.s. 70		

Stamford

5701 yards; par 70; s.s.s. 68

The refreshment room at Stalybridge station will be remembered with affection and gratitude by countless travellers who sheltered there from the bitter wind which always seemed to bring the threat of snow while waiting for the arrival of an express train to Leeds, York or Newcastle. It constantly amazed me that this industrial valley town, dark satanic mills and all, was in Cheshire, its soot-blackened stone-walled cottages so Yorkshire in feel. But Cheshire it *was* and its golf club, Stamford, still *is,* dramatically clinging to its hillside high above those satanic mills.

It is a wild moorland place, tumbling from time to time into secret valleys, wooded glades or craggy crevices. Heathery outcrops and thin lines of gale-battered trees mark the edges of the higher fairways, hardly a bunker being necessary on such easily defended country. The start, then, is remarkably easy going, a broad par-5 running gently downhill. Guesswork will be necessary if the pitch is blind on the 2nd, only a strong hit passing the summit marker post.

The 3rd is enchanting, exceedingly narrow though it is at the bottom of its own private valley. From there we work our way back up the hill until, on the 6th green, we are once again by the clubhouse. Suddenly everything tightens up, the 7th drive needing to hold a narrow strip of land to the right of a dragonfly pond, the approach shot clearing the stream draining from it to find the green on the far bank.

That hole is surpassed in potential for disaster, however, by the 8th. From a tee up in the heather the fairway in front careers drunkenly down a hillside tipping over to the left towards a black wood. Fortunately there is room out to the right on the 5th fairway but the further right you go the more demanding will be the carry on the second shot, possibly even blind, over trees to an ever narrowing fairway far below. Local knowledge is imperative to ensure a level stance for that second shot, as, indeed, it is on the mildly eccentric 9th with its extraordinary swing to the left 170 yards out. Choose enough club to clear the ditch and give a sight of the green but take care not to strike it too well, plunging into the trees straight in front.

There is a narrow, tree-lined drive on the 10th but thereafter things quieten down until the 13th tee at the opposite end of the course. It would seem that the principal necessity is to clear the chasm directly in front, but the fairway is lined with trees and bushes down the left while the right falls away into the wildest of rough. The real fun comes with the approach shot, played downhill, very possibly off a hanging lie, which must cross a ravine in the bottom of which trickles a little beck. The green is up the opposite bank, a mere shelf above the stream. It is absolutely ghastly if you miss on any side even by inches.

The 13th may be a hole to concede, however, to give yourself a moment or two longer in which to get your breath back after ascending the mountain track to the back tee on the 14th. This is a hole all about length and direction, so easily misjudged, even on such a short hole, when playing steeply downhill and across a slope. Direction, too, is vital off the 15th tee with all manner of evils on the right. The pitch is tricky to judge, played over a little ridge to a green in its own shallow punchbowl. Avoid the chasm on the 16th and it is plainer sailing to the end, though the final green is no easy target at the bottom of a narrow, sloping fairway. Mountain golf is not to everyone's taste but it rarely fails to uplift my spirits.

Overleaf: the 13th hole

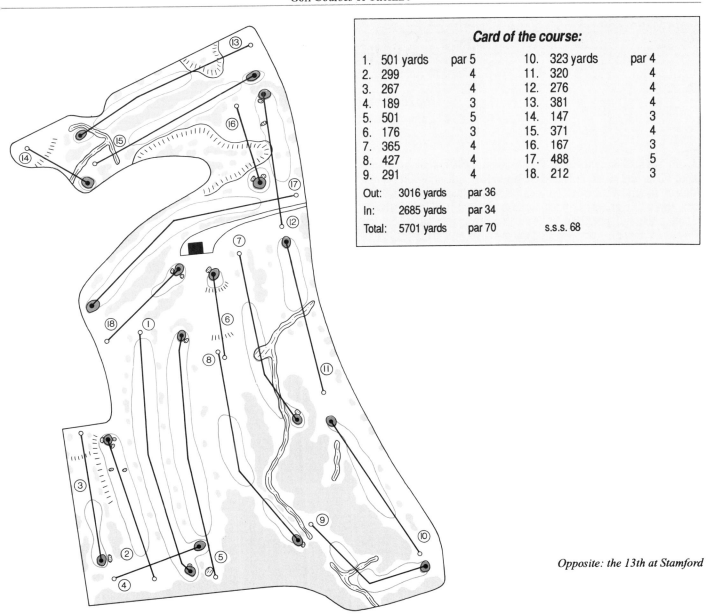

Card of the course:

1.	501 yards	par 5	10.	323 yards	par 4
2.	299	4	11.	320	4
3.	267	4	12.	276	4
4.	189	3	13.	381	4
5.	501	5	14.	147	3
6.	176	3	15.	371	4
7.	365	4	16.	167	3
8.	427	4	17.	488	5
9.	291	4	18.	212	3

Out:	3016 yards	par 36		
In:	2685 yards	par 34		
Total:	5701 yards	par 70		s.s.s. 68

Opposite: the 13th at Stamford

Stockport

6326 yards; par 71; s.s.s. 71

Tom Watson once decreed that aspiring golf course architects should live and work at Ballybunion before inflicting their creations on others. That is not, of course, to say that all courses must have links-like characteristics, but simply that it is imperative to uncover the full potential of a site before construction begins. Nowadays that means topographical surveys, soil analysis, Plasticine mock-ups and the rest. In the old days instinct and cunning separated the imaginative architects from the also-rans. Stockport's distinction and charm are largely due to Peter Barrie, the club's professional, who laid out the course when the club moved here in 1908. He was advised by Sandy Herd, who, six years earlier, had finished off the *gutta percha* ball for good by demolishing a classy Open Championship field using the new *Haskell* ball. Barrie, too, seems to have been quite an innovator being, it is thought, the first club-maker to produce *Jumbo*-size woods on the premise that "wood drives further and better than lead".

The 18th hole

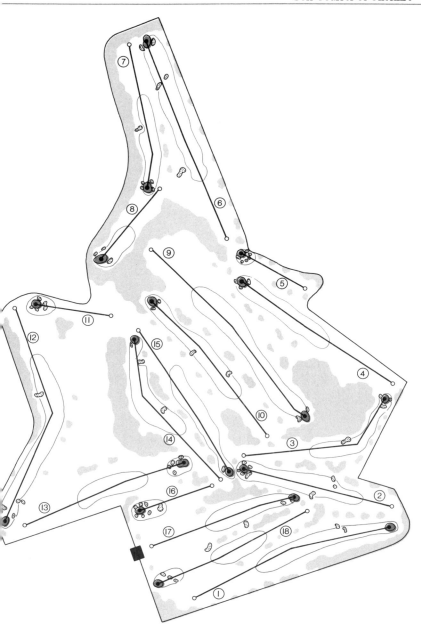

It is, for the most part, their original course which is played today, a few alterations (notably the 3rd hole) being carried out by James Braid in 1935. Yet if Braid were to return today he would hardly recognise the place. Then it was an open heath, almost moorland, the whole course visible from the clubhouse. Thirty-five years ago a great many conifers were planted and while they are rarely part of the strategy of play they now frame each hole gloriously, giving privacy to many of them and materially reducing the impact of surrounding housing and industry. Given also that the ground is riven with gullies, craters, punch-bowls and beef-tubs, in best seaside fashion, it will be obvious enough why this is one of my very favourite Cheshire courses.

I suppose it could be said that it is a weakness that there is only one long par-4 and that comes at the beginning. It may not survive for ever as there are plans for road-building which might devour it but for the moment the course opens in savage style with a long and difficult drive needed to carry the first big depression of the round. Even then the second shot is played flat out slightly blind downhill with a useful pylon as a sighter. The green is bunkerless. There will not be another until the final green. The pretty 2nd is a matter of avoiding the fairway bunkers left and right off the tee and the five sandy graves surrounding the green.

James Braid's 3rd hole is today complicated by the growth of dense trees which narrow the drive and effectively cut off the green from the left side of the fairway. A big, long, straight drive leaves a gentle pitch uphill to the plateau green. Anything less can mean taking quite a gamble with the approach high and blind over the trees.

The course runs anti-clockwise around the boundary fence for the first eight holes and perpetual slicers will be very conscious of the proximity of that fence on the 4th and 5th holes, slightly more open and heath-like in character. They are followed by the first (and only) real glimpse of industry, a majestic example of Victorian factory design dominating the hill beyond the 6th green. The hole itself is one of those give-away birdie opportunities for the low-handicap player and a treacherous card-wrecker for the less gifted. We have the problem of driving over, round, or (most likely) into a number of troughs which would not be out of place at Delamere and then, from an uncertain lie, trying to avoid the two prominent cross-bunkers perfectly positioned for our class of play.

The 7th is immediately attractive, too, with a lovely second shot in past a mound and trough on the left to hold a plateau green whose slippery slopes send the errant approach inevitably into sand or, worse, trees. In its way the 8th is the one-shot equivalent, and equally fetching in its wooded setting. Ending the half, the 9th green is slightly hidden behind a bank on the left.

Yet another picturesque green set off by big trees and white sand awaits at the end of the 10th, and there is a teasing shot over a cross-bunker to reach the domed 11th green, once again close to a slicer's fence. Then comes the 12th drive which can only be described as cruel as the fairway makes a 90-degree right turn about 200 yards out from the tee. Only giants would contemplate clearing the trees to cut the corner while the rest of us must labour with our fairway woods first to turn the corner and then to try not to fall short into the sizeable bunkers 50 yards short of the green.

The 13th may be the 1st Stroke Hole and it does have a fine second shot over a shallow valley but I confess that my mind is already on the 14th, another of my favourite holes. The drive seems straightforward enough, down an avenue of trees towards a distant marker post, but the fairway leans to the right and from that side there may be a sight only of the top of the flag hidden behind a bunkered mound or, if your luck is really out, completely cut off by the trees around which the fairway bends.

A yawning chasm lurks to the right of the drive on the 15th and there is yet another to clear on the short 16th though the greater problem may well be avoiding the seven bunkers which surround this raised green overlooked by the clubhouse. You are under examination from the bar, too, as you drive at the 17th, as ever, over deep depressions, but the rest is gentle unless the hole has been cut on the right hand side of the narrow green when it is then attended by a green-front bunker and mound. Enjoy the respite for you will be made to work over the last hole.

From the final tee you drive into a series of heaving mounds and troughs exceeding even the turbulence of *Crosbie* at Royal Troon. You can only pray for a favourable lie from which to pitch uphill over more depressions and a line of cross-bunkers before reaching the tranquillity of the green.

Card of the course:

1.	463 yards	par 4	10.	395 yards	par 4
2.	339	4	11.	153	3
3.	367	4	12.	510	5
4.	405	4	13.	384	4
5.	159	3	14.	386	4
6.	480	5	15.	379	4
7.	327	4	16.	172	3
8.	201	3	17.	334	4
9.	504	5	18.	368	4
Out:	3245 yards	par 36			
In:	3081 yards	par 35			
Total:	6326 yards	par 71	s.s.s. 71		

Tytherington

6767 yards; par 72; s.s.s. 72

How long does it take for a golf course to become established, to feel as if it has always been there, and is not simply waiting for nature to take its hand over a century or so? The answer at The Tytherington would seem to be well under ten years. Part of a leisure and housing development opened in the second half of the 1980s, the course has quickly acquired its own reputation as a good test of golf. The land over which the course was built clearly had much to offer, rolling down towards the main Manchester-London railway line, with ponds here and there and a plentiful array of mature trees.

Never the less the architect has to make good use of the available resources or he has failed in his primary duty. At Tytherington David Thomas and Patrick Dawson have provided the sort of course that keeps the player thinking on every shot without necessarily intimidating him. There are a couple of tough drives on the back nine but generally speaking those afraid of trouble to the sides are free to opt for an iron from the tee even if this means no prospect of reaching the green with the next shot. If my memory serves me correctly there are only four holes on which you are forced to carry water. On a modern course such conservatism is rare and to be applauded.

Almost every green is imaginatively sculptured, many of them vigorously active, and a great deal of difference to play is made simply by the siting of the flag. While this is of great interest to the golfer who has an eye to the shape of the greens on which he is putting it must, at times, give a headache or two to the greenkeeper responsible for positioning the flags. Each ridge or hump reduces the available pin positions, and so does a narrow or angled putting surface. At Tytherington many greens have all three characteristics. The abundant bunkers are every bit as artistic in shape and form, but at least they are not filled to excess with fluffy sand and from some of them a full shot can be made by a clean striker of the ball.

As an opener the 1st is a tough proposition with a narrow fairway close to the out-of-bounds fence on the left and with trees and a sizeable depression on the right. Length is vital, for the second shot is made over a dip and up the other side to a plateau green. Trees to either side again affect the drive on the 2nd, but it will be position that matters most, the fairway turning sharply to the left past a couple of prominent bunkers about 200 yards out. Gentle progress down the middle followed by a high pitch are all that the golfer playing within himself need do to reach the thin, domed green perched up above big bunkers. Tigers, however, have first to clear the fairway bunkers with their drives in order to cut off some of the dog-leg and then contrive a long, high fade (a Nicklaus speciality) not only to climb to the green but also to approach it on the right axis.

Pete Dye's idiosyncratic architecture is brought to mind on the 3rd with a huge cross bunker boarded the whole way across, beyond which a shallow but wide green awaits. In contrast the old championship courses are recalled on the 4th, the railway forming the left-hand boundary of the hole. Trees again narrow the drive and there is a pond on the right to catch the fade. The green, with its deep pot-bunkers all down the right could well have been lifted straight from Prestwick. The downhill 5th is not forbidding, though the entrance to the green between a pair of bunkers is narrow enough.

A woodland walk is needed to reach the 6th hole, a straightforward uphill, if narrow, par-4. The parallel 7th, downhill, is a blatant appeal to the vanity of all golfers. Surely that Sunday-best drive will roll onto the green and give a putt for an eagle! The architects thought of that and utilised a depression 70 yards from the green that is not easily spotted from the tee. In it they have put a bunker and a swale of semi-rough through which little will pass unimpeded. Further fortification in the form of four left-hand and five right-hand bunkers is given to the green, entirely appropriate for a hole of this length. A swale of semi-rough interrupts the 8th, too,

The 12th hole

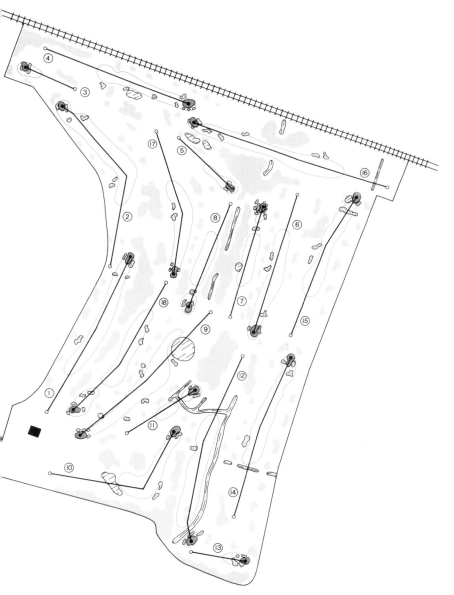

in the gap between trees to either side – just where a decent drive ought to finish. From there the pitch is gently uphill to the green, though with a noteworthy hump on the middle left of the green havoc can be created with all sorts of long putts.

The first forced water-carry is encountered on the 9th, short perhaps as par-5s go, but a fair handful for handicap golfers. We are asked to carry 170 or 180 yards of lily pond simply to make the fairway. We can, in theory, bottle out on the right but we are probably too vain. If we make the carry we have to contain our drives within the narrow confines of a fairway which runs across the line to the left, adequately bunkered for star players, too. It would seem that bunkers line the fairway all the way to the green, climbing slowly and curling gently now to the right. At the far end the green is raised up in moundwork above three deep bunkers, angled even more to the right.

Water is again on the agenda for the 10th, though the real imperative is to reach the high ground at the summit of the hill in front. Bunkers are set into the hillside on the right and trees inhabit the left. Around them the hole bends sharply left downhill to the green. Just as in a Civil War battle, everything depends on position on that summit.

The third enforced water carry follows on the 11th, with a ditch in front of the green and another on the left. In practice, from the yellow tees of the day, even these are hardly significant, but from the back it is quite possible to reach the lily pond we drove over on the 9th and another tributary of the ditch running down the right. All these are but preparatory exercises for the rigours of the 12th.

The drive is tough, albeit downhill, but it is along a narrow corridor over one ditch and then bounded by another, far more threatening, on the left. If that is successfully negotiated the next shot has to be played uphill towards a couple of trees in the middle of the fairway. All too easily that shot finishes directly under them leaving a very testing low pitch over a dammed stretch of the ditch that has now grown to a stream (if not a pond), over the cross-bunkers beyond and thence to the green. I suspect the 13th at Augusta National was in the minds of the architects when this hole was conceived.

The 13th is a gentle hole into the corner. The 14th, however, is far from gentle, the narrow fairway squeezed between a bunker on the left and occasional but important trees on the right. The second shot has to climb over an ever narrowing mown fairway to reach the hilly, extravagantly moulded green, itself rising treacherously beyond the narrowest of entrances between bunkers. The 14th is accorded the dubious privilege of being 1st Stroke Hole.

Another downhill drive follows, on the 15th, seemingly directly into the prestigious drawing rooms of Prestbury homes, but this time the pitch requires less in the way of muscle, even though it must cross a huge cross-bunker spanning the entire fairway. Of greater threat is the little pond which adjoins the green on the left. Now we are back by the railway, and the 16th runs alongside it. It is no threat, the major hazard being the narrowness of the fairway

in driving range as it is squeezed between big trees on both sides. Thereafter the fairway climbs steeply before winding a narrow path in through a chain of bunkers to the green. The closing holes are plainer, both right-handed dog-legs, the 18th distinguished by the succession of steps in the fairway as it climbs in the latter stages to a ledge green, like so many here angled provocatively.

The Tytherington Club has become home to the Women's European Tour, details of which are to be found towards the end of this book.

Card of the course:					
1.	465 yards	par 4	10.	420 yards	par 4
2.	507	5	11.	217	3
3.	164	3	12.	520	5
4.	401	4	13.	156	3
5.	196	3	14.	439	4
6.	382	4	15.	402	4
7.	301	4	16.	540	5
8.	350	4	17.	412	4
9.	480	5	18.	415	4
Out:	3246 yards	par 36			
In:	3521 yards	par 36			
Total:	6767 yards	par 72	s.s.s. 72		

Upton-by-Chester

5808 yards; par 69; s.s.s. 68

On the front of a great many golf scorecards is a photograph of the clubhouse. Unfortunately, as far as Cheshire is concerned, while most of these clubhouses are comfortable and satisfactorily functional few could be described as handsome. Upton-by-Chester was one of the exceptions, standing proudly like some rural vicarage overlooking its 100-acre arboretum through which the course wanders.

Around the parkland site on three sides the boundary is formed of attractive houses and their equally attractive (to the golf ball, at least) gardens, their tone much in keeping with that of the course itself. As on the fourth side runs the Chester-Wirral railway there is no room for manoeuvre in the disposition of the holes themselves and it could be said that the site is very fully occupied. It does mean that improperly wayward tee shots stand some chance of finding a satisfactory lie on an adjoining fairway, though further tree planting in recent years will before long plug the few remaining gaps in the defences.

As an opening hole a par-3, short at that, can be quite a teaser, but you will need to be on song for the demanding 2nd, the first of two holes over the road. Prominent ahead of you on the left is a tall wire fence keeping the occupants of a big house free from bombardment. The house, as luck would have it, is more or less on the direct line between tee and green, so the hole must be played as a dog-leg turning quite sharply to the left. Its companion on this annex, the 3rd, is a gentle downhill par-4 which might be driven when the wind is favourable. The setting of its green, right by a church, would have a Betjeman purring!

The 5th appeals in an old-fashioned way with the green almost hidden from view in the bottom of a big dip and the 6th with a raised green on the far side of a big cross-bunker presents a narrow target. Then the shoulders must be fully turned on the 7th, the drive down an avenue of trees to a fairway leaning to the left and a second shot between a couple of sentinel trees to a green raised up just sufficiently to repulse the dying approach.

The 8th may well be driven, if the plentiful bunkers are avoided, and its rolling green makes putts interesting if they are of any length. It is an aphorism of much links golf that all greens break towards the sea. At Upton for sea read railway.

The course trundles back and forth through the centre of the park until the 14th changes direction starting out alongside the 5th. It is a fine hole, dog-legged to the left around trees and a pond, with a stiff second shot to be played over a couple of boggy depressions and past a steep-faced bunker to climb onto the distinctly shallow green. Upton has moved up a gear.

Into a wind the 15th can be quite a handful, particularly if the pin is cut on the left part of the green in behind a recently added bunker. The pond immediately in front of the tee should, of course, have no part in the golf but its very presence is often sufficient to induce the first topped-shot of the day. The 16th is straightforward enough but there is no fudging the 17th a long, long par-3 across a huge depression, the green rolling to the right but with any number of local variations in the borrows and slopes. Upton finishes in style with a tidy carry over another pond, trees tightening things up on either side, and then a delicate pitch up over a yawning cross-bunker to reach the green so picturesquely set below the clubhouse, the obligatory monkey-puzzle completing the vicarage garden.

The 18th hole at Upton-by-Chester

Card of the course:

1.	162 yards	par 3	10.	147 yards	par 3
2.	416	4	11.	351	4
3.	285	4	12.	423	4
4.	153	3	13.	478	5
5.	349	4	14.	401	4
6.	174	3	15.	198	3
7.	417	4	16.	509	5
8.	266	4	17.	240	3
9.	518	5	18.	321	4

Out:	2740 yards	par 34
In:	3068 yards	par 35
Total:	5808 yards	par 69

s.s.s. 68

Vicars Cross

6243 yards; par 72; s.s.s. 70

The name Eric Parr is unfamiliar to me, but he was professional at Blacon Point, a course near Chester requisitioned by the RAF in 1938. He designed and constructed the first 11 holes at Vicars Cross, its successor as a club, in the months leading up to the outbreak of war and saw to the 18-hole reconstruction after its use as a smallholding during hostilities. It is the more to be pitied that his name is not more frequently encountered. At Vicars Cross, it must be said, he made the fullest and most imaginative use of a site that is gently rolling but hardly spectacular, his creative use of the contours preventing the least element of dullness and, in fact, ensuring a stimulating round for golfers of most abilities.

The 9th hole

The card is unusual: the first par-3 not coming until the 8th hole; a par of 72 despite the course's being no longer than 6243 yards; and, the reason for the previous statement, only one par-4 over 400 yards. So the modest hitter will not be embarrassed here, though on such meadowland the fairway grass is lush and holding, giving little or no roll once the ball has landed, especially after rain. Trees and shrubs planted regularly over the years give the course a parkland feel and in many cases are now sufficiently mature to be very real parts of the strategic design. They can interfere with erratic play, yet nowhere is one discouraged from opening the shoulders. Add to this frequent distant views of the Cheshire outcrops from Beeston to Helsby via Delamere and it is soon clear that this is no suburban course despite its proximity to Chester.

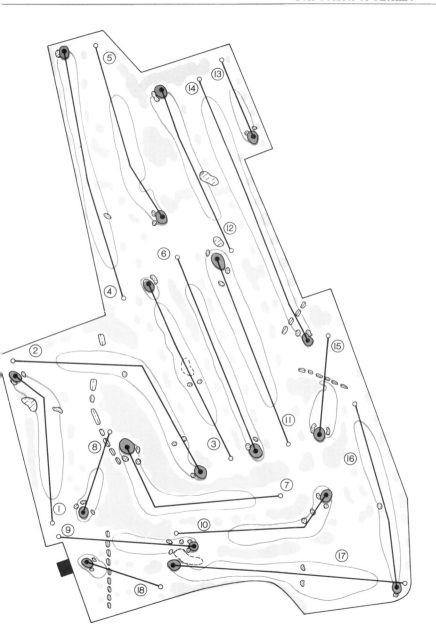

The opening hole is encouraging at only just over 300 yards but a pond to the left is easily driven and there is a bunker on the right where we would have preferred our drive to finish, for the green is tucked round sharply to the left behind the pond. The 2nd drive is no less encouraging down into a valley and up the other side, preferably just to the right of the marker post if one is hopeful of reaching the green in two. But that is not simply a matter of making lengthy progress, the green again being tucked in, hiding behind a tree on the left and guarded by a big depression only just in front of the green. Par-5s do not need to be well over 500 yards to be of interest, and this is a fair example.

Again there is a hollow to contend with on the 3rd, a big rolling affair starting about 180 yards out, tempting many a player to lay up short. That means, of course, that it will take a shot of some 200 yards or so to reach the green and a further obstacle awaits in the form of a second, smaller depression a few yards short of the green, quite invisible from afar. Following a plain par-5, the 5th swings significantly to the left after passing trees and a dip on the left at very driveable distance. The 6th returns play to the central high ground with a narrow drive through big trees and a sweeping second shot uphill to the green.

The next drive, that on the 7th, is, if anything, even tighter, for the hole bends inexorably to the right through an avenue of trees. So great is the bend that the marker post is set almost in the left hand rough and even then there is not much view to be obtained of the green far below to the right. The continuous downward slope of the fairway exaggerates any directional laxity making this very much a test of positional play. A short par-3 semi-blind over a hedge and bunkers returns play to the clubhouse area.

There are similarities with nearby Sandiway in that it is the 9th hole which begins the second part of the round, and what an enticing hole it is, almost short enough to be a par-3! The tee shot is uphill, invitingly so despite the prominent display of at least five bunkers. What is not so apparent from the tee is the amphitheatre depression out to the right, which comes into play again on the 17th.

If the play seems gentler for a few holes it is no criticism and there are sufficient hidden depressions and little ponds to keep interest alive. A big tree *is* the 15th, and from the back tee (which was a rabbits' playground on my early morning visit) the challenge of clearing the tree — over it with a *spoon* shot or round it with a long, controlled fade — is considerable.

The 16th is more remarkable for its panoramic view than its golf, but the 17th is another example of an enjoyable short par-5. The yardage alone would qualify this hole as a par-4 but few will drive sufficiently far up the hill in front to stand a realistic chance of making the green with their seconds. Not too many of us will get past the pair of bunkers 180 yards out (this is uphill, remember) and then our second shots look remarkably forbidding with a hedge encroaching rapidly from the left and sufficient trees on the right to make the fairway appear impossibly narrow. It curves round behind the hedge to the left, and it is only as we approach the green itself that we can see the big depression out to the right that was shared with the 9th and the plateau on which the green sits — no over-clubbing here.

There is another similarity with Sandiway in that the round ends with a par-3, this one being considerably shorter and tricky only in the need to find the correct part of the two-level green.

Card of the course:

1.	324 yards	par 4	10.	333 yards	par 4
2.	485	5	11.	393	4
3.	386	4	12.	335	4
4.	514	5	13.	169	3
5.	336	4	14.	553	5
6.	416	4	15.	200	3
7.	386	4	16.	379	4
8.	161	3	17.	470	5
9.	262	4	18.	141	3
Out:	3270 yards	par 37			
In:	2973 yards	par 35			
Total:	6243 yards	par 72		s.s.s. 70	

Wallasey

6607 yards; par 72; s.s.s. 73

How the spirits of Tom Morris must have been uplifted at the sight of the tumbling dunes on which he was to work when commissioned to lay out the first golf course at Wallasey! Changes have been made over the years and little, if any, of Morris's work remains but the essential character of the course is unaltered, the mammoth sandhills unsurpassed even at neighbouring Hoylake. There is a marvellous variety about the holes, with plenty of change of pace, the golf from time to time moving down off the dunes to flatter ground by the sea wall or inland onto plainer country. The sandy sub-soil means that there are no problems of drainage and the golf will be every bit as good in mid-winter as it is in June. But, before you rush out to the first tee, take time to look at some of the photographs hanging in the upstairs card-room, part of a considerable collection of memorabilia: R.T. "Bobby" Jones qualifying here for the 1930 Open, a vital part of his unique *Grand Slam*; and one of Sam Snead (surprisingly) losing in the final of the Seniors' Championship – not that one should be inspired to lose, but that one might attempt to emulate in some small way that most graceful and relaxed of swings. Take a look, too, in the lounge where the only portrait Bobby Jones signed (by J.A.A. Berrie, R.A.) hangs, a portrait familiar to us all from the many reproductions of it in books and other clubhouses around the world.

Straight away we are thrown into the best (and thick) of things with an opening fairway which almost heaves its way to the green cocked up drunkenly beyond guardian bunkers. It is followed by a stern hole, a long slow dog-leg to the right up its own private valley with dense willow scrub awaiting the slightest mishit. And, as if to give us a sample of everything in the first three holes, we are then sent out onto the tops of the dunes to experience the full force of the wind, steering our drives down into a narrow valley before pitching uphill to the green. If the 2nd hole seems to have escaped from Birkdale the 3rd must have been stolen from Ballybunion.

There is no tee on the coast of North-West England to compare with that on Wallasey's 4th. From its vantage point command may be taken of the entire shipping traffic from Morecambe Bay right round the Welsh coast as far as Anglesey. The hole itself is not unduly spectacular provided care is taken not to stray over the fence on the right and onto the beach. A bobbling short hole with a none too generous green takes us to the end of the course, and the end of the dunes for a while.

It is to be hoped that any tendency to slice early in the round has been cured because a deep ditch runs close in all the way down the right side of the drive-and-pitch 6th, and a fence down the right of the par-5 7th, flat holes both of them, though not without their unforgiving natures. The 8th, too, would be unremarkable if it were not for a tree-covered hillock 120 yards in front of the green around or over which the approach shot must be played to a tiny green well protected by moundwork.

In a *Stableford* competition, that form of golf so valuable to societies and so well suited to golfers of mixed abilities, 7/8ths of the handicap is the allowance. So, as the par-3 9th hole is relatively simple and is rated only 17 in the stroke index, few players will be allowed a stroke here. By one of the quirks which abound in golf this is the hole named after Dr. Stableford, inventor of the competition and most famous old member of Wallasey.

The dunes call again loudly and the 10th returns us to them in mischievous fashion with a short but sharp dog-leg to the right up to a viciously contoured domed green. All manner of trouble from willow scrub to a deep abyss deters anyone from attempting to shorten the route. The 11th, too, is a fairly short par-4 somewhat reminiscent of the 3rd (and therefore archetypal links golf at its best).

Little more than a chip-shot at the 12th lowers us to the flat land across which the 13th and 14th wend a rather mundane (if bunker-strewn) path before the pitch to the 15th raises our hopes

Wallasey, 18th hole

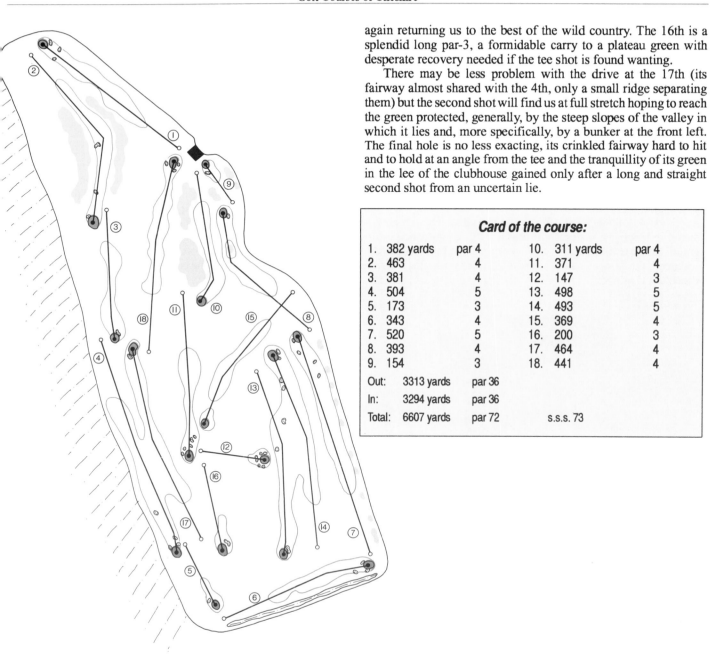

again returning us to the best of the wild country. The 16th is a splendid long par-3, a formidable carry to a plateau green with desperate recovery needed if the tee shot is found wanting.

There may be less problem with the drive at the 17th (its fairway almost shared with the 4th, only a small ridge separating them) but the second shot will find us at full stretch hoping to reach the green protected, generally, by the steep slopes of the valley in which it lies and, more specifically, by a bunker at the front left. The final hole is no less exacting, its crinkled fairway hard to hit and to hold at an angle from the tee and the tranquillity of its green in the lee of the clubhouse gained only after a long and straight second shot from an uncertain lie.

Card of the course:

1.	382 yards	par 4	10.	311 yards	par 4
2.	463	4	11.	371	4
3.	381	4	12.	147	3
4.	504	5	13.	498	5
5.	173	3	14.	493	5
6.	343	4	15.	369	4
7.	520	5	16.	200	3
8.	393	4	17.	464	4
9.	154	3	18.	441	4

Out:	3313 yards	par 36
In:	3294 yards	par 36
Total:	6607 yards	par 72 s.s.s. 73

Walton Hall

6692 yards; par 72; s.s.s. 73

Wandering over handsome parkland with fine mature trees framing most holes this is country house golf, albeit a municipally run facility for the poor of the parish. When I first played here some years ago it measured 6849 yards from the back plates, full by any standards and hugely long for a public course. Though now reduced in length very slightly it is still a big course, the gestures grand, the greens expansive and sweeping, the bunkers plentiful and deep, the fairways amply separated from each other, maintenance not skimped.

Going out I rate the 6th and 9th highly, the 6th a big dog-leg up a hill and round past trees. If the third shot played is a putt at least one stunning shot must have been played before it. The 9th is some 10 yards shorter than it once was and is all the more likely to tempt the big-hitter into trying to blast his way home in two. His drive must then pierce the gap between a vestigial hedge on the right and an intrusive ditch on the left. The second shot crosses a depression and must hold the centre of the green or risk sliding off to the right into a damp coppice.

Coming back, you are allowed two strokes fewer for 12 yards

The 13th hole

greater length—serious golf. I shudder to think what happens when a competent two-ball gets stuck behind a beginners' four-ball over this stretch, and the 11th is a hole to test even the best players, easy enough if you make the carry accurately over the intervening gully. If not.....

Curling left up a hill the 12th is a scenic three-shotter, while the 13th is heady stuff, down past a fairway bunker and then down again to find a plateau green. Not only are you required to know how far you hit the ball consistently, but also you should be well appraised of the differences made by rises and falls, and of the necessity to stop the ball.

The 16th is a stiff par-3 from the back tee, a huge carry over a couple of depressions to reach a long, but narrow, green. The 18th, too, demands a big thump, from the back tees at least, in order to cut off some of the dog-leg on this splendid finishing hole.

Dig this up, sod by sod, and re-assemble it in Hertfordshire or Surrey and you could charge a five-figure joining fee, four-figure subscription, and three-figure daily green fee.

Card of the course:

No.	Yards	Par		No.	Yards	Par
1.	306 yards	par 4		10.	430 yards	par 4
2.	476	5		11.	211	3
3.	330	4		12.	510	5
4.	175	3		13.	397	4
5.	429	4		14.	389	4
6.	453	4		15.	341	4
7.	201	3		16.	218	3
8.	476	5		17.	400	4
9.	494	5		18.	456	4

Out:	3340 yards	par 37	
In:	3352 yards	par 35	
Total:	6692 yards	par 72	s.s.s. 73

Warren Park

5890 yards; par 72; s.s.s. 69

Earlier in this book I mentioned how lucky the residents of the Wirral are in their municipal golf provision. At Warren Park in Wallasey they have nine holes of genuine links golf first established in 1909. Strangely enough the course is situated somewhat further inland than one or two less links-like courses further along the coast, inland and uphill from the railway. It is characterised by tiny greens and humps and hollows everywhere, but perhaps the residents of Prestwick would most readily identify with the capricious 5th with a totally blind pitch shot over a marker post on a ridge down to a tiny, bunker-beset green hard up against a fence. There was nothing fair about golf in its formative years!

The 5th hole

Card of the course:

1.	281 yards	par 4		
2.	263	4		
3.	434	4		
4.	315	4		
5.	286	4		
6.	164	3		
7.	328	4		
8.	370	4		
9.	504	5		
Out:	2945 yards	par 36		
Total (18 holes):	5890 yards	par 72	s.s.s. 6	

Warrington

6305 yards; par 72; s.s.s. 70

T ravelling to Warrington by bus in the years shortly after the last war there were two potential excitements for a small boy: the possibility of being stopped at the swing bridge as a vast tanker or banana boat slid majestically along the Manchester Ship Canal, or the sighting of a military plane, camouflaged and bristling with guns (or so I liked to think), at Stretton. In those days I gave not a glance to The Warrington Golf Club, plainly enough to be seen on its hillside perch beside the A49 at Appleton. The course has been there a long time, over 90 years, though I am told it used, in its

earliest days, to occupy a site on both sides of the main road. Nowadays that road enters the mind of habitual slicers only on the 1st and 18th holes, the rest of the course circling a central tree-clad hillock which does multiple service as a reservoir, host for umpteen masts and aerials, and mount for an obelisk commemorating the family which once owned the estate in these parts.

The 15th hole

James Braid's name, as so often in Cheshire, is associated with the design, and there are several period features to suggest that his work has not been totally obliterated over the years. The recurrent theme of the design is the plateau or ledge green, almost every one of Warrington's 19 falling away steeply on one side, being complemented on the other side by a bunker-riddled slope. That figure of 19 is perhaps pedantic, but correct, there being a totally separate winter green on the 4th, its bunkers adding to the driving hazards of the hole when played in its par-4 summer version. I note, too, another quirk of the card, which is that from the yellow tees there are back-to-back par-3s and par-5s, putting it in the select company of Cypress Point and Ballybunion. The reason that is not true of the medal card is that the 12th hole then becomes a gentle, very short, par-4 instead of the muscular and daunting long one-shotter it is from the yellow plates.

The round begins earnestly with a long par-4, broad enough, but reachable in two shots only if the drive is sufficiently long to gain the advantage of a distant downslope. Bunkers well short of the green threaten the second shots of those who did not drive so successfully. Placing of the drive is fundamental to the outcome of events on the 2nd, a wicked hole for ever climbing and curling to the right. Trees and an out-of-bounds on that side compel an approach to the green from the left, but a bunker over there is ideally placed. No bunker is necessary around the green, the entrance being exceedingly narrow between trees, while a little channel runs up to the green and along its right flank gathering a great many approach shots, particularly mine.

I cannot recall another hole in Cheshire (or anywhere else, for that matter) where the drive is played blind across a hilltop pond, the ground falling away past a marker post beyond, but that is what happens on the charming 3rd, the golf enhanced by fine views over the Cheshire countryside towards Frodsham and Helsby. A pond must be driven on the 4th, too, and if you get in trouble off the tee you might also be conscious of another pool which lurks threateningly within trees on the right, well in range of many second shots. A final twist is the closeness of the green to the hedge and ditch on the right towards which the faded approach shot will unerringly drift.

Returning to Warrington after many years, standing on the 5th tee I was immediately reminded of my first outing here: for a moment I felt completely disorientated, the fairway sloping to the left but bending right, the trees leaning away from the prevailing wind and against the slope, and nothing level or strictly upright immediately visible to confirm that I was actually sober! In reality it is quite a teasing hole, demanding a long and accurately placed drive to allow a full second shot round the corner and up the hill to the right, big trees in the angle contributing enormously to the strategy. A short hole continues the climb to the top of the course and to the two very different tees for the 7th.

This is one of those holes to which you look forward even before leaving the sanctuary of the 1st tee, an exhilarating plunge down the hillside further enhanced with the views it affords northwards to Pendle Hill and Bowland. From the yellow tee it is straightaway, albeit through a gap in the trees, but any airborne shot must make reasonable progress. From the white tee, however, half-way back along the 6th, the drive is largely blind and quite testing, curving all the time to the left, strong hitters needing to calculate exactly how much of the curve they dare attempt to cut off, a bunker on the left about 200 yards out and another on the right 50 yards further on lurking in wait.

Gentler, but at least as handsome, the 8th fairway beckons as it leads up to a strange green up on a mound – strange in that it is much further away than it looks. So cunningly is the mound shaped that there is effectively room for another green in front of the real one, three bunkers short on the right adding to the illusion. It needs wisdom and courage to take sufficient club to carry all the way to the flag, neither to err to the left! It is no less imperative to be authoritative on the short 9th, the green no more than a narrow ledge on the side of a steep hill, guarded by no fewer than eight bunkers some of which are real seaside horrors.

After driving at the 10th the golf is for a hole or two rather less exciting, though if you can reach the 11th in two shots you are no slouch, uphill as the fairway is over the last part of the run in to the ledge green, dropping away on the left and, inevitably, bunkered on the right. The 12th, as already stated, varies according to the tee in use, and the 13th takes play back to the central hillock.

From here on there is plenty of length, almost a mile and a quarter in five holes, a good thump needed on the 14th tee if the drive is to make the higher part of the fairway in front, the job made a little more difficult by a big tree which has been allowed to remain on the edge of the fairway 220 yards out. If anything, the views are even better from here than they were on the earlier visits to the high ground, particularly of the shapely road bridge across river and canal at Runcorn. The 15th curves round in a similar fashion to its

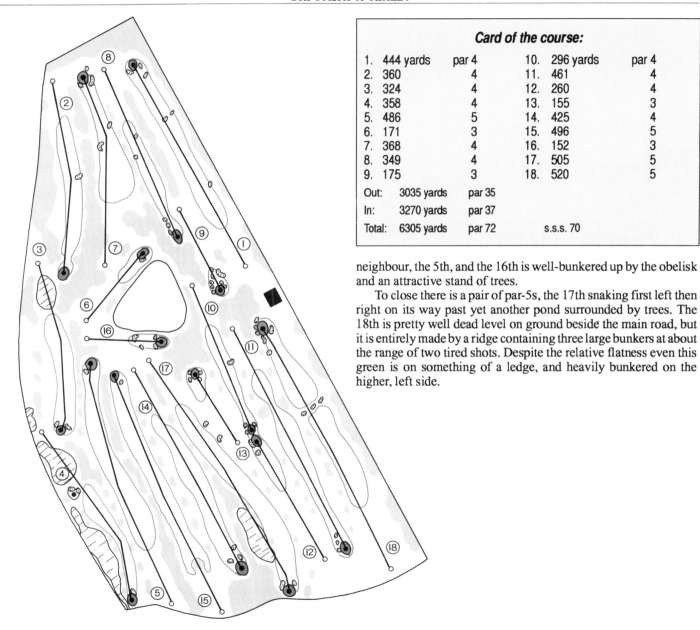

Card of the course:

1.	444 yards	par 4	10.	296 yards	par 4
2.	360	4	11.	461	4
3.	324	4	12.	260	4
4.	358	4	13.	155	3
5.	486	5	14.	425	4
6.	171	3	15.	496	5
7.	368	4	16.	152	3
8.	349	4	17.	505	5
9.	175	3	18.	520	5

Out:	3035 yards	par 35		
In:	3270 yards	par 37		
Total:	6305 yards	par 72	s.s.s. 70	

neighbour, the 5th, and the 16th is well-bunkered up by the obelisk and an attractive stand of trees.

To close there is a pair of par-5s, the 17th snaking first left then right on its way past yet another pond surrounded by trees. The 18th is pretty well dead level on ground beside the main road, but it is entirely made by a ridge containing three large bunkers at about the range of two tired shots. Despite the relative flatness even this green is on something of a ledge, and heavily bunkered on the higher, left side.

Werneth Low

5888 yards; par 71; s.s.s. 68

Walk into a pub, football ground, cathedral, concert hall or fun fair: some communicate atmosphere immediately, others never will, however hard their proprietors work at it. In the case of golf clubs, many set their tone in the clubhouse, while others are lucky enough to possess a course exuding character and feel. Werneth Low is just such a place, and it comes as no surprise to find that it is one of that elite band of 9-hole Cheshire courses.

This is moorland golf at its primaeval best, reminiscent of those unsung gems of Scottish inland golf, Lanark and Paisley. For sure you will get a number of unkind bounces on heaving fairways, wicked blind shots to greens, and occasional punishment out of all proportion to the nature of the crime committed. But isn't that just what early golf was?

Take the 1st hole, with its drive out over a damp pit to a fairway curling to the right, tipping that way, too. All too easily the ball hurtles off down the slope out-of-bounds or crashes into the low run of stone cottages lining the latter part of the fairway. Even after a good drive the pitch is demanding, over a cross-bunker on the left and in to a ledge green right by the fence.

The 2nd is currently a short par-4 played blind over a ridge to a little green, but a new ledge green by the present 9th tee has been constructed to convert this into a par-3. Two completely new holes are under construction downhill of this panoramic fairway, one of them ending in a fiendish pitch over a hedge and gully to a ridged green. Before long this will be played as an 11-hole course (7 on the clubhouse side, 4 over the road, and the clubhouse 7 again to make 18), and it is hoped to extend to 18 by the end of the century.

Pounding back up the hill towards the clubhouse the 3rd is played as a par-4 first time round and as a par-5 when it reappears as the 12th. The stone wall on the right must be courted if the drive is to hold the sloping fairway, and the green will only be found with an immaculate approach shot, uphill, bunkers everywhere, and the omnipresent threat of out-of-bounds on the favourable side of the hill.

Over the road the distant views may soften but the golf retains its ruggedness, not least on the 4th, which I am assured is simple enough, but on a nodding acquaintance commands considerable respect. There is a marker post for the drive and if that is reached the pitch is sharply to the right, downhill, and inch-perfect to the green on the line of a stone memorial. If any of these requirements is not met the ball is likely to founder in a muddy pit on the left or an all-consuming gully on the right. After that matters calm down for a hole or two, given fair weather, until the return to nobler things by the clubhouse.

The 8th is a glorious hole, in golfing terms driving down to the bottom of a hill and pitching up the other side to a two-level plateau green, but in the visual sense assuredly handsome. At the bottom of the hill there is a very Scottish hazard in the form of a shallow well, hardly more than a drain, bounded by an immaculately built stone wall. The round finishes on another marvellously springy fairway first beating a narrow path between bunkers and then leading, somewhat blind, over a little ridge to a green nestling before a hedge under the clubhouse. Moorland golf may not appeal to those who like their creature comforts around them as they play, but it appeals most strongly to my anachronistic mind!

Opposite: the 3rd hole

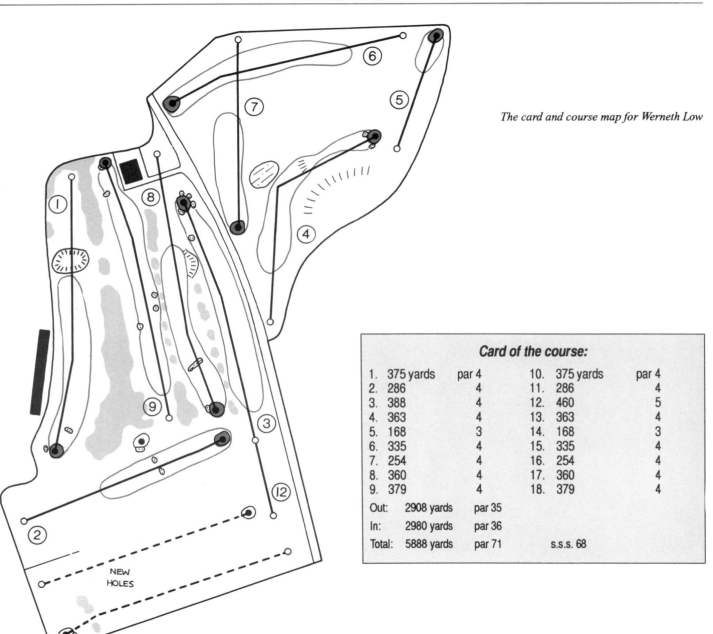

The card and course map for Werneth Low

Card of the course:

1.	375 yards	par 4		10.	375 yards	par 4
2.	286	4		11.	286	4
3.	388	4		12.	460	5
4.	363	4		13.	363	4
5.	168	3		14.	168	3
6.	335	4		15.	335	4
7.	254	4		16.	254	4
8.	360	4		17.	360	4
9.	379	4		18.	379	4

Out:	2908 yards	par 35
In:	2980 yards	par 36
Total:	5888 yards	par 71 s.s.s. 68

Widnes

5719 yards; par 69; s.s.s. 68

Those purists who would point out that Widnes is not a Cheshire golf club because it is not in the Cheshire Union should just look back to my introduction where they will find that geography, too, s a reason for inclusion, even if that geography is as recent as the ast lot of boundary changes. Widnes, a town once proudly in Lancashire and joined to Cheshire only by a stately railway bridge and miraculous transporter bridge, now finds itself in Cheshire *tout court*. It is not for me to reiterate the rights and wrongs of officialdom. I am only too happy to include Widnes in my collection.

The approaches are hardly auspicious, past the Rugby League ground and in through a gap in the houses. Houses, indeed, are prominently visible over the first two or three holes, but thereafter the golf is remarkably peaceful for such a land-locked site. Few acres are available to the club for their course and, inevitably, that means a good number of parallel holes and resultant safe landings for truly wild drives, but trees planted some years ago are now maturing into sober contributors to the overall strategy of play here. Take the 4th, for instance, once so gentle a dog-leg to the left that hardly anyone would notice. Now trees either side of the tee narrow the drive critically and some of those unable to hit a gentle draw will find themselves playing their seconds from among the saplings more recently planted on the right.

Trees are not so much of a hazard on the 5th where the main problem is keeping the drive out of a bunker on the right just where the fairway begins to turn sharply right. There is plenty of room on the left though it seems otherwise for the hedge on that side curves round to the right as the fairway does. The 6th also enjoys the partnership of a hedge, encroaching on the left as the hole progresses. The main threat to good scoring is, however, the ditch which crosses the hole fifty yards in front of the green before running down the left all the way past the green.

The 7th hole

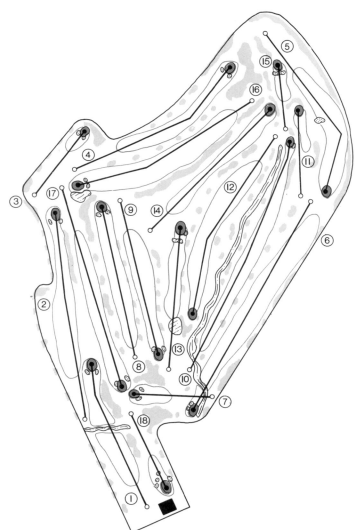

The other potentially ruinous hole is the 10th, also a par-5. The drive is interesting enough with a pond on the left, but it is as the distance increases that the fairway narrows, with first a ditch and then, also, a hedge ever nearer to the line of play, the green awfully close to both of them. Check that you are about to play the correct hole when you leave that green! It is only too easy to step straight onto the 15th tee, again running alongside the hedge, this time over a cross-bunker to a gently undulating green whose surface was still remarkably true on a miserably wet day at the end of the greyest July I can remember. The green at the 16th is one to hit accurately, with a narrow entrance between bunkers and a pond enclosed in willows just through the back of the green.

Card of the course:

1.	310 yards	par 4		10.	503 yards	par 5
2.	417	4		11.	172	3
3.	166	3		12.	401	4
4.	377	4		13.	293	4
5.	366	4		14.	344	4
6.	479	5		15.	136	3
7.	151	3		16.	383	4
8.	313	4		17.	420	4
9.	324	4		18.	164	3

Out:	2903 yards	par 35	
In:	2816 yards	par 34	
Total:	5719 yards	par 69	s.s.s. 68

Wilmslow

6607 yards; par 72; s.s.s. 72

There is a sub-plot to this book – that which is written between the lines, as it were. We all look at our home courses and imagine filling every hollow with water, lengthening the imperative carry from each tee to at least 200 yards, raising all greens by 20 feet and incorporating unreadable borrows into their incredibly rapid surfaces. Before engineering your election to the Greens Committee take yourself round Wilmslow to experience the art of understatement. It is a course capable of withstanding the onslaughts of the European Tour players who came here a decade ago for the Martini International and Greater Manchester tournaments. Open Championship aspirants cut their teeth here almost annually in the first qualifying round. Yet this is a members' course which will not embarrass the industrial or commercial chief whose professional and family commitments allow him no more than one round every other month and for whom practice consists of reading the latest golf magazine on an energy-sapping flight to the far side of the known earth.

The 17th green

The Wilmslow Golf Club celebrated its centenary back in 1989 though it has occupied its present site only since 1903. Not only have great players struck the golf ball on it but also some of the greatest of them have had a hand in its design and redesign over the years: Sandy Herd, James Braid, Tom Simpson, George Duncan and Fred Hawtree before the war; Cotton, Pennink, Lawrie and Partners and David Thomas more recently. Nothing too revolutionary has been undertaken at any one time so that the course retains many of its most endearing features (such as plentiful cross-bunkers in an age which seeks to remove them) while it is able to accommodate all the trappings of the corporate and business golf currently so much in vogue.

Wilmslow's 1st is a majestic start to any round, even if it does induce more than a touch of anxiety with a big carry called for over a deep valley containing the final green and a stream. The real art, though, is in positioning the drive not only to make the *Elysium* of the high ground but more particularly to give a view of the green round the corner of the trees on the left. All too frequently approach shots fall foul of the little depression just in front of the putting surface, running off into an all-gathering bunker.

One of Wilmslow's greatest attractions is the variety of hole lengths, the encouraging change of pace. The two longest par-4s come in the front nine, and at 442 yards the 2nd is just the longer of them. It involves a slightly uphill drive towards a little mound in which a couple of *Principal's Nose* bunkers are cut and just beyond there is a little plantation around which the fairway turns abruptly to the left for the long flat beat to the green. The 3rd continues in the same general direction heading for a double green shared with the 6th. It is a short par-5, easy enough as that, but distinctly exciting for the birdie seeker. Then the drive must clear three prominent fairway bunkers, leaving a long second shot over the first of Wilmslow's cross-bunkers to the narrow green guarded by three bunkers while a stand of trees effectively cuts out approaches from the left.

The next two holes run out into the fields, the short 6th somewhat at the mercy of the winds, and then it is time to return to the clubhouse keeping company (not too close, it is to be hoped) with the road to the David Lewis Centre. The 7th is another potential birdie hole for the strong, involving a carry over cross-bunkers short of the green, while the 8th is similar and gloriously old-fashioned. The drive is somewhat tighter with a bend in the road eating into the left edge of the fairway and a bunker on the

right placed to catch those who err too greatly on the side of safety. The second shot is difficult to judge, again over cross-bunkers, but downhill to the green. The top of the flag is plainly visible but it is hard to estimate just how far short of it to drop the long approach shot. The turn is reached in mischievous style with a little drop shot down to a tiny green just the other side of the brook, the remaining three sides of the putting surface almost completely bounded by sand.

Driving off from a tee just outside the door to the Professional's shop the 10th provides an admirable alternative starting point, a much gentler affair than the 1st. A drive of good length is needed to give a reasonable line in to the green perched, in similar fashion to the 4th, beyond a line of trees on a ridge out to the right. As so often at Wilmslow the green is narrow and angled across the line of approach.

At first glance it appears as if the 11th is the same hole in reverse, back to a green by the Professional's shop, but it is not as simple as that. The gully which crossed the 10th is now much wider and the carry to the far side substantial. There is an alternative route out to the right but the green is shielded from approaches from that side by a tree. It is protected more particularly by a second gully just short of the putting surface, and the customary bunkers.

After the long curve of the 12th, the 13th tee is set down in a damp corner, the drive needing to avoid overhanging branches as well as a number of ponds. In former times the green was a little way beyond yet another set of cross-bunkers making the hole a par-4 of manageable proportions. Now it is an attractive par-5 swinging left past a big tree at the end of the practice ground to a green more heavily contoured than most at Wilmslow and well bunkered to boot.

From there it is back into the trees at the 14th, a short hole of the all-or-nothing kind. "All" is a gently rising green, while "nothing" is the trees tight in to either side and the deep valley to be crossed at the bottom of which are the double indignities of a stream and a hedge. Open though the next two holes may be they demonstrate the positional subtlety of the course, notably on the approach to the 16th green, and then it is back across the ravine on the 17th.

I like the closing hole with its testing drive towards a couple of bunkers on the high ground to the right (veer left and the ball disappears into the trees or stream). Thereafter the fairway sweeps down, first left then right, until it flattens out just before the green.

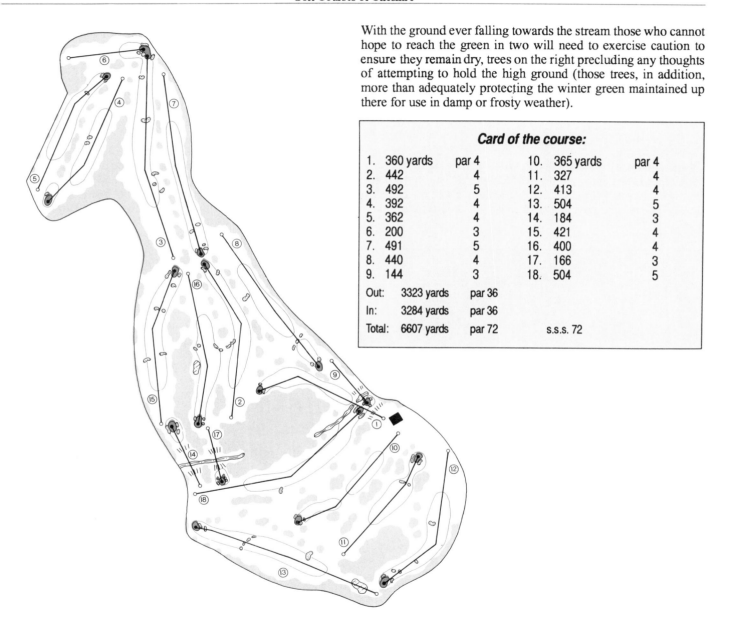

With the ground ever falling towards the stream those who cannot hope to reach the green in two will need to exercise caution to ensure they remain dry, trees on the right precluding any thoughts of attempting to hold the high ground (those trees, in addition, more than adequately protecting the winter green maintained up there for use in damp or frosty weather).

Card of the course:

1.	360 yards	par 4		10.	365 yards	par 4
2.	442	4		11.	327	4
3.	492	5		12.	413	4
4.	392	4		13.	504	5
5.	362	4		14.	184	3
6.	200	3		15.	421	4
7.	491	5		16.	400	4
8.	440	4		17.	166	3
9.	144	3		18.	504	5

Out:	3323 yards	par 36	
In:	3284 yards	par 36	
Total:	6607 yards	par 72	s.s.s. 72

Wirral Ladies'

4966 yards; par 70; L.G.U. scratch score 70

Natural curiosity drew me first to Wirral Ladies'. After all, how many other ladies clubs are there in the world? But this a book about the courses themselves, not particularly about the clubs as such, unique or otherwise, and a splendid little course it is, too.

The 11th hole

Harold Hilton, the great Hoylake amateur and twice Open Champion, advised on the first 9-hole circuit laid out a century ago when a number of wives of Royal Liverpool members wished to take up the game, found themselves thwarted at Hoylake, and persuaded their husbands to invest in a site on the Bidston Road. Turning the other cheek, as it were, they also sanctioned the formation of a men's section within the club and were happy enough to take the professional advice of an (until recently) all-male Advisory Committee. One of their wisest decisions was to purchase the Freehold of the land from the Earl of Shrewsbury in 1927.

The course is very traditional, clearly in the spirit of Hilton's original nine holes. Little, if any, of his work remains and the present course is essentially that redesigned just after the Second World War, one or two par-3s since lengthened into short two-shotters. It is an extraordinary place, a tiny piece of archetypal heath-and-heather lifted bodily from Surrey to the Wirral. And if you assume that a ladies' course must have negligible carries and gentle rough you will be in for a dreadful shock: these are some of the most demanding tee shots in the county, very tight, the rough frequently immensely punitive, the greens invariably subtly contoured and raised in such a manner as to test approach work severely. Forget the woods, take an iron off the tee and expect to run your pitches in to the green in the best old seaside manner. Look out for the mischievous fox which has taken to roaming the course in daylight, even, I am told, on Captain's Day, and if you stray into the rough in early August you may be fortunate enough to espy the rare Marsh Gentian which has been taken as the club's emblem.

The ladies have an advantage over the men on the 1st for they play it as a par-5, the men as a par-4. As this course goes the fairway is comparatively generous but it is quite possible to make a first encounter with the heather in endeavouring to keep away from the out-of-bounds gardens on the left. No fewer than six bunkers surround the 2nd green and the greenkeeper is afforded a number of wicked pin positions on this undulating surface, a luxury he is given on almost every green.

The first real test of touch comes on the downhill approach to the 3rd green. The ball must be run onto the putting surface but the last part of the fairway is very narrow and there are two seaside bunkers lurking in a clearing behind the bushes on the left. Aim left, up towards a green shed, off the 4th tee and the green is opened up. From the right there may be no shot to the green, the ball breaking left on, or past, a mound on the right. What a joy a good short par-4 can still be to all but the tigers!

All the time the course is tightening up, trees on either side constricting the landing zone on the 5th fairway, the slight right-handed dog-leg further turning the screw. The green is set in a wooded glade on the far side of a couple of cross-bunkers at the bottom of a gentle slope – handsome stuff. Breaking out from the trees the 6th fairway reminds me of Sunningdale as it winds gently uphill, curving as it does so to the left, and the 7th is similar.

Up in a corner the 8th keeps the pressure up despite its being only just over 100 yards distant. A monster bunker down at the front left is balanced by a second on the right, but so shallow is the green that the ideal tee shot pitches on the upslope to it, just creeping on to the putting surface to leave an uphill putt to the hole. From bitter experience I can vouch for the difficulties of putting downhill here.

It would seem that the ladies do not care to make life easy for themselves. A sizeable carry over gorse is called for on the 9th, the

tee being set back in a narrow chute of trees. While the green is best approached from the right of the fairway a line of white posts down that side indicates the risks to be taken. The 10th is one of those holes lengthened from a par-3 to a par-4, apparently because the very narrow entrance to the green was felt to be too penal for a long one-shotter. It goes without saying that it is almost as vicious in its new form with dense gorse on both sides and a further clump in front of the tee just in case anyone should develop a taste for topping.

I shudder at the thought of topping a drive at the 11th, a big carry over savage rough for any standard of golfer. The pitch, too, is tricky with the green tipping away on the left. A long carry, especially so for the women, over all sorts of rough and three bunkers, trees to either side, makes the 12th a difficult par-3, the more so as there is a little step up to the green deflecting the feeble approach off to one side or the other.

Invigorating as a men's par-4, the 13th plays as a par-5 for the ladies. The drive is wide open, but the last 100 yards or so of fairway are narrow with trees on the right, a wilderness of gorse on the left, and three seaside fairway bunkers to be negotiated by those still in play. The 14th is altogether less severe, though from the ladies' tee the drive is made towards an out-of-bounds fence.

The 15th, running alongside the 5th is almost a mirror image of it, and the 16th, turning back up the hill, is yet another of those teasing short par-4s. The teasing takes place around the green, a domed affair with a bunker on the right and a mischievous slope at the rear left down which all too many approaches disappear and from which not too many pitches reappear successfully.

The 17th is a beauty, the only bunkerless green on the course nestling in trees. Bunkers return, and with a vengeance, on the final hole, either side of a rolling seaside green, and all within the close scrutiny of the members looking on knowledgeably from the comfort of the bar. For the record I quote the ladies' card (the men's course being some 200 yards longer for a par of 68 and Standard Scratch Score of 66).

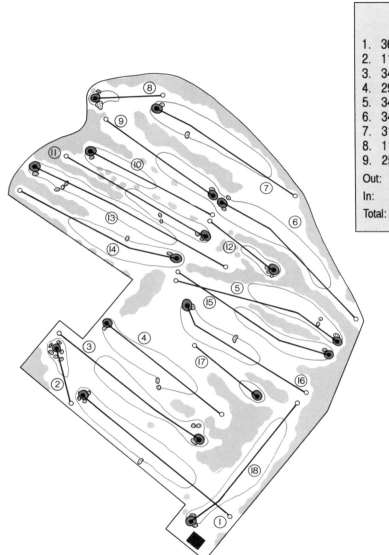

Card of the course:

1.	367 yards	par 5	10.	257 yards	par 4
2.	113	3	11.	274	4
3.	345	4	12.	162	3
4.	291	4	13.	418	5
5.	345	4	14.	345	4
6.	346	4	15.	346	4
7.	316	4	16.	238	4
8.	115	3	17.	144	3
9.	252	4	18.	292	4

Out: 2490 yards   par 35

In: 2476 yards   par 35

Total: 4966 yards   par 70   L.G.U. Scratch Score 70

Opposite: the 15th hole at Withington

Withington

6411 yards; par 71; s.s.s. 71

It falls to Withington to wrap up this account of golf in Cheshire as it stands in 1993. It does so unostentatiously, yet another of the clubs occupying that unpromising strip of flat land bordering the Mersey, dominated by the roaring presence of the M63 and sinister fizzing of its accompanying high-voltage wires on their ugly pylons. Typically, Withington has its fair share of decent holes, one or two of which might put a worried frown even on the normally inscrutable countenance of a Hogan, and managing to keep a surprise or two up its sleeve right to the end. If I have learned anything from visiting so many courses in so concentrated a spell it is that no Cheshire course can be summed up simply from a glance from the clubhouse terrace or a fleeting glimpse over a hedge while speeding past. How often I have glanced enviously at the lucky players just teeing off at Withington's 1st as I have crawled nose-to-tail down Palatine Road trying (in vain) to avoid some monumental tail-back on the M56! What you see from the road is a teasing par-3, only the shortest of irons away, but the green is shallow, perched up on a hillock behind a trio of bunkers

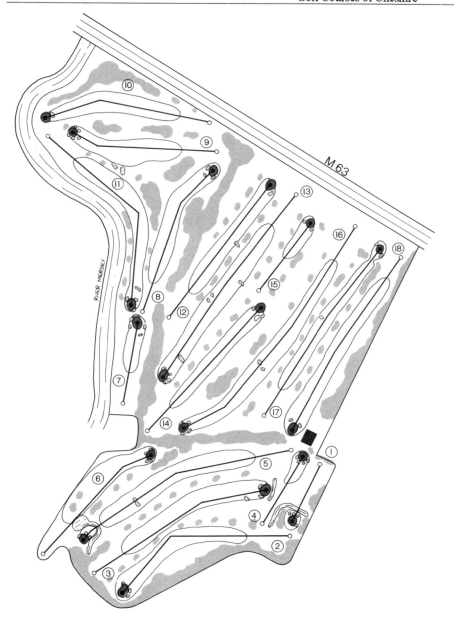

additionally guarded to the right by overhanging branches. Then, before we are quite sure of our form, we are made to drive through a narrow gap in the trees in order to find the 2nd fairway.

For a while things are straightforward, until the final stages of the 5th in fact. Here we must lay up short of a little stream crossing the fairway or else summon up the strength for a towering second shot, for what appears from a distance to be no more than a ditch broadens out on the right into a pond while on the left the stream sneaks round to constitute a real threat close by the green. The next drive would be a doddle if it were not for the two imposing trees left to grow in the very centre of the fairway. A slow fade would curve round ideally onto the fairway, but a slow fade can easily turn into a slice and then there may be no shot to the green raised up by a hedge. The tidy rows of weed-free vegetables in the allotments by the tee reminded me of the neglect my garden has suffered while researching this book!

Over the next few holes one is made readily aware of the restrictions of a site bounded by a river and a motorway. None the less one can admire the way a routine hole is enlivened by the simple expedient of planting a few trees, eight poplars turning the otherwise plain 8th into a tactical dog-leg. The 9th, too, is a good dog-leg to a narrow green encircled with bunkers. A local Rotary Club is to be applauded for planting further trees on this and other holes as part of an environmental project.

How many social matches, I wonder, award themselves a half for the 10th, thus avoiding the excessive walk back to the 10th tee? If they do make the journey they embark on a back nine of 3643 yards, the kind of length more usually associated with courses tricked up for the U.S. Open, and it was the 11th hole in particular of which I was thinking when I made my earlier reference to Ben Hogan. I can visualise his rifling a 280-yard drive down between the river bank on the right and the trees on the left, adding a little touch of fade to the last few yards of flight to turn the corner towards the green. The rest of us, incapable of that kind of length with accuracy will be faced with a complicated second shot which must fade right past tall trees on the river bank beyond which the green lies, well-bunkered at that. A devilish hole for the high-handicapper, and just the sort of thing one imagines might be built amidst the dijks of Holland.

After that the course runs back and forth to the motorway, making the most of what little nature has provided until suddenly moving up a gear over the last two and a half holes. A *Principal's Nose* bunker comes into play on the second shot if the drive has been timid. Then, very late in the day, the hole swings round to the right to a well-trapped green tight up to a hedge. The 17th also appeals with a narrow fairway further narrowed by a well-positioned fairway bunker. A good hit is then required if it is to clear the little ridge which makes the green seem a little nearer than it really is. The 18th, too, needs plenty of muscle but it is wider with only the threat of hooking into the clubhouse or hedge beyond the green left to embarrass the inept.

Card of the course:					
1.	137 yards	par 3	10.	371 yards	par 4
2.	409	4	11.	449	4
3.	409	4	12.	358	4
4.	170	3	13.	478	5
5.	489	5	14.	354	4
6.	316	4	15.	184	3
7.	179	3	16.	574	5
8.	348	4	17.	433	4
9.	311	4	18.	442	4
Out:	2768 yards	par 34			
In:	3643 yards	par 37			
Total:	6411 yards	par 71		s.s.s. 71	

The Architects

However basic a golf course somebody has chosen the site, laid it out, or perhaps altered someone else's existing work. I do not pretend that I have managed, or in some cases even attempted, to identify the architects responsible for the construction of each course in this book. One or two architects, though, stand out for the quality of their invention, for the lasting challenge they give to succeeding generations of aspirant golfers. I offer my immediate apologies to anyone omitted from this list through my ignorance.

Peter Alliss

Son of Percy Alliss, himself one of the finest European professionals in the inter-war years, Peter was a leading tournament player in the 1950s and '60s, playing in eight Ryder Cup teams, and winning Spanish (three times), Italian and Portuguese Opens in addition to many British trophies. As the principal British television commentator he is the successor to Henry Longhurst. His many commercial golfing enterprises include course design and construction, of which The Belfry (in partnership with David Thomas) is the most prominent.

James Braid

One of "The Great Triumvirate" (with J.H. Taylor and Harry Vardon) who dominated golf in the first twenty years of this century, he won the Open Championship five times between 1901 and 1910. He was subsequently in considerable demand as an architect but, as he suffered from travel sickness, entrusted much of his on-site work to John R. Stutt who himself became an architect of note.

Harry Colt

Colt, born in 1869, was a Cambridge law graduate. He is reckoned to have been the first designer not to come from the professional ranks, the first to use the drawing board, the first to prepare plans for tree planting, and, most importantly, the first international designer. His contributions to Cheshire golf are few, but significant, amongst them Prestbury, most notably, and his revisions to Royal Liverpool and Sandiway.

Herbert Fowler

Fowler did not even take up golf until he was 35 (in 1891), yet rapidly became a scratch amateur. In the early 1900s he designed and built what we now call The Old Course at Walton Heath (at the request of his brother-in-law whose consortium financed the project). It received immense critical acclaim and led to his partnership with the equally distinguished Tom Simpson in a design and construction company. Saunton, The New Course at Walton Heath, and The Berkshire are amongst the more famous of his British courses (there are several impressive layouts in the USA), but his style is just as evident in the less well-known Beau Desert, Huddersfield, and Delamere Forest.

The Hawtree Family

Frederick G. Hawtree began designing golf-courses back before the First World War. Afterwards he joined forces with the great J.H. Taylor. He is particularly noted for laying out the Royal Birkdale course in 1932 (at which course both his son and grandson have made small but significant changes). He made considerable alterations to Wilmslow in 1935, and was an early advocate of "pay-and-play" courses. His son, Frederick W. Hawtree took over the firm in 1955 and, though he, too, worked on a number of famous courses the world over, it is the skill with which he created interest and challenge on unfavourable sites for which he is particularly noted, a good example being the original 9-holes at Eastham Lodge. In turn his son, Martin, continues the dynasty from a base in Oxfordshire and has been at work in Cheshire on recent alterations and reconstructions at Crewe, Davenport, Macclesfield, Prenton and Prestbury.

Alan Higgins

He started in the business of designing and constructing golf courses in 1960 with the extension to the Hillside course at Southport. In the ensuing years he has worked for the Robert Trent Jones, Snr. Organisation on courses for King Hassan II of Morocco at Rabat, Marrakech and Agadir, as well as Switzerland and the Ivory Coast.

Since becoming independent in 1976 he has been involved with projects in Europe, South America and Britain. He is presently working on developments in Spain, Greece, Abu Dhabi, France and Britain, after completing Carden Park, an impressive contribution to Cheshire golf.

He is especially interested in the aspect of conservation.

George Lowe

Born near Carnoustie back in 1856, Lowe is one of the least celebrated of golf architects, yet he is reputed to have laid out at least 120 courses, overseeing the construction of the new course at Royal Lytham which, while by no means unaltered, remains one of the most complete tests of golf in the land. Consultant to many early courses in Cheshire, sadly little of his original work is left intact in the county. He was a capable professional player, fine teacher, and renowned clubmaker (he patented the first "matched set" of iron clubs in 1896). Clearly a man of multifarious talents he emigrated to Australian 1920, becoming a J.P. in Queensland.

T.J.A. Macauley

Thomas Macauley founded a successful civil engineering consultancy practice in 1961, and by 1969 had expanded his services to include golf course architecture. This became his sole interest within ten years, and now works throughout the EC, and occasionally further afield. The Birchwood course is a good example of his work, while his most recent project in Cheshire has been the reconstruction of Hazel Grove. One of the few architects competent in computer aided design, Macauley introduced the USGA Greens Specification to England with his 1973 layout at Birchwood.

Alexander (Alister) Mackenzie

Born in Yorkshire in 1870 (and thus a contemporary of "The Great Triumvirate") he studied natural sciences and medicine at Cambridge. During service as a surgeon in the Boer War he became an expert in camouflage, a discipline to which he returned in the First World War and through which he is credited with saving many thousands of lives. He claimed that successful camouflage, like the best golf course architecture, is a matter of discerning observation, utilising nature fully, and, where necessary, imitating it.

As Honorary Secretary of Alwoodley he took an interest in course design in his 30s and soon attracted the attention of the established architect, H.S. Colt. He also entered, and won, an important competition for the design of a golf hole in the United States. As soon as hostilities ceased he was then able to join Colt and Alison in the USA, first in partnership with them and later independently. But it was his spectacular design for the Cypress Point Club in California that attracted the greatest acclaim and led to his being chosen to collaborate with Bobby Jones in the design of Augusta National. These and other important courses such as Royal Melbourne and New South Wales make him easily the most influential golf course architect of the years between the wars.

Tom Morris

As a player "Old Tom" won the Open Championship in 1861, '62, '64, and '67, the last of them after he had returned to his native St Andrews as greenkeeper and professional. Architecture as such in those days involved making the most of the natural features available as almost no earth moving was possible. His skills in this area were passed on to Donald Ross who in turn took them to the USA, influencing architects there to this day.

Morris's noblest monuments are at Muirfield and the Royal County Down, both of which forsook the out-and-back layout almost obligatory on links courses up to that time, the 1890s. It is worth remembering that his designs were for play with clubs and balls very different from those in use today. How well they stand the passage of time! Westward Ho!, Lahinch and Wallaseyare further testament to his skills.

Frank Pennink

One of the outstanding amateur players in the years just prior to the outbreak of the Second World War, he joined the firm of C.K. Cotton after the war, a firm which has bred a good number of designers who subsequently went on to become big names in their own right. While he has been responsible for revisions to such important courses as Royal St George's and Royal Liverpool prior to important tournaments his less prominent work has included a number of very stylish municipal courses such as Walton Hall.

Edward (Ted) Ray

Winner of the Open Championship in 1912, Ray figured in the U.S. Open the following year when he and Harry Vardon were surprisingly beaten in a fairy tale play off at The Country Club by the local boy, Francis Ouimet. He triumphed, though, in the 1920 U.S. Open at The Inverness Club and was the last overseas winner of that championship until Gary Player in 1965, and the last Briton until Tony Jacklin in 1970.

T.G. Renouf

Professional at Manchester Golf Club for twenty years, and (towards the end of an illustrious career) at Stockport, Renouf laid out a number of Cheshire courses, some of his work surviving unaltered to the present day. Like his contemporary and rival, Harry Vardon, "Tommy" was a native of Jersey and, amazingly, spoke little or no English when first he arrived in this country. Without ever challenging Vardon's record at the highest level, the ever dapper Renouf was a competitive match player and could claim the great Walter Hagen amongst his distinguished scalps. He was also a teacher of the highest calibre, attracting Fred Astaire and his sister, Adele, to the Manchester Club for tuition.

Donald Steel

One of the busiest architects of our own time, Donald Steel is a great scholar of the game. Golf correspondent of *The Sunday Telegraph* for nearly 30 years and author of a number of authoritative golf books (not least the definitive study, *Classic Golf Links of Great Britain and Ireland*), Steel is able to draw on an immensely wide experience in his course design. At Vila Sol in Portugal and Barseback in Sweden his courses have been played by the European Tour, and as adviser to the Royal and Ancient he has supervised the alterations made to Royal St George's, Turnberry, Muirfield, Royal Birkdale and Royal Lytham for recent Open Championships.

In Cheshire few golfers will not have experienced his work, that at Portal and Shrigley Hall being most prominent, and Eaton the most recent. Less prominent, but no less influential, is the advice given to Royal Liverpool, Wallasey, Caldy, Heswall, Chester, Delamere Forest, Dunham Forest, Lymm, Romiley, Sale, Sandiway, Vicars Cross and Wilmslow.

David Thomas

After an impressive career as a tournament player (2nd twice in the Open, winner of three Opens in Europe) Thomas began in course design with Peter Alliss. Their joint efforts included The Belfry, host to three Ryder Cups and a host of other important events. In more recent years his name alone has been associated with certain courses, several of which feature in this book.

The Cheshire Union of Golf Clubs

Amateur golf is co-ordinated and promoted at county level by the Cheshire Union, founded in 1920. It organises the many county championships and inter-county matches, through its various committees selects representative teams, sets standard scratch scores and regulates handicaps. Its members, incidentally, are entitled to generous concessionary green fees at Cheshire courses subject to one or two quite reasonable conditions. For the 75th anniversary of the Union in 1995 a celebratory history is currently in preparation under the authorship of Eric Illingworth of Upton-by-Chester.

Women Professional Golfers' European Tour

Formed as the WPGA back in 1978 this was originally almost a bolt-on addition to the men's tour. They set themselves up independently only as recently as 1988, in due course establishing an administrative base at the Tytherington Club near Macclesfield. Inevitably, and particularly so in recessionary times, there have been set-backs, but the Solheim Cup win over the USA at Dalmahoy in 1992 demonstrated the burgeoning strength in depth of the current crop of European players. They are now winning tour events in the USA following the example of Laura Davies, arguably the female counterpart to Severiano Ballesteros, not only in the innovative quality and improvisatory nature of her powerful play but also in her inspirational presence in such events as the Solheim Cup. Fittingly, in 1993 Laura Davies retained her Ladies' English Open title at the tour's home at Tytherington.

The Eclectic Course

We all have our alternatives to counting sheep when sleep proves elusive. Unlikely to induce slumber because it exercises the grey cells rather too vigorously, but a favourite nocturnal pursuit of mine, none the less, is the creation of an eclectic course made up of holes chosen from courses I have played. There is no reason why it should not be the 18 toughest or prettiest holes I have ever encountered joined end to end, but I have made my own rules for a selection drawn only from courses in Cheshire:

◻ The course has to be one I would enjoy playing if it were the only course on which I was permitted to play from this day on.

◻ Holes must keep their place on the course — a cracking good course could be constructed consisting entirely of marvellous 8th or 17th holes, for the sake of argument — because approaching a hole at the beginning of the round differs from hanging on grimly over the closing stretch or consolidating things in the middle of the round.

◻ There must be a reasonable balance to the course, not too many unreachable par-4s, and the more difficult drives and short holes arranged in such a way that thought must be given to who drives first in that most pleasant of golfing pastimes, foursomes play.

◻ Only one hole per course is allowed — and that causes the biggest problems!

I do not pretend that this is the finest course in Cheshire, but I should not complain if restricted to it alone for the rest of my golfing life. If it provokes the reader into devising a better one, it has more than served its purpose.

One of the hardest decisions was choosing between so many excellent opening holes: Caldy, Delamere, Hazel Grove, Heswall, Knutsford, Stockport, Tytherington, Wilmslow, and so on. It is impossible to define it, but the 1st at Sandiway has something extra special which appeals to me, though it is probably the most straightforward of those quoted, gloriously downhill from the tee and not too exhaustingly uphill to follow.

What attracts me to the 2nd at Vicars Cross is the manner in which the tee shot accommodates a left-hander who tends to draw the ball early in the round. I am given a slight chance of getting on the green in two if that drawn drive runs on better than usual allowing me to take a lofted enough club to climb the final stage to the green.

Having climbed, I relax, playing downhill at Heswall's 3rd. There is every chance I will dunk my second shot in the pond beyond which the little green twists and turns, but I am unlikely to get too cross with the cries of curlew, redshank, and oystercatcher drawing my attention far away to the beckoning salt marsh.

With Prenton's 4th I confirm my insanity, the sort of lunatic hole on which the better the drive the more likely it is to perish in the stream which crosses the hole. It is a great exercise in brinkmanship, however, but not so extreme that you cannot take the soft option when pessimism is the order of the day.

The Eclectic Course Card

1. Sandiway	405 yards	par 4	10. Bromborough	160 yards	par 3
2. Vicars Cross	485 yards	par 5	11. Birchwood	569 yards	par 5
3. Heswall	337 yards	par 4	12. Royal Liverpool	395 yards	par 4
4. Prenton	368 yards	par 4	13. Reddish Vale	456 yards	par 4
5. Avro	220 yards	par 3	14. Delamere Forest	373 yards	par 4
6. Caldy	377 yards	par 4	15. Mere	393 yards	par 4
7. Bramhall	500 yards	par 5	16. Wallasey	200 yards	par 3
8. Alderley Edge	175 yards	par 3	17. Portal	439 yards	par 4
9. Prestbury	455 yards	par 4	18. Wilmslow	504 yards	par 5

Out:	3322 yards	par 36
In:	3489 yards	par 36
Total:	6811 yards	par 72

It is not essential to have an extremely long par-3 on a golf course, but the 5th at Avro is played from a substantially elevated tee, encouraging a full shoulder turn. In addition, I have an unhealthy liking for those curiously prehistoric greens sunken in treacherous hollows. Golf courses aim to expunge them. I enjoy my encounters with tradition.

I think I am right in saying that the closest you are likely to get to the sea in Cheshire golf is in the three-hole stretch at Caldy ending on the 6th green. The 6th may not be Caldy's toughest or most teasing hole, but it is its most maritime and the best golf is played with the scent of seaweed and salt in the air.

Moving back inland, the 7th at Bramhall brings out the vanity in most of us, trying for that big drive which manages to get the best bounce off the hill in front, thus avoiding the prominent bunker before us. Then there is the prospect of a raking second shot over intermediate bunkers to the green angled in from the right. What joy we get as we clang the bell to call those behind to continue when we are marching forward to putt!

It pleases me to be able to include a couple of holes from 9-hole courses, Cheshire being so well supplied with ones of quality. Alderley's 8th is a bit of a brute if you get it just a little wrong, but I have given myself plenty of leeway thus far.

No golfer standing on the high ground of Prestbury's 9th tee, surveying the glorious view of so much of the rest of the course and of Cheshire in general, could resist playing this majestic, sweeping hole. True, he might come to the most awful grief on the perilous slopes, in the cavernous bunkers, or under the darkest of fir trees, but the hole is simply too inviting to be left unplayed.

"But you called for a wicked tee shot across a gaping void to Alderley's 8th, and you'll demand something similar on the 16th at Wallasey. Now you do the same with Bromborough's 10th — even numbered holes, the lot of them. Is that really a course fit for match play?" That, of course, is the essence of match play at my level, dovetailing individual strengths and trying to hide weaknesses, much discussion and negotiation being necessary in the locker room prior to that first definitive tee shot's being taken.

Birchwood's 11th is fiendish, foul, immoral, malicious, pitiless or savage, yet it can be played safely and tactically and for the purposes of my eclectic course has been stripped of its urban surroundings, thus allowing play to take place as the architect intended in the sort of surroundings my dreams afford me.

Had I been expected to play Royal Liverpool's 12th hole from the Championship tees it would certainly not have found its way into my selection, but from the club medal tee it becomes a charming hole encapsulating all that is best in links golf: deep sandy pits to trap drives and approaches; fairway turf at once springy and speedy, the well-struck drive bounding on prodigiously; grasping, wiry rough just beyond the fairway; tumbling dunes all around the green sheltering its delicate putting surface from the worst ravages of the wind and granting those who come to watch our amateur golf a perfect grandstand with magnificent sea views to hold their attention when our golf does not.

Having opted out of the sternest of challenges on the 12th, I elect to punish myself inexcusably on the 13th at Reddish Vale, a hole of unremitting vindictiveness in its latest stages. There is little prospect at my time of life of reaching this green in two, and even with a wedge in hand I shall be pitching with trepidation, fully aware of the perils of plunging on into the woods above the hole or the witches' cauldron low down to the right.

Delamere Forest is one of those courses from which one might select any number of strong holes for an eclectic, but the sublime 14th is the equal of any. The prospect of pitching down to that green in front of the trees is one of the half dozen experiences I anticipate most eagerly before any round at Delamere and I have not been disappointed so far.

The opulence of Mere probably does not sit comfortably in the company of the rest of these holes, but the 15th is just so beguiling that it cannot be resisted: holes on which all is visible from the tee, sweeping first down over a stream, then up the other side are hard to resist. When there is a handsome tree strategically left to grow in mid-fairway and it dictates play so completely the final shreds of such resistance as may remain are torn away.

Stern, unforgiving and immensely attractive, the 16th is but one of Wallasey's many star holes worthy of inclusion in any collection. I cannot say I would rather play this hole than the first-rate 3rd, 11th or 18th on the same course, but neither do they outshine it. After all, excellence cannot be exceeded.

Masochism prompts me to reserve a place for the 17th, this most demanding of Portal's holes. It would be tiring enough to climb the two hills involved (and being a traditionalist I carry my own bag — no trolley, and *certainly* no golf cart!) at this stage of the round, but it is necessary also to avoid the plural perils of lily ponds and the wildfowl seeking shelter and sustenance thereon.

What a list of candidates might be prepared for suit~

to close a round of this kind! Wilmslow's may not be an obvious choice – a rather short par-5 with little to trouble the drive. But that is the whole point. I can cruise home with three iron shots if I wish to protect a good score or I can let fly with the *Jumbo* driver I hope to buy with the proceeds of this book in the hope of scuttling my second onto the green, successfully defying the slopes and stream to get there. And if my opponent has already won both the match and the bye we can opt for the upper ground of the winter green, the more swiftly to speed our passage to the solace of the bar.